CRACKPOT TEXTS
ABSURD EXPLORATIONS IN MODERN AND POSTMODERN LITERATURE

First published in Great Britain by Zoilus Press, 1997
ISBN 0 9522028 5 9

Printed by Antony Rowe Ltd., Chippenham, Wiltshire

First Edition

CRACKPOT TEXTS

ABSURD EXPLORATIONS IN MODERN AND POSTMODERN LITERATURE

MAC DALY

with a Preamble by Panjandrum Deadwood

Zoilus Press
London
1997

For
ROGER C., CHRIS F. and JOHN H.

Longum iter est per præcepta, breve et efficax per exempla
Veritatis absolutus sermo ac semper est simplex
Monstrum, nullâ virtute redemptum a vitiis
Non ego ventosæ venor suffrigia plebis
Sæpe intereunt aliis meditantes necem
Qui nescit dissimulare nescit vivere
Præfervidum ingenium Scotorum
Dum relego, scripsisse pudet
Quæ supra nos nihil ad nos
Legimus, ne legantur
Splendide mendax
Pabulum

Preamble

This work is not literature or criticism, but a Hebridean satellite of both, likely to transform the conventional understanding of neither. Indeed, in its numerous earlier incarnations it was to be called (its author informs me) *A Metafictional Galimatias, or a Journal of a Tour to the Hebrides of Literature and Criticism.*

Metafiction here was to be understood in two perhaps complementary, perchance contradictory, senses: (a) as fiction which is self-consciously aware of its status as fiction and continually draws attention to such status; (b) as writing which is "beyond", which "transcends", fiction (by analogy with the misapprehended meaning of "metaphysics").

Galimatias is a French term used by Montaigne to denote "confused language, meaningless talk, gibberish". In English it is a singular noun, as in Walpole's transferred usage, "her dress, like her language, is a galimatias of several countries" (*OED*).

A Metafictional Galimatias would thus signify either "meaningless talk about metafiction" or "gibberish which is itself metafictional". It was thus a conscious design of this book to maintain, by its cunning deployment of confused language, both of these possible interpretations in permanent suspension. The final choice of *Crackpot Texts* admirably rids the volume of these titular felicities.

The contents of this execrable work comprise: a futuristic vision of literary education within a European socialist republic; a proletarian monologue with glances at Michel Foucault and Hegelian philosophy; a verbal hunt for a unicorn written for seven speakers; the sensational exposé of the most scandalous literary plagiarism of recent times; a search for a missing apostrophe which crosses five continents; an anatomy of nonsense; a dissection of the political utterances of two major Scottish novelists; a keen-as-mustard appraisal of a sharp-as-a-razor writer; a pragmatic plea for the retention of a doctrine universally despised; the electoral programme of a new politico-literary formation, which is also an apology for itself; a farrago of found documents from which the present preambler emerges as hero; epistolary chastisements; and a cultural health warning.

In its engagement with avant-garde and rear bumper modernists and postmodernists alike, it takes in James Kelman, Franz Kafka, Alasdair Gray, Frank Kuppner, W.H.Auden, Walter Benjamin, Hugh MacDiarmid, F.T.Marinetti, Roland Barthes, T.S.Eliot, Jacques Derrida, Ellis Sharp, Doris Lessing, and Sidney Ouvrier. In other words, too many and too few.

Dr Panjandrum Deadwood
Reader in Literary Reading
University of Odium
1 April 1997 (a.m.)

Examiner's Report

La Commission Européenne d'Examen
British Division
GCSE Examination 2005
Subject: Texts and Textuality (Syllabus A)

The number of Centres offering Texts and Textuality A reached an all-time high this year. This was perhaps coincident with the completion in 2004 of the five year transnational phasing-out of all "Literature" syllabi which the Commission inherited on its inauguration in the late 1990s. It was therefore necessary to convene a dozen Review Panels, all of whose meetings were successfully decentred from the English capital, although it still remains a matter of some regret that only one Review Panel can be located offshore.

Conflict, internecine struggle and the exposure of the internal contradictions of the syllabus (and its concomitant assessment procedures) throughout the lengthy review process were ensured by the removal of time limits for Review Panel meetings, as well as the introduction, hitherto unhazarded with this syllabus, of Chairpersons. The increasing popularity of the syllabus was reflected in the composition of the Review Panels themselves, in which seasoned T&T savants rubbed shoulders with self-conscious "Eng. Lit." exiles, a conjunction which reportedly intensified the atmosphere of embattled plurality in the meetings. Disputes were usually overridden (and the Division's deadlines eventually met) by resort to caucuses. The commitment of practising classroom teachers in ensuring that all aspects of reviewing are conscientiously questioned, deconstructed, challenged and, on the odd occasion, subverted, continues to be an impressive feature of the scheme.

Some Centres once again submitted grades late, despite a recently renationalised postal service. More gravely (but perhaps not unexpectedly, given the booming number of Centres coming into T&T A from the ex-pseudo-discipline of "English Literature"), there were an excessive number of instances this year of Centres which had badly misinterpreted the syllabus. These problems seemed to be collective rather than individual (although, in any final analysis, the two obviously cannot be thus falsely dichotomised) as they usually involved the whole of a Centre's entry rather than small groups of candidates who were the responsibility of a single teacher. Centres are again advised that, although the syllabus is designed to encourage and promote radical and revolutionary sentiments and action, it is not with the intention of these being directed wholesale against the syllabus itself. Centres which followed this somewhat reactionary line were shown no leniency this year. Indeed, it is necessary to record here that one Centre, which refused to withdraw an assignment inviting candidates to envisage a text as having an "author", had, as a last resort, to be forcibly prevented from offering T&T A for a five year period. While the British Division welcomes the increasing numbers of Centres coming into T&T A as a result of the enforced demise of "Eng. Lit.", it wishes to make it entirely clear that T&T A from its very inception has been intended as an ideological buttress for European Socialism, and that the techniques and procedures of late capitalist pedagogy have, almost by definition, no place in this order. Centres wishing to offer "English Literature" are still not legally forbidden to do so in the context of correspondence courses with fee-paying citizens of the U.S.A, Japan, and certain other surviving plutocracies. To anticipate being able to do so in the European Republic under the guise of T&T A is to invite rude disappointment.

This much should be clear from a reading of the text which is the syllabus itself, but it is evident that many Centres new to the scheme, and certain Centres which have been with us for a few years but have remained entrenched in various unreconstructed ideological bad habits, seem never to have read the syllabus, much to the detriment of their candidates in the final assessment. Whilst it would be heretical to go so far as to claim that the syllabus possesses something which might be called a unitary meaning, as Chief Examiner I have been instructed to remind recalcitrant Centres here, where they may have less opportunity of ignoring them, of its explicit demands.

Candidates are required to submit a minimum of seven assignments, as follows:

1)   an iconoclastic commentary belittling, ridiculing or satirising any item of "canonical Literature" which the late capitalist education system tended to promote as an object of reverence (a variety of techniques are encouraged here, from direct and full-blooded critical assault on the chosen "work of Literature" and/or its pre-socialist upholders, to spoof and pastiche designed to expose and explode the "artistic" pretensions of "the literary" as an epistemological category);

2)   a written analysis deconstructing the "text" of a given cultural object or entity (e.g., a reading of contemporary or historical styles of lingerie, "Sexual Implications in the Design of Manual/Automatic Automobiles") [done under controlled conditions in which provision is usually made for the candidate to observe or experience the given object or entity];

3) a self-consciously ideological polemic on an issue of topical importance (e.g., "Ten Steps Towards the Abolition of The Family", or a piece attacking the employment of non-union-ised labour);

4) a sociological enquiry which promotes the political rights and material interests of a socially prioritised minority (which includes ethnics, gays, disabled people and the like, but not dispossessed shareholders) or an historically exploited majority (e.g., women, non-westerners, the working class);

5) an examination of a text of the student's choice from the pre-socialist era which emphasises the overwhelmingly historical determinations at work in any sample of textuality (e.g., a study exploring how the Cold War "wrote" the assembly of 1960s and 1970s "poetic" texts assigned the name "Ted Hughes", or "Historical Materialism and Madonna");

6) a "phonetic" text (written or spoken) which transliterates or reproduces the candidate's regional accent (RP speakers are obliged to assume an accent other than their own for the purposes of this assignment, but any difficulties caused by this enforced adjustment are disregarded in making an assessment); and

7) an investigation (presented in any appropriate form of the candidate's choice) which reveals the internal textual contradictions of Texts and Textuality Syllabus A itself.

It must be stressed that seven *separate* assignments are required (assignment no. 7, notably, is "compulsory and optional"). The submission of an assignment written in Scouse, which comprises both a cultural analysis of and a polemical attack on current designs in hearing aids, and additionally explores the consequent problems experienced by people with hearing difficulties, would not in itself satisfy the demands of (2), (3), (4) and (6) above. This example is fictional. Most actual attempts by centres to conflate assignments in this way are usually much more bizarre.

Nor, as long as an example of each of the seven is included in the candidate's final folder, is it forbidden to submit extra pieces which are germane to the cultural concerns of, and material practices promoted by, the syllabus. However, Centres are advised that matters are rendered administratively difficult for the Division if these extra assignments are not kept entirely distinct from the others. Some candidates from one Centre were unfortunately penalised quite heavily this year, despite a clever and laudable attempt to inscribe an extra assignment *across* each of the seven submitted assignments. (The extra assignment in question was entitled

"Palimpsest" and consisted of printing various symbolic shapes - e.g., Dr
Marten bootprints - on sheets of paper, on which were then written each
of the candidate's seven required assignments. While this showed a
primitive but commendable grasp of the concept of a "subtext", it also
rendered virtually all of the assignments completely indecipherable.)

Once again this year, work of a high standard was presented in all
grades, although it was perhaps to be anticipated that Centres which have
in solidarity offered the syllabus since its inception have continued to
achieve the best results while, at the other end of the scale, Centres which
came into the syllabus only this year typically spent most of it (if the
sometimes frenzied correspondence with Divisional advisers is an accurate
indicator) struggling to reach some basic understanding of what the syllabus
actually means. The Division is pleased to be able to confirm press and
media predictions that candidates of "working class" origin would generally
achieve considerably greater success than their "bourgeois" competitors in
this syllabus. By means of T&T A we therefore continue admirably to fulfil
one of the key aims of the Commission's charter, namely "to redress
historical wrongs" (*Un Bâton Avec Lequell On Frappe Les Salops Riches:
La Charte de la Commission Européenne d'Examen* [Strasbourg, 1998], p.
6).

Given the self-consciously transitional nature of the syllabus at the
present historical juncture, it would seem imperative and useful that
detailed comment be offered here to guide Centres in their planning and
presentation of work leading to the production of each of the required
assignments listed above.

The variety, quality and sheer mercilessness of candidates' continuing
ideological *blitzkrieg* on "English Literature" continues to provoke official
admiration of the highest order. Assignments set by British Centres
continue to be circulated by the Commission throughout the European
Republic as exemplar material which other national Divisions endeavour
to emulate. Indeed it must be said, at the risk even of sounding patriotic,
that no other national "Literature" seems capable of provoking a response
of such venomous and vitriolic dimensions as "English Literature" has
among candidates taking T&T A this year.

Some words of caution ought, nonetheless, to be offered. In particular,
iconoclastic techniques which may have seemed pioneering in the early
years of the syllabus now seem distinctly *passé*. For instance, it should be
noted that "manic footnoting", in which vast acres of patently absurd
scholarly apparatus are painstakingly attached to each square inch of a
canonical "literary work", was originally introduced into English poetry by
Alexander Pope in his eighteenth century mock-epic, *The Dunciad*. The
general feeling in Review Panel meetings regarding this matter was that the
use of a technique perfected by an "author" who was himself a member of

the capitalist "Eng. Lit." canon was ideologically dubious. Although candidates were not penalised this year for indulging in this practice, the Division has decided henceforth actively to discourage it. On the other hand, "cartoon" versions of "literary classics" were marked down this year, as it was indicated in last year's report that such versions had belatedly been used by the declining imperialist "Eng. Lit." establishment in a desperate last ditch manoeuvre to popularise its bankrupt concept of "the literary". (For instance, Martin Rowson's comic strip, *The Waste Land*, published by Penguin Books in 1990, appeared on a list of prescribed texts in a JMB English Literature A-level syllabus seven years later, whereas the T. S. Eliot poem which inspired it did not.) Again, the Review Panels felt that a practice sanctified by the cultural dogmatism of the twentieth century *literati* must not be permitted in the context of a syllabus designed (among other things) to expose this group as profoundly anti-social, and that those Centres which had ignored the clarion call in last year's report to desist from doodling needed to be chastened.

Two innovatory iconoclastic textual strategies, one signally ingenious and the other devastatingly simple, deserve to be recommended. The first took the form of a stream-of-consciousness interior monologue of "the author" at the time of composition of one of "his" works. As this unfolded, it usually became obvious that "the author" was indulging in precisely the behaviour which "his" work was expressly moralising against, so that, for instance, Walt Whitman was presented as experiencing a masturbatory climax at the exact moment of writing the line about "grey sick faces of onanists". Even more remarkable, however, was an assignment submitted by a candidate from Eagletonshire, which simply reproduced *in toto* and without comment the entire extant verse of Philip Larkin as an illustration of how self-evidently absurd and ridiculous "English Literature" always was.

So much for the excellent work of candidates which celebrated the death of "Eng. Lit." (assignment no. 1). Can praise of the same order be applied to the work of candidates undertaken in controlled conditions (assignment no. 2)? The general model for this assignment is, of course, Roland Barthes' revolutionary *Mythologies* of 1957, and it was thus perhaps predictable that a number of Centres should encourage candidates to analyse the "text" of the life-size inflatable effigies of Barthes which have become commercially available in this, the year in which the ninetieth anniversary of his birth has been so widely celebrated. While many of the resultant assignments were quite innocent, a number of teachers who employed these artefacts to encourage their pupils in an assignment entitled "Barthes Meets the Bread Van: the Conjunction of High and Low Culture in Paris in 1980" should perhaps have foreseen that questions of taste and propriety were at issue in re-enacting before their charges the conspiracy by which the Sunblest company assassinated one of capitalism's most trenchant adversaries. It is also at least arguable that diesel fumes in the exam hall will have rendered the conditions uncontrolled. In any case, the stimulus and the assignment seem unnecessarily elaborate. The effigy alone, inflated or deflated, dressed or undressed, and perhaps wearing a Roman hairpiece, would have provided quite adequate inspiration. As this suggests, the simpler the stimulus, the more focused the assignment tended to be. This was especially true of obviously Freudian offerings (analyses of bananas, uprooted trees, gushing fountains, etc.) which, though a century out of date, remain as reliable as ever.

Assignment no. 3 caused a number of problems for Centres new to the syllabus. Here, a somewhat unforgivable historical ignorance was at work in an over-reliance on left wing textbooks left over from the late capitalist era. Polemics whose anachronistic content is indicated by titles such as "Troops Out of Ireland" and "Trident Must Go", however salutary their politics, have very little currency in a demilitarised twenty-first century European Socialist Republic. Some Centres seem not to have been keeping an eye on the newspapers over the last decade or so! However, it is pleasing to note that few similar blunders were made overall in work conducted for assignment no. 4. The implicit threat in last year's examiner's report (to quote: "the notion that *animals* constitute an historically exploited majority is indisputably undialectical") seems to have been universally heeded, so that this frankly boring and tiresome topic seems irreversibly to have bitten the dust. New pseudo-categories continue to emerge (e.g., "Lecturers in English Literature" and "RP speakers" as currently victimised minorities and "Pedestrians" and "The Unborn" [??!!] as historically oppressed majorities). Despite - indeed, because of - their laughable absurdity, appeals in favour of these groups were usually not penalised on the assumption that they were intentionally parodic (i.e., originating in irreverent impulses which are seen to be concordant with the aims of the syllabus).

The prevalence of "poetic" samples of textuality in assignment no. 5 remains worrying, as does the pool of "poetic" texts chosen. Seamus Heaney, Roger McGough and Wilfred Owen are all still alive and kicking in this corner of the syllabus. This is not in itself objectionable (although chief moderators in some regions would disagree), but concern was voiced on several of the Review Panels that the full range of past and contemporary textuality was seldom reflected in submissions for this assignment: across the entire year, indeed, there was not one single submission dealing with *Class War*, *The Little Red School Book* or the S.C.U.M. [Society for Cutting Up Men] *Manifesto*, all firm favourites in earlier years of the syllabus. Anarchism, it seems, is out of favour among secondary school teachers, even within the rather secure confines of a rule-bound GCSE syllabus. Moreover, while several centres did choose to analyse a videotext, only a handful of these continued to uphold an honourable tradition indicated by assignment titles such as "Following the Thatcherite Agenda: GCSE Examining Boards' Oral Communication Internal Trial Marking Videos, 1991". Fewer than usual chose to expose the historical determinations at work in GCSE subject syllabi of the pre-socialist era, although one candidate did submit an accomplished analysis (since published in *The English Magazine*) of rampant capitalist values in the Examiner's Report on the Northern Examining Association's English Literature Syllabus B GCSE Examination 1990 (and even this submission moved, notably, on the fringes of the subculture signified by the word "literature"). The Division is unable to propose a means, short of prohibiting "literary" texts in this assignment category, of ensuring that a fuller range of texts is treated. It will be launching a consultation exercise on the issue among avowedly socialist teachers in the near future.

The extremely poor performance of RP speakers in the "phonetic" category (assignment no. 6) continues, which, given the erstwhile social ascendancy of the class which RP speakers represent, is hardly a matter for concern. Indeed, attempts by RP speaking candidates to ape the language of their regionally accented colleagues seem, as ever, to have provided much comic relief during the serious business of final moderation. However, it is pleasing to record that grading was as ruthless as usual, and that no assignment in this category from an RP speaker was awarded higher than F+. It is equally a matter for congratulation that no regional speaker received lower than C-, suggesting that the nature of this assignment, nationally, has by now been well and truly understood. Quotation from a Glaswegian candidate's work evidences the liberatory effects of both this assignment and T&T A in general:

> lichricher is deid ya bam
> in stannard english snookered
> a kin tok the way ah whant
> withoot mi bein "choochterd"
>
> r.p.'s like a turd oan ma heel
> ma newscaster's fae devon
> oxbridge seems tae be a hell
> in bangor sounds lik heaven
>
> geez ma sontag in eisenstein!
> geez ma aphra behn!
> leonard fur laureate, kelman fur king
> in god bless walter benjamin!

marxismo's sure a braw thing
beats daily worship hawns doon
who'd read hughes ur gunn before
ra textuality a pontoon?

it's whit wiv always whantit
it's whit wiv always needit
in noo wiv bloody goat it
in it's no even oan credit

some folks whant some mare a it
bit that's ridic, a say
whit kin texts in textuality be
if no Texts and Textuality A?

giz *the pooh perplex* in derrida!
geeza bitta gramsci!
vocabolario internazionale
helps find a rhyme fur tumshie!

While this exemplifies the historical watershed which T&T A has
effected, one notices the contradiction of the first line and the
(caledoniased, yes, but unmistakeable) echoes of William Blake's "Preface"
to *Milton* in the third and seventh stanzas. The candidate's unbridled
enthusiasm for T&T A is also somewhat ironic, given the "compulsory and
optional" assignment (no. 7) in which candidates analyse the internal
contradictions of the T&T A syllabus itself. As usual, candidates who
identified implicit as well as explicit contradiction were rewarded for this,
while candidates who showed an appreciation of, enthusiasm for and a
genuine personal response to syllabic contradictions earned the highest
grades of all. Extensive comment on candidates' work in this area is,
however, unnecessary, as most of the assignments were highly competent
and themselves replete with internal contradictions which only a
navel-gazing examiner would wish to elaborate. Centres will in any case
have noticed that this year's revised syllabus permits candidates to expound
and examine the internal contradictions of this examiner's report instead of
the syllabus, if they so wish.

Your Average Working Kelman

What a pile of fucking shite! What a pile of absolute gibbers! The very idea
that such forms of conflict can be so resolved! This is straight bourgeois
intellectual wank. These fucking liberal excesses taken to the very limits of
fucking hyping hypocritical tollie.
— James Kelman, *A Disaffection* (London, Secker and Warburg, 1989),
p. 306

What I try and do ... I try and make them angry. ... Because making them
angry's a start. That's something. Even just making them angry.
— *ibid.*, p. 320

Ah fuck off, fuck off.
— *ibid.*, p. 337

Noo, whit ah mean is, fuck. Ah mean, fuckit, ye know, there ye are, in
the public library, ben the fiction section, scourin fur juridical stroke prison
fictions by geniuses of the early century, middle Europeans because yer
none too keen oan Jimmy Boyle and other recent homegrowns and
    There ye are then. Oan yer hunkers, Kafka in the left haun, the right
reachin oot fur Koestler, an ye see it. Kelman. Whit was the name a the
book — A DISINFECTANT? Naw. There it is. A DISAFFECTION.
Thats right. Kelman. Another homegrowner. Oan the telly the other night.
THE LATE SHOW, drivin roon in a Sierra mind ye, bit maybe they hired
it fur the day. It disni matter. He wis lookin anaemic an hardbitten, ergo
wan of us, ye think. A decent fella. Ordinary. A bit shy. Actually a bit of
a mumbler. As far fae Sarah Dunant as Pluto is fae Mercury. In fact, half
of whit he said completely·indecipherable. And thats good, shows he's the
real thing. Airs and graces have I none, shortlisted for the Booker though
I be. An something in ye relents, there, haufway tae the carpet in Stirlings
wi the fruits of the imaginative universe all aroon ye, something melts in
that iceberg at the centre of ye which sails proud and hard evry day against
the provincialism and small-mindedness of this city, and ye think, maybe
ahll give it a try. It says ONE IS TEMPTED TO MENTION ZOLA AND
BECKETT oan the cover, efter aw (quaint phrasing, THE
INDEPENDENT), which makes it a bit easier, a bit more palatable. And
no reviews from the GLASGOW HERALD either. Perhaps this is what yev
been waiting for all these years, a Scottish writer of truly international
standing or potential. Maybe Kafka and Koestler can wait. Ye get oot yer
card. The lassie at the issue desk says yer lucky to get a haud a this, it's
the wan evrybiddys readin. Specially since he wis oan telly the other night.

Aye. And then ye tuck it under yer arm till yer oan the bus. Ye huv a
quick look there, and yer no sure aboot it. Hell but, gie it a chance. So ye
take it hame and ye read it ower the next three days and ye finish it. And
ye realise it's complete absolute unadulterated fuckin shite.

Fooled again by the Scottish literary establishment. The bastards.

Whit dae ah mean? The beginnin, furra start. *Patrick Doyle was a*
teacher and he *found himself round the back of the premises* of his local
arts centre *for a pish*. Ah mean, fuck, eh? The usual. The usual impression
of Glasga. Ah mean, the arts centre's a licensed premises. It legally must
have a bog. So why's he roon the back, eh? Why isni he usin the nice
clean urinals in the bog like evry other cunt? Ahll tell ye why. Cause this
is a fuckin Glasga novel, that's why. And fictional Glaswegians canni be
bothered usin toilets. They'd much rather go doon the stairs and oot in the
cauld tae risk frostbite oan the bell-end than walk five yards tae the
antiseptic utopia of a postmodern water closet. This novel's not not called
A DISINFECTANT fur nothin. Either that or there is no bog, which
corroborates all the usual stereotypes of Glasga as a city in which laws are
not enacted (in this case legal enforcement of hygiene standards), or there
is a bog but Doyle is the example *par excellence* of the kind of wanker and
misfit who lives in this city in which, even when the legal *minima* are
provided, the locals refuse to take the opportunities thus presented. Ah ask
ye. Whit next, eh?

Ahll tell ye whit next. Doyle finds a pair a pipes. Industrial pipes. The
kind electricians use. Bit guess whit? Ye know that Magritte painting, the
wan that has oan it the slogan *Ceci n'est pas une pipe*? The wan of which
Michel Foucault said *Rien de tout cela n'est une pipe; mais un texte qui*
simule un texte; un dessin d'une pipe qui simule un dessin d'une pipe; une
pipe (dessinée comme n'étant pas un dessin) qui est la simulacre d'une pipe
(dessinée à la manière d'une pipe qui ne serait pas elle-même un dessin).
Sept discours dans un seul énoncé? Aye. Well then. The same holds. These
urni fuckin pipes either. Oh no. They *could be looked upon as a surrogate*
pet. Even better! a surrogate child! Or wife for god sake! In fact, these
pipes represented the whole wide world. With these pipes in tow anything
was possible. Nay! Probable! An there ye huv it. Doyle is lonely, sex-
starved, an a fuckin loony wi delusions a grandeur. A typical fuckin
Glaswegian. The Glaswegian known tae us all from evry other fuckin
representation a west a Scotland manhood. Compare wan Duncan Thaw in
wan *Lanark. Mister Patrick Doyle — Mister Patrick Doyle, a wee boy, not*
yet a man, not yet a husband and/or father, a bachelor, a single chap.
What a life. What a fucking life. Ah mean, eh — eh?

An don't forget Patrick Doyle is as Irish a name as ye could get and so
the Irish are coppin it in the neck wi this representation as well. As well
as evry Glesga Joe.

Aye, Patrick Doyle, a specimen of sheer negativity, full of hate, a malcontent supreme, god knows what he'd do in a Camus novel. But there's no fear of things ever goin that far. Oh and by the way, nearly evry bastard smokes in this book. And they drink like fuckin sperm whales. The imaginative territory of the book is wan that seems never to have been invaded by central heating either. An evry bastart swears evry fuckin second sentence.

Doyle takes most of whit he's only himsel tae blame fur oot oan the kids he teaches (able tae translate Latin at eleven, by the by, in a Glasga comp!). He quotes Pythagoras at them (the *Pears Cyclopaedia* knowledge of the great pre-Socratic Eleatic really grates here), thinks aboot Goya instead of teaching them (Thames & Hudson Goya consulted), has them reciting vacuous political propaganda: *The present government, in suppressing the poor, is suppressing our parents — Our parents, who are the poor, are suffering from an acute poverty of the mind — We are being fenced in by the teachers at the behest of a dictatorship government in explicit simulation of our parents the silly bastards viz. the suppressed poor.* Pure projection, mind ye. It's Doyle who's suppressed, mentally poor, fenced in, and a silly bastard. Maybe the whole thing's a fable about this kind of way of projectin meanins oanti a community fae the particular vantage point of the spiritual cretinism Doyle enjoys. Himsel, Doyle says his favourite job would be a *beachcomber*, which suggests a certain level of romantic pissed-affedness wi his lot past and present: *When Patrick's parents forced him into going to university because let's face it they hadnt done that at all although having said this of course he had in no sense desired to attend that institution, especially because he had or had not wanted to go in the first fucking place.* Which makes ye want tae sae it's make yer fuckin mind up time Kelman. *This stuff is only palatable with vodka.*

Oan it goes, is it must tae be a book, fur, fuck me, three hunnern thirty seven pages a tripe like this. Nae real story, mind ye, nuthin ye could analyse in a properly Proppian way, if ye ask me, though that's only ma personal opinion, it might stand correction. Doyle's goat an unhealthy sexual obsession wi a colleague, Alison Houston (wi characteristic sexist bastardry — characteristic of this modality of the Glasgow novel, I should say — she gets referred tae as *Mirs Houston*) that makes him behave wi worse juvenility than his first yearers. Which may be why he says *one of the dangers inherent to the teaching racket is starting to act out the character parts of the topics you get paid to encounter*, although he maybe means *pupils you get paid to encounter*. Either that or this is a code tae help us decipher wankpig Patrick Doyle himsel, who's obviously read sa many Glasga novels that he actually thinks, talks and behaves the way their protagonists do. Life imitatin art, ye might say. More accurately, strife

imitatin fart (*Salvador Dali: better to fart in company than die in a corner*).
But not somethin tae take it face value anyways and ye know ye know

Next thing, still Friday night, old paper Doyley's oan the em seventy
fuckin four headin south fur Sassenachtopia, leavin it aw behind. Gets as
far as Motherwell but by that time the references tae philosophers are
drappin oot a the text like birdshit oot the sky oan a spring mornin.
Heraclitus gets short shrift (*fuck Heraclitus* it says), ye might think because
he wrote sa impenetrably that only aristocrats and scholars could
understawn him. Bit this might be true a Kelman himsel, fur aw his surface
intelligibility. Efter aw, what's understandin worth when ye canni actually
see the point? (While ahm oan this though, ye don't huv tae huv read *The
Psychopathology of Everyday Life*, though ah huv, tae make sense a *fuck
Hera-clit-us*, don't ye think. Obvious as fuckin sunshine. Tae coin a
phrase.) There's a pretty patent Heraclitean point bein made here, mind ye,
aboot the illusion a Doyle's surface unity beneath which seethes a flux a
prejudice, inadequacy an sheer drab wankery, but that disnae get
emphasised. Heraclitus is just fucked in favour a Kierkegaard, Dostoievski,
a sly wee pseudo-ignorant reference tae Nietzsche (*So God is dead is he,
well well well. Where did that come from?*) an meditations oan suicide.
Welcome welcome all to existentialdom. Roll up roll up get yer Beckett
and bollocks, Camus and candy floss, de Beauvoir and Bovril. Sartre-and-
shite-sandwiches two furra pound. Existential literature has rolled inti
Glasga and no fur the first time. Keech ur whit — eh — eh? Patrick Doyle
MA (HONS) did his wan year a undergraduate philosophy awright. Drap
in the names Kelbo. Sprinkle oan the glitter. As Karl Jaspers said, go an
fuckin wank yersel.

Next thing owl Paddy's reached his existential crisis, a wee bit of a
premature ejaculation tae be honest. *It is these types of facts that Patrick
wishes to be capable of admitting. It is these types of facts he must be
capable of admitting, if ever he is to achieve a genuine vision, a genuine
honesty in his method of continuing.* Noo isn't that just whit ye wid call a
bubble a smegma, eh? The Problem of Authentic Existence. Who gives a
fucking camel's hump fur that these days eh? No fuckin me. An no you
either if ye were honest. Whit bastard wants tae be bothered wi a *method
of continuing*? Who the fuck's goat the time tae be fucked wi this fuckin
kind a fuck nooafuckindays? Ah mean, Paddy jist canni get his hole, an
that's the problem. He's a plain wanker an nuthin mare. Nae bastard needs
an existential philosopher tae tell them that. Most existential philosophers
couldnae get their holes often enough either. Whit is the myth of Sisyphus
anyway if no a wanker's allegory? Ah mean.

So instead a wankin himsel Paddy turns tae wankin the pipes,
manipulatin them aw kinds a ways an havin inane adolescent fantasies
centred roon these replacements fur his dick. Wan wish fulfilled is that

dream a evryman — of havin a big enough prick tae be able tae stick it in yer ain gub, an urgent male need not enough womenfolk seem prepared tae slake. Much masculine dissatisfaction in the early years of puberty oan this account, like dogs chasing their own tails, lasting until death unless compliant partner is located. A bad analogy that, the dog wan, though. Ever watched wi fascination and jealousy yer common or garden mongrel givin his ain knob-end a lavish tongue job? You bet Patrick has too. So he gets these pipes and he plays them. That's the verb, *plays*. He *blows* down them. Not a far cry from *playing with* them and giving them a *blow job*. All fuckin Freud-for-beginners stuff this (remember that line aboot the pipes bein *a surrogate pet!*). He's even got two so he can choose between a *fat* wan and a *thin* wan as his mood dictates. And then yer basic infantile exhibitionism creeps in: *he had fancied the idea of reaching such a pitch/level that he could put on a sort of performance, just of him and the pipes. A type of arty crafty avant-garde affair but so what, fuck off with your fucking inverted snobbery. What he could do was hire a large room somewhere and send out invitations to folk. It wouldni be too difficult.* Oh aye. Patrick Doyle MA (HONS) invites ye to a lunchtime session in which he will symbolically nibble his own dong. Entrance free. RSVP. Oh aye.

This in fact is whi he dis wi Alison Houston — gets her up in his hoose wan Sunday efternin an gets the ding an the dong oot and asks her tae admire them. Which she manages with great discretion. A fine woman, sorely compromised by the Doyle fella who's been huvin aw kinds a sordid imaginins about her tits, orifices et al. The explanation he gies her's a rather damn obvious rationale for the novel itself, by the way: *what I'm actually doing is blowing on them, getting sort of musical sounds out of them, a bit like eh — I dont really know, the concept I suppose is to do with improvisation, the way people take and use what they see lying about and I don't know just bloody christ use them, make music.* Aye. An excuse for sheer lack of craft, that wan. A bit like throwin a chimpanzee intae a world ping pong championship, publishin a book like this, if ye ask me. Shortlisted for the Booker Prize, criterion invoked: pity. Alison asks him if he's painted the pipes and he says *Aye. But I've never been quite sure about that either, about whether I would have been best to just leave them in their natural state.* An Alison asks *Though who's to say what their natural state really is* and Doyle goes *Aye christ, exactly.* For *them* and *their* here read *characters in this novel* and for *I* read Kelbo, the author, posturing unsure as to whether to craft his characters *à la* aesthetic form or recycle a dubiously understood reality with all its excesses and redundancies, and when aw's said an done daein neither but fudgin the issue page in page oot. *Not to worry too much about events over which you exercise no control. Over which you have lost control is more like it. In fact that sums it up. Control has been had and eschewed so fuck it. Really.*

Ye can accuse me a vulgarly wantin tae know where I stawn, a wantin tae be securely positioned bi the narrative, *fenced in by the* author *at the behest of a dictatorship* diegesis, ye can say that if ye want bit bit

Fuck this Doyle character.

He's informed by the heidie of the school that his transfer's come through — a transfer he disni remember applyin fur. Foolish conversation wi headie and kids follows. Pukes up aw ower the classroom floor and sawdusts it. Goes pretty fuckin mental that night. Phones up Alison. Meets her in a pub, tries tae force the issue till eventually she says whit the reader has been feelin aw this time: *I don't want to have a relationship with ye.* Good fur you hen. Kick him in the chucks as well! *I just can't have a relationship with ye Pat.* Even efter that he tries a snog in a doorway, the pathetic bastard, an gets a big bloody hard on. Poor wummin eventually histi dive in a taxi tae make an escape.

Next day he fucks aff oota school at lunch time withoot tellin anybiddy, pisses aff up tae his brother's hoose, Gavin. Boozes like hell aw efternin wi Gavin an Davie and Arthur. *They got on fine together. They were friends. And they were not all making him feel excluded; that was one thing, they were not making him feel awkward. That's two things.* This belongingness is purely momentary, needless tae say. *Things were alright before I came. Now that I am here things are not alright. I should not have come and then things would still be fine; yous three neighbours would be fine. Instead of that in came myself and fucked up the proceedings, the atmosphere, clouded things over, making things go awry.* Too fucking right Doyley. Me an Kafka an Koestler wid a goat oan jist fine if you hadni butted yer neb in. Nae wonder Gavin gets wicked aff wi this bastard of a brother (*Imagine calling your brother a bastard! Strange statement!*), this embourgeoisified alienated dickchugger of a brother (*Do you mean me? Are you fucking calling me a middle-class wanker?*), tellin the unemployed Gavin he's packin his joab in. More maudlin self-pity heaped oan an already engorged bitterness (*I mean I canni understand people who arent awful bitter*). Cunt needs executed, encouraged in his suicide bids. Then he goes hame. End.

Whit the whole thing desperately lacks is a Hegelian conceptual framework, a bit a dialectics. Apart fae Pythagoras, Hegel is the philosopher maist mentioned. Unlike Doyle *Hegel was never near to insanity. He never was. Or so we are given to understand. He had a good cheery lifestyle as a student. He caroused with women and drink.* Aye, good auld G.W.F. Between writin those great indigestible chunks a *The Phenomenology a Mind* he found time tae plentifully shag his landlady and father a son. Then he married a wummin half his age and had a further two. The new wife even took in the bastard eftir the landlady died. Doyle could a learned so much fae a man like that. *Hegel was fucking good,*

*good, a good ordinary man amongst men who enjoyed a bevy and a screw
and a carousing singsong with all his cronies.* Doyle so much wants tae be
a man like that, in fact. Bit he disnae hiv the mental equipment that can
cope wi the *Phenomenology*, that's the problem. *Hegel is a devilishly hard
fellow to comprehend. Some of what he has to say for himself is so
positively disbelievably believable, disbelievably believable.* ONE IS
TEMPTED TO MENTION Hegel's own acknowledgment in the Preface
to the *Phenomenology* of the *complaints regarding the unintelligibility of
philosophical writings from individuals who otherwise possess the
educational requirements for understanding them.* ONE IS TEMPTED TO
QUOTE G.W.F.'s humorous observation (*loc. cit.*) of the same persons'
*complaint so often made against [philosophical writings]: that so much has
to be read over and over before it can be understood — a complaint whose
burden is presumed to be quite outrageous, and, if justified, to admit of no
defence.* If only Mr Doyle knew the difference between the determinate
negation of the Hegelian dialectic and the empty scepticism of his own
windbaggery. ONE IS above all TEMPTED TO CITE the great thinker's
pure fucking magic analysis of self-consciousness, desire, lordship and
bondage, master and slave (*vide* the *Phenomenology*, chapter IV [A]) as a
way of understanding poor Mr Doyle's existential plight. The philosopher
Ivan Soll complains aboot the *extreme fuckin opacity* of Hegel's text here
(actually ahm no sure if he swore) and another yin, Richard Norman,
remarks that *since I find large parts of it unintelligible, I shall say little
about it.* Ha ha. The world's full a cop-oot merchants. A shame that Doyle
seems to have listened tae them rather than Hegel himsel. For slavery is a
word Patrick's overfond of using unreflectively (*It's always the bosses that
have the dialogue and then arrive at the decisions for them — well in fact
it's for themselves really but they kid on it's for the slaves they're doing it*).
Hegel, but, teaches us that the master is enslaved by slavery. It's all to do
with bloody *Selbstbewusstein*, self-consciousness, intit? Self-consciousness
depends oan recognition a the self bi others, but others threaten tae put a
limit tae the self, and so the self finds itself (if ye see whit ah mean) in
perpetual combat for domination a other selves. The self strives tae be
fucking lord and master over other selves, get it? Tae make other selves
slaves tae it, the master self. Clear enough. This is, after all, whit Doyle
wants tae dae tae Mirs Houston, and whit he does dae tae the kids in his
classes. It's also whit he hates having done tae himself by the likes of Old
Milne, the heidie, and maist a the world in general. Problem is (back tae
Hegel) neither category — master, slave — remains fixed. The master
needs tae be acknowledged, eftir aw. Thing is, the acknowledgment a
slaves is fuck all use. A slave stops bein a self eftir a while an becomes a
mere thing, an artefact incapable of anything that wid count as
acknowledgment. Ergo slaver enslaved because there's fuck all to give

enslaver acknowledgment. Fuckin simple. Mirs Houston, refusing to be enslaved, does Doyle a favour by rejecting him. When she says *I don't want to have a relationship with ye* she is turning down the slavery of being impaled oan Doyle's dong, being *fenced in* by his fantasies. She is thus preventing Doyle's own enslavement, which'd be consequent oan his enslavement of her. Doyle thus remains truly free, although it is a condition a that freedom tae remain unsatisfied, because of his lack of mastery (*I dont understand ye. You're clever and you've got a good well-paid job. You've only got yourself to look after. You can do whatever ye want. If ye dont like something ye can just get up and leave. You're free. And yet you're still no satisfied. That's what I think's wrong. But that's always how things are: the ones that want something never get it and the ones that get it areni satisfied, they just want something else.*) Booker prize shortlist, category: Hegelian theme. If only Doyle knew it. When he says/thinks/feels *Ah fuck off, fuck off* at the end, he frees the world by telling it to fuck aff, prevents its enslavement, which'd be the consequence of it enslaving him.

Ah fuck off, fuck off — the precise words ah flung the fuckin book at the wall with eftir finishin the fuckin thing. Ah thus refuse tae be fuckin enslaved by this stream a Glasga gibbers. Ah reject those acknowledgments, those fuckin blurbs, which swagger as lord and master over the book itself (*His style is endlessly inventive, his characters have huge souls and his point of view is uncompromising. If people don't start listening, they have only themselves to blame.* Maureen Freely, *Observer*. Is that a joke name, by the way — Freely? In this context? Must be.) In other fuckin words, ah liberated the text by refusing tae be enslaved by it, forced the fuckin thing tae be free.

Whit pissed me aff most wis wan fuckin remark near the end. It said: *The Red Road Flats is an awful place to live. When I was at school in Balornock I had a friend and she had a cousin living there and her mother killed herself.* Noo what I want tae say tae this is: *This is straight bourgeois intellectual wank.* How dae ah know? Cause ah fuckin lived in the Red Road fuckin Flats masel. Ah remember the chill day we moved in. Seventh a January sixty seven. A wis three an a quarter. Thirty three Petershill Drive, flat three stroke wan. Ah remember the warm day we left. Eleventh a May seventy nine. Ah wis fifteen an a hauf. Ah went tae school in Balornock — first Saint Martha's primary, then All Saints secondary. An ahll tell ye this, it was sheer virtually unmixed bloody pleasure fae beginnin tae fuckin end. The complete reverse, in other words, of this totally shitey book.

Only the Names
Have Been Changed

This is where the subject's basic institutional justification must be found. I can read books perfectly well outside the institution; if I am to be within the institution it must be in order to discuss my reading of those books with others — peers or experts. Given that, by definition, my reading will have been private and idiosyncratic, my need and desire is to negotiate that reading with others and thereby to learn more about the text which occasioned the reading, about myself, about others, and about my relation to all that.

> — Colin Evans, *English People: The Experience of Teaching and Learning English in British Universities* (Buckingham, Open University Press, 1993), p. 63

Being versus Having — that's the battle that's been going on since the year dot; and every time an artist's scored to win the match for Being, the shouts haven't died down but the critics have equalised. But the critics still have to fight it out amongst themselves to decide who scored the equaliser, and the university functions by "training" people in spotting who did. Existentially a student is a kind of reserve for the Having team, and the "ability" required to get a degree is to show one can negate any assaults that Being might make.

> — Tom Leonard, "The Proof of the Mince Pie", *Intimate Voices: Selected Work 1965-1983* (Newcastle upon Tyne, Galloping Dog Press, 1984), p. 66

Dear Student [...] why don't you read what I have written and make up your own mind about what you think, testing it against your own life, your own experience. Never mind about Professors White and Black.

> — Doris Lessing, Preface to *The Golden Notebook*

I can't go on, I'll go on.

> — Samuel Beckett, last words of *The Unnamable*

PRESENT: ALISON, CAROLE, DARREN, DR DALY, FRANCES, JENNY, ROBERT.

DR DALY   Well, good morning everybody. Okay. Now then. *The Golden Notebook*. Right. Now I'm going to say what I have to say about this novel in this afternoon's lecture, so what I'm wanting to hear this morning is what you, eh, what you think about it. Now then, Jenny here has, I think — **[laughs]** I hope! — prepared something —

JENNY   Yeah —

DR DALY   To start us off.

	[Pause.]
JENNY	Shall I — ?
DR DALY	Away you go!
JENNY	Right.

[Pause.]

I don't know how much of this'll make sense, but, er, I'm going to, to talk about Lessing's book and realism. I'm only following notes — haven't written it down — fingers crossed it won't be too garbled.

[Pause. Takes breath.]

Okay. Basically, the protagonist of *The Golden Notebook*, Anna Wulf, tells her psychoanalyst, a woman with the rather strange name of Mother Sugar, on page, er, four five eight, "I believe I'm living the kind of life women never lived before." She — i.e. Anna — thinks that as a female communist living in modern England she is experiencing something entirely new. Now, whether or not this is actually true, Lessing, er, seems to be suggesting that the conventional realist novel is incapable of conveying the whole experience of women, like Anna, in this kind of, um, situation. What *The Golden Notebook* seems to be, I think, is an example of a new form which will at least *attempt* to do this, to get across this kind of new experience, whatever it is. This new form is an example of — bit of jargon here — metafiction. According to Patricia Waugh, in her book *Metafiction*, which is about metafictions — sorry, that's a bit obvious — Waugh, she says that a metafictional text quote explores a theory of fiction through the *practice* of writing fiction unquote. That's from page two of the book. So in *The Golden Notebook* we find a text which does this. It puts an example of a realist novel — *Free Women* — side by side with, um, the four notebooks ... um ...

DARREN	Four ... ?
JENNY	Four ... yes, four ... there're four notebooks.
DARREN	Five. There's five. Isn't there five?
JENNY	Black, um, Red, Yellow, er, and Blue ... four ...
DARREN	There's a Golden one too.
JENNY	**[laughing nervously]** Oh, yeah, but I'm not counting that just yet.
DARREN	Oh, right, sorry.

[Pause.]

Didn't mean to interrupt.

[Pause.]

DR DALY	Okay?
JENNY	You want me to go on?
DR DALY	**[eager]** Mm!
JENNY	Okay, where was I? Yeah, these four notebooks try, eh, to convey the fragmentation of modern female experience. Now, eh — I've forgotten what point I was trying to get across — yes, and so the notebooks demonstrate the inadequacies of the realist novel, while simultaneously offering us an example of a new literary form. Is that all right? Everybody, um, with me so far?

[Silence.]

Okay.

[Pause.]

Right. Well, before examining how this is achieved, maybe we should perhaps first consider the basic structure of the novel. If you look at the Contents Page of the book, if you've got it, you'll see one way of representing it. Here's another way — a diagram I drew up. Sorry I've only got one copy but I'll, er, hold it up, like this, and point at it. This diagram is a bit different. From the Contents Page you'll see that *The Golden Notebook* — oh, I mean the whole novel, of course, not the actual Golden notebook Anna writes in, the one I forgot to mention earlier ... The book is structured on a cycle of five chapters of *Free Women* (which is a normal novel written in the third person), and it's interrupted by sections from the Black, Red, Yellow and Blue notebooks, which Anna Wulf keeps. This cycle is, eh, repeated in the same order four times and is followed by the contents of the, um, Golden notebook. See, I told you I'd get to it. The novel ends with a final section from *Free Women*. Now my diagram — hang on, er, I'll come back to that ...

[Pause while she shuffles her file cards.]

Yes, got it. The notebooks cover a seven year period beginning — I think! — in nineteen fifty, although their chronology is all mixed up — bit of a scrambled egg this book — with *Free Women*. Now, if I'm reading it right, we find out at the end that *Free Women* is the work of Anna herself. So although it's placed first in the text, it's actually composed last, if you see what I mean. That's why it appears at the bottom of my diagram, 'cause my diagram shows all the bits of the book in the order in which Anna writes them — well, almost — which is different from what you get on the Contents Page, which is the order we read the book in. So that kind of order, the order we read it in, is what you might call an assembled illusion. All the bits of the book were apparently written by Anna, but the order we read them in isn't the order she composed them in. My diagram shows you that. Sorry, I'm repeating myself, aren't I?

[Several reaction noises.]

DR DALY That's all right.

JENNY Oh, all right then. Now — yes — a lot of this novel's effect depends on the way it *disorders* all these bits. That's really important.

[Pause.]

Sorry, I seem to be a card short.

[Rummages in bag.]

Oh, I'm really sorry.

DR DALY It's interesting …

JENNY It's okay. It doesn't matter. I think I can remember the rest. Sorry. Right, there wasn't much more anyway.

DR DALY Okay …

JENNY I sort of wanted to end on a question and suggest an answer to it. The question was, er, if Lessing truly wanted to establish a new form to express modern experience, why did she bother including *Free Women*? Why didn't she just forget about realism altogether? 'Cause there are real problems with *Free Women* being the culmination of Anna's struggles, because by writing it she ends up writing the kind of novel which she has been condemning for most of the notebooks — the kind of novel which she says is inadequate, and she keeps going on about how if she doesn't find a language for her new experience she feels she's going to go bonkers. Well, Waugh says on page twelve of *Metafiction* that new literary forms are unlikely to, er, satisfy the reader unless they combine the new element with something familiar and conventional. So that might explain *Free Women*. Maybe Lessing also thought that in order to establish a new form the inadequacies of the old form must first be demonstrated. She does say in the Preface, er, page, em … sorry … something about a wordless statement, the book making a wordless statement. You know the bit I mean? Oh —

DR DALY I think it's page fourteen —

JENNY Well, anyway, the basic point I want to make is that putting

Free Women next to the notebooks works quite well in showing up the inadequacies of the realist novel. Apart from that I think the book's okay, but a bit depressing. Not the kind of book you'd take to bed with you.

DR DALY	Great, well —
ROBERT	I dunno —
DR DALY	Sorry?
ROBERT	It kept putting me to sleep anyway.
	[Pause.]
DR DALY	That bad?
ROBERT	**[wearily]** Mm.
	[Long silence.]
JENNY	Does it make sense?
	[General noises — "oh","er","um", etc.]
	[Pause. The clock in the quadrangle strikes the quarter hour.]
ALISON	It —
DARREN	It reminds me —
ALISON	Sorry! Er —
DARREN	Sorry. You know — it reminds me — you know that song, "Strange Brew"?
	[Pause.]
ROBERT	What, you mean the lager advert?
DARREN	**[guffawing]** No!
ROBERT	Eh?
ALISON	No, you mean Cream.
DARREN	Yes!
ROBERT	A cream advert?
ALISON	The band Cream, like **[beatnik imitation]** *in the sixties, MAN*!
ROBERT	Aw ...
CAROLE	Oh, you mean the one that — **[sings]** "Strange Brew, do what's inside-a you"?
DARREN	Yes.
JENNY	Oh yeah ...
ALISON	Yes!
CAROLE	Yes?
ROBERT	Nope ...
DARREN	Well, this book reminds me of that.
CAROLE	Really?
ALISON	But this is set in the fifties.
ROBERT	How d'you mean?
DARREN	Well, it's all mixed up, this book, innit? A strange brew.

	[Pause.]
ROBERT	Yes?
DR DALY	Uh-huh?
DARREN	Well — that's all.
	[Long silence.]
ROBERT	What does that mean?
JENNY	**[with sarcasm]** Deep!
DARREN	**[snorts]** Well, you called it a scrambled egg. Why can't I call it a strange brew?
JENNY	Yeah, but —
DARREN	In fact, when T.S.Eliot was asked to explain what some of his lines meant he just repeated them. Saying this is a strange brew is a bit better than just repeating it.
JENNY	**[protesting]** I didn't just repeat it!
CAROLE	It would take an *awful long time* to repeat this book ...
DARREN	And actually, actually, what you were saying, in this Preface here. She says, she says, actually, *actually*, that she wants the book to make a quote wordless statement unquote. *A wordless statement*. "Strange brew" is two words more than that.
ROBERT	Ah, um, but she takes six hundred pages to make a wordless statement, though.
DR DALY	Maybe this Preface — maybe what we should do is look at this Preface. What do you think?
DARREN	Good for a laugh.
DR DALY	But, no, I mean, it's saying some quite interesting things, wouldn't you say?
DARREN	**[so deadpan that he may be serious]** In my last essay I said something was "interesting" and you wrote "boring word" in the margin.
ALISON	This is a seminar, not an essay.
DARREN	It's a verbal —
CAROLE	I liked this Preface —
DARREN	— construction —
CAROLE	— better than the book.
DARREN	— all the same.
DR DALY	Uh-huh. Why was that?
CAROLE	Well ... well ... I —
DR DALY	Was it —
CAROLE	I, I agreed with it, yes.
DR DALY	Uh-huh. You mean you agreed with all of it, or, or — ?
ALISON	Yes, I liked it.
CAROLE	Well, this bit here for instance, page fifteen, where's she's,

	er, well, she's slagging off reviewers and critics and teachers. People like you, really.
DR DALY	Like me?
CAROLE	Mm, you know, no disrespect, like, but, yeah.
DR DALY	And so what did you agree with there?
CAROLE	Well, I thought she was right. She says, "It is not possible for reviewers and critics to provide what they purport to provide and for which writers so ridiculously and childishly yearn. This is because the critics are not educated for it; their training is in the opposite direction." I agreed with that.
DR DALY	Okay, but why? That's what I'm interested in. **[Pause.]**
CAROLE	Mm. Well, it just had the ring of truth about it.
DR DALY	D'you mean, er, that, that — well, that it answers to your own experience of reviewers and critics? Is that it?
CAROLE	Maybe. **[Pause.]** She goes on, doesn't she, to have a go at schools and indoctrination and all that?
DR DALY	Yes, yes — yes, she does ...
ALISON	Next page.
CAROLE	I agreed with all that as well.
DR DALY	Uh-huh. **[Long silence.]**
ROBERT	You mean — d'you mean this bit here, page seventeen, "You are in the process of being indoctrinated. We have not yet evolved a system of education that is not a system of indoctrination" blah blah blah? 'Cause if that's the bit you mean, I thought that was drivel, to be honest.
DR DALY	You did?
ROBERT	Oh God, yeah. Sounds like a lot of right wing ranting.
DR DALY	So you disagreed with the politics of it?
DARREN	What's right wing about it?
ROBERT	Sort of thing you hear from a Tory Cabinet minister.
DARREN	Oh, hang on a minute. On page fourteen — look at page fourteen: "I got intelligent criticism from people who were, or who had been, marxists. They saw what I was trying to do. This is because Marxism looks at things as a whole and in relation to each other".
CAROLE	Mm. Why has "marxists" got a little em and "Marxism" a big em there? Is that — is that important?
DR DALY	I don't think so.
DARREN	So it's left wing ranting, not right wing ranting. **[Pause.]**

ROBERT	You can have right wing Marxists, you know.
DARREN	Sorry?
JENNY	But I don't think it is ranting, you know — I think it's reasonable. It sounds just like my school.
DR DALY	Righto — so somebody *does* think it answers their own experience.

[Long silence.]

ALISON	What kind of school was that then?
JENNY	Cath-
DARREN	Aw, but, come on —
JENNY	-olic.
DARREN	— I mean, listen to this bit 'ere: "Those of you who are more robust and individual than others, will be encouraged to leave and find ways of educating yourself — educating your own judgement. Those that stay must remember, always and all the time, that they are being moulded and patterned to fit into the narrow and particular needs of this particular society." She's just a grumpy author annoyed at not having a degree.

[Pause.]

ROBERT	The bit that gets me is about educating yourself — "your own judgement". The idea that you just toddle off and have thoughts all on your own. But how can you, er, think at all outside of society? Brain in a vat.
DR DALY	You find that idea too Romantic?
ROBERT	Definitely. She says the ones who stay are being fitted up for society. I suppose that's us, university students. But she's got this screwy idea that the ones who leave school earlier do so because they're brighter and, um, that they then spend the rest of the time educating themselves! Well, my big brother left school at sixteen and he's a complete moron.

[Laughter.]

JENNY	Ah, but that's just your opinion. He probably thinks you're a moron as well.
ROBERT	Uh-huh. But I'm right.
JENNY	Well, how d'you know? She says you don't have thoughts of your own. Not real thoughts, anyway.
ROBERT	[laughs] 'Cause I'm better educated than he is!
DR DALY	Well, that's a bit of a circular argument, but — I mean, can we perhaps try to talk about this in slightly less anecdotal terms? You know, like, how does this fit in with the novel, what's going on in the novel? Why has she bothered to

write this Preface? What has this got to do with the kind of
ideas in the book, 'cause, because — well, it's a kind of
defence of the book, against the ways it was being read in
those ten years or so before she wrote the Preface, isn't it?
She says that on page fourteen again, she's complaining
about what she calls quote the parochialism of our culture
unquote, and so maybe we'd do well to be a little less
parochial ourselves in discussing this, no? She's saying that
nobody really noticed the central theme of the book — or
what she sees as the central theme of the book — that's on
page eight — where she says that the main theme is
"breakdown": quote sometimes when people crack up it is
a way of self-healing, of the inner self's dismissing false
dichotomies and divisions unquote. Now, okay, she's saying
that people didn't understand this theme, isn't she, because,
yes, alright, they've been educated to read books in
extremely narrow ways, so that's that point. And she spends
a lot of time complaining in the Preface about the dreary
ways in which critics and reviewers fail utterly to register
when a new kind of text appears on the scene, how they're
the last people you should expect to have the kind of mental
equipment to deal with that kind of novelty, that kind of
novel. Okay. So the Preface is kind of clearing the decks of
the obstacles placed in the text's way, really, isn't it? Well,
okay, fine — what next? Do you think the book is actually
doing what she thinks it's doing?
[Long silence.]
What about this idea of "breakdown"? What's the text
saying about that?
[Long silence.]
Any ideas?
[Pause.]
Has it got anything to do with this kind of formal
experiment that Jenny mentioned in her talk?
[Long silence.]
Frances?
[Pause.]
What do you think?
[Long silence.]

FRANCES   [her first utterance] Er ...
ROBERT   It nearly gave *me* a breakdown, I can tell you that.
CAROLE   Yeah. Yeah. I mean, liked the Preface, okay, but — the
           rest of it, cor, slog or what, you know?

DR DALY	Uh-huh.
DARREN	She's a manic depressive, really, isn't she?
DR DALY	You mean Anna? Is it as simple as that?
DARREN	No, I mean Doris Lessing.
DR DALY	Oh.
ALISON	But you can't just deduce something about the author because of what the book's about. I mean — well, um, whatsisname, I mean, wasn't necessarily in a good mood when he was writing his comedies.
CAROLE	Well, they're not very funny, are they?
ROBERT	Shakespeare? Didn't he have a dark period or something?
DARREN	Tell you what, I think Doris Lessing was having a period when she wrote this!

[DARREN is the only one who laughs, and far too rumbustiously. Sounds of tutting from all of the women, except FRANCES. Long silence before DARREN tries to rehabilitate himself.]

Aw, okay, bad taste, bad taste. Sorry, but, I mean, you know, only someone on a real downer could have written this, if you ask me. Not a happy camper.

[Pause.]

DR DALY	Don't you think you're reading too much of Anna into the author? I mean, Anna isn't depressed all the time, and they can be separated, can't they? What do you think?
DARREN	I'll take a lot of convincing.
JENNY	Thing is, Darren, right, you've made your mind up already, haven't you? And nothing's going to change it.
DARREN	What's wrong with making your mind up? If nobody ever made their mind up we'd be in a right mess.
JENNY	Yeah, but we're meant to be *discussing* it.
DARREN	I *am* discussing it. I'm just not likely to change my mind discussing it.
ROBERT	I think you don't like this book because it's by a woman. You never like books by women.
DARREN	I never said I didn't like it! I said she was a manic depressive. *You* were the one who said you didn't like it.
ROBERT	I said it nearly gave me a breakdown. I didn't say I didn't like it.
CAROLE	Oh …
DARREN	But you don't like it, do you?
ALISON	Huh —
ROBERT	No, but —
DARREN	See!

ROBERT	— do you, then? Are you seriously saying you like this book?
DARREN	No.
ROBERT	Ah-ha!
CAROLE	Oh ...
DR DALY	Alright, okay, look, what I'm — what I'm really not clear about — not clear about at all — is the reasons for you both disliking it.
ROBERT	He doesn't like it because it's by a woman.
DARREN	That is NOT TRUE!
ROBERT	God, you liked that Joyce *Portrait* thing and that was totally depressing. And Kafka, blooming hell —
DARREN	But you can't — hah, you *just can't* — say Joyce and Kafka in the same breath as Lessing! Come on. Can you? *Can you?*
	[Pause.]
JENNY	Okay then, so *why* don't you like it?
DR DALY	Can I —
CAROLE	I don't like it either.
DR DALY	Maybe —
ALISON	Actually —
JENNY	Yeah?
ALISON	— I have to agree.
DR DALY	Maybe we aren't getting anywhere just giving personal — what was that, Alison?
ALISON	Pretty grim. Hated it. And the other thing is, well, so *old-fashioned*. Not old-fashioned, exactly — er, outdated ... out of date ...
	[Pause.]
DR DALY	Go on. What do you mean, exactly?
ALISON	Er, well —
CAROLE	I know what you mean. Nobody could get worked up about these things any more — communism, single mothers, all that *angst* —
DARREN	Yeah, vaginal orgasms.
	[Embarrassed silence.]
	There *is a bit in here* where she goes on about vaginal orgasms. I asked my girlfriend about that. She does psychology. Said Lessing must have got it from Freud. Says it's a lot of crap.
JENNY	**[venomously]** Surprised your girlfriend has any orgasms *at all*.
	[Another lengthy, ponderous silence. This last remark

	has raised the temperature.]
DR DALY	**[with what may be irony, but primarily trying to douse the flames]** Well, this is interesting. Interesting to see that a simple novel really can get people debating so excitedly. Says something about the text itself, that, don't you think? **[Pause. Some clearing of throats.]**
FRANCES	**[her second utterance]** Er … **[She coughs.]**
DR DALY	Mm?

[Silence. The clock in the quadrangle strikes the half hour.]

Has anybody read anything else by Doris Lessing by any chance?

[Negative reaction noises.]

Oh well.

[Pause.]

I'm still not at all certain, and I'd like to know, really I would, the *basis* for the universal dislike of the book. That is, I want to know what kind of criteria are working behind that judgment, what kinds of assumptions you've been bringing to the book, what kind of expectations it disappointed. I'm not sure we've got very far with those questions. Whatever we think of a book, I suppose that's what we're here for, to try and get to the root of *why* we think that way. I think we need to dig a little bit more. At the moment we're hardly getting beyond the expression of dislike. Okay, we've said something about it being out of date in inverted commas but we could say that about Charles Dickens or Jane Austen. And it wouldn't, on reflection, be a very impressive argument. There has to be a stronger basis than that.

JENNY	Tell us why *you* like it then.
DR DALY	Well, no, that would compromise the seminar. I'll say what I have to say in the lecture. This is your discussion time, not mine.
CAROLE	Oh, go on!

[A silence of refusal from DR DALY.]

FRANCES	**[her third utterance]** Er …

[An expectant pause. She continues, nervously.]

I've been doing a subsidiary course in Business Management.

DR DALY	**[having left a gap which was not filled]** Uh-huh?
FRANCES	We've read a book by someone called Hampden-Turner. *Charting the Corporate Mind*. He's got a chapter in it called

"The Hunt for the Unicorn".

DR DALY   **[wary]** Mm, yes?

FRANCES   There's a quote in it I remember. It's a study of big, really big companies, computers, petrol, electronics, that kind of thing. It's all about what he calls *dilemmas*, how most of these companies have two major ways of thinking or seeing. They should follow both at once but can't because they think they're incompatible. They end up getting stuck on one of the two horns.

[Several mystified noises.]

DR DALY   Right. I see.

FRANCES   **[sighing with relief]** Do you? Oh, good.

DR DALY   I mean — **[he rouses himself]** — *no*, I don't see. Please go on.

FRANCES   Oh. Well, er, er, the thing is, I've been listening to what everybody's been saying and this Hampden-Turner thing seems to fit it.

ALISON   You've lost me. Completely. I'm very suspicious of all this business guff.

FRANCES   **[starting to withdraw]** Uh huh —

CAROLE   Me too.

ROBERT   Capitalist conspiracy.

[DARREN tuts.]

FRANCES   **[deciding to try once more]** It's just that there seemed to be two horns in what you were saying, Dr Daly.

[Everybody bridles at "Dr Daly", including DR DALY. We may also assume some uneasiness about the word "horn". FRANCES does not notice, or seems not to.]

One the one hand — on the one *horn* — a lot of what's been said in reaction to the book has been — "anecdotal", you called it, I think. People have given sort of gut reactions to the book, negative ones. On the other horn, what you're asking for is an explanation, an elaboration of the reasons behind these reactions, the causes, the ideas that govern them.

DR DALY   **[getting interested]** Right.

FRANCES   But the thing is, as soon as those reasons are worked out and explained the reaction is no longer a gut reaction. We're on the other horn of the dilemma then.

DR DALY   So ... so ... really what you're saying is — it's a well-known dilemma really — the first horn is the affective faculty and the other the cognitive.

FRANCES   Er ...

[Several sounds of bafflement.]

DR DALY   You aren't familiar with those terms, cognitive, affective? Sorry, then. Never mind. Call one *feeling*, the other *thinking*.

CAROLE   Which is which?

ALISON   Affective — feeling. Cognitive — thinking.

ROBERT   I've no idea where all of this is leading. I get the gist — you want us to think instead of feel about the text, right?

DARREN   But we don't feel like thinking.

[He chuckles but no one is impressed.]

FRANCES   **[excited]** Yes, think *instead of* feel. In other words, you get pulled off the horn of feeling and impaled on the horn of thinking. One or the other. Now the quote I remember from the Hampden-Turner book is "any one value or criterion of excellence pursued in isolation is almost bound to steer you into trouble". The trouble is that these two kinds of reading can't be matched up. In private, reading is about feeling — and gut reactions. In public, accounts of reading are about thinking — or thinking in a way that cancels out, I mean, fails to recognise, those feelings. I know this is kind of theoretical — well, maybe even a meta-theory.

CAROLE   **[who has evidently lost the thread some time ago]** Eh?

DARREN   I once met a theory. Its name eludes me now.

[ROBERT groans.]

DR DALY   I see what you're driving at, Frances, but I can't help thinking the dichotomy is a false one. Gut reactions aren't feelings *separate from* thought. You must be thinking to *have* gut reactions in the first place. What I was asking for —what no one was revealing, or making the effort to find out — were the thought processes that *led to* the gut reactions.

FRANCES   I wasn't saying that. I wasn't saying, er, there are no thoughts at that stage. What I was saying was that concentrating on the thoughts — or what you're prepared to *recognise* as thoughts — might, can, does ignore the actual complexity of the feelings, including what goes into the feelings *as well as* thought. I think that's the kind of narrow reading Lessing's attacking in the Preface. Maybe the feelings are to do with things, as well as thoughts, that can't actually *be talked about*.

DR DALY   But if they can't be talked about ... I can't ask you to talk about them ... I can only ask you to talk about what you can talk about ... if I want you to talk ...

FRANCES	Yes.
DR DALY	So the hunt for the unicorn —
DARREN	**[impatiently]** There is no such thing as a unicorn! It's an entirely mythical creature! **[Pause.]**
ROBERT	And, er, a bit phallic as well, isn't it?
FRANCES	There may be things about this novel which we cannot say. Which we cannot say here or, if we can, only each to ourselves.
ALISON	Yeah, I see what you mean.
JENNY	"My major aim was to shape a book which would make its own comment, a wordless statement: to talk through the way it was shaped." Yeah.
CAROLE	Help, somebody, what has that got to do with it? I'm completely in the dark.
DR DALY	These rejections of the book, then — that it's boring, mixed up, depressing — these are all — what? — statements in words concealing the wordless statements? Methods of repressing the actual turbulence of feeling a novel like this sets off?
FRANCES	Maybe. Maybe.
DR DALY	The problem I have with that is that it turns the reading of a text into a desperately private thing, almost incommunicable, only partly communicable.
FRANCES	Why should that be a problem?
DR DALY	It's a problem for this kind of —
CAROLE	Turbulence of feeling? Nobody said they had any turbulence of feeling.
JENNY	Nobody *admitted* they had.
DARREN	All right then, let's put it to the test. Quite simple. Anyone who experienced a turbulence of feeling when they read this book put up their hands. **[Silence.]** No hands. No turbulence of feeling.
ALISON	You know that doesn't follow. **[Pause.]**
ROBERT	"Turbulence of feeling" — that's Raymond Williams, isn't it?
FRANCES	I was reading an article in the library this morning by — what was it — Punter. It's about teachers and students in university English departments.
DR DALY	Punter?
DARREN	Imagine being called Punter!

FRANCES   David Punter.

CAROLE   How do you find time to read all these other things? I'm up to my ears in crits all day.

FRANCES   I don't read crits.

CAROLE   None at all?

FRANCES   Not really. I'm more interested in the theory and pedagogy of the subject.

CAROLE   Oh ... um ...

FRANCES   There was a good bit in this article on the "development of critical ability" that doing an English degree seems to be all about. I wrote it down.

ROBERT   Go on then. Sock it to us.

FRANCES   "There is only a very distant correlation between the nature of the psychological investment effected in fictions by people between the ages of fourteen and eighteen, which has much to do with the vicarious experiencing of alternative selves and ways of being, and with the evasion of aspects of familial authority, and that kind of investment which is presumed by English departments, which has more to do with induction into various largely unstated authority structures through the dual medium of text and faculty member."
           [Pause.]

ROBERT   Was there a full stop in any of that? I bet there wasn't. It really annoys me how they always deliberately write in long sentences. Ought to do a class in prose style.

CAROLE   That last bit again. Read the last bit.

FRANCES   " ... induction into various largely unstated authority structures through the dual medium of text and faculty member" — i.e., in this case, the novel and Dr Daly.
           [More discomfort at FRANCES' formality of designation.]

CAROLE   So, am I getting this right, those are the two horns then, are they, the book and —

ALISON   A sort of double-pronged attack on us, it makes out.

DR DALY   Let's —

FRANCES   No, those two things together make up *one* of the horns.

CAROLE   *One* of the horns? Oh dear.

DARREN   It's a blinkin' *foghorn* we're going to need to get us out of this, I'm telling you.

ROBERT   **[laughing]** That's a good 'un.

FRANCES   The two horns are two different ways of reading. I'll go over it. The first horn is quote the psychological investment effected in fictions by people between the ages of fourteen and eighteen unquote. The second horn is quote that kind of investment which is presumed by English departments unquote.

DR DALY   Which horn does Lessing want to impale us on?

JENNY   **[excited]** I've got it!

DR DALY   Sorry?

JENNY   There are two horns in this novel too, aren't there?

FRANCES   Are there? I've only read the Preface.

JENNY   Yes, I mean —

DR DALY   **[cottoning on, incredulous]** *You've only* — **[but he is swept aside by JENNY's spilling of her file cards onto the desk.]**

JENNY   The horn of realism and the horn of — horn of —

DARREN   Plenty?

JENNY   — of, well, non-realism. I was wondering why she bothered with the realism at all and now I see that it's so that we get tossed from one horn to the other — realism, non-realism, realism, non-realism —

DARREN   You could say, then, that it's a pretty horny book.

JENNY   — and that's the "breakdown", the "crack-up" Anna keeps talking about — the novel enacts it until we, as well as Anna, come to desire the single horn, the what was it — the horn of the unicorn. Is that what the Golden notebook section is then, the unicorn's horn?

FRANCES   Er …

[Long silence.]

DARREN   Look, alright, serious point here — really — isn't the Golden notebook section the one where she goes on about the vaginal orgasms?

[Pause.]

Honest. Serious point. Isn't it?

DR DALY   I can't remember.

DARREN   I think it is. I think it is, you know.

ROBERT   So?

JENNY   Yeah, what about it?

DARREN   Well, it makes sense then. She's impaled on the unicorn's horn and she has a vaginal orgasm. Perfectly understandable.

[Pause.]

ROBERT   They do say that *rhinoceros* horn is an aphrodisiac.

[Pause.]

CAROLE   But I don't think that *is* the bit where she goes on about —

	um …
ALISON	It isn't.

[Silence. The clock in the quadrangle strikes three quarters of an hour.]

| DR DALY | I'm not sure where we've got to. We hardly seem to have discussed the novel at all. And I didn't really follow the connections you were making, Jenny, about the form of the novel. I can see there's something in what you were saying but I wonder if we haven't become distracted by this horn metaphor altogether. I'm not convinced that it's helpful. |

[Pause.]

We've only got ten minutes left. Perhaps we could examine a particular passage?

[Pause, without assent or dissent.]

How about if we look briefly at the first Yellow notebook section, starting on page a hundred and seventy seven.

[Flicking of pages. General noises.]

We're told in the square brackets there that "The yellow notebook looked like the manuscript of a novel, for it was called *The Shadow of the Third*. It certainly began like a novel." Now a question I'd like you to think about is, who's speaking in those square brackets — whose words are they?

[Silence.]

Where are they written?

DARREN	**[suspicious]** Is that a trick question?
DR DALY	No. Not at all.
DARREN	**[still untrusting]** Well, they're written on page one seven seven, obviously.
DR DALY	**[consternated]** I mean, *are they written in any of the notebooks*?
DARREN	Ah.
DR DALY	They appear at the end of the first section of the Black notebook.

[Pause.]

| JENNY | But they aren't in the Black notebook. |
| DR DALY | All right. They appear at the beginning of the first Yellow notebook section. |

[Pause.]

| ALISON | They don't belong to it, though. |
| DR DALY | So? Where are they? |

[Pause.]

| ROBERT | Er, in the No Man's Land between the two? |

JENNY	No *Man*'s Land?
ROBERT	**[exasperated]** Oh, alright, No Woman's Land.
	[Pause.]
DR DALY	Really? No woman? There's no woman there? There is a woman there, isn't there? Between the notebooks.
	[Pause.]
CAROLE	You mean … ?
	[Pause.]
JENNY	You mean —
CAROLE	Doris … Lessing?
DR DALY	Presumably. No?
	[Silence.]
CAROLE	**[heartened]** Yes!
ALISON	Yeah. Alright, yeah.
DR DALY	What's she doing there?
	[Pause.]
ROBERT	Maybe still looking for the unicorn.
DR DALY	**[sighing]** What kind of *function* would you say she is performing?
	[Silence.]
	Would you agree that she is performing an *explanatory* function?
	[Silence.]
	Would it be going too far to say that she is performing an *editorial* function?
	[Silence.]
	What are the implications of that?
	[Silence.]
	An editor can cut things as well as explain them. In fact, these square brackets often appear to indicate that there are contents of the notebooks we haven't been given. On page five hundred and ten the last section of the Red notebook is introduced with a summary explaining that it's full of newspaper cuttings from nineteen fifty six and nineteen fifty seven which contain six hundred and seventy nine references to the word freedom which Anna has underlined in red pencil and yet we aren't presented with those cuttings or what they contained apart from the word freedom. One of Lessing's many cuttings are Anna's cuttings. And those are just the cuttings she confesses to. How do we know there aren't more cuttings that she hasn't told us about or that she hasn't added up properly?
	[Silence.]

Are the contents of these square brackets to be trusted?
[Silence.]
Here we have one of the many paradoxes of this novel.
Doris Lessing reveals herself to be cutting out of the novel
bits of text that Anna has cut out of newspapers. And, going
back to this *Shadow of the Third* thing which has the
appearance of a novel — but is it? — and is this? — well,
what's it about? The heroine is a woman called Anna who's
writing a novel, we find out on page two hundred and
thirteen, about suicide. So at this point we have Doris
Lessing writing a novel called *The Golden Notebook* about
Anna Wulf writing a novel called *The Shadow of the Third*
about a woman called Ella writing a novel about suicide.
Now, I ask again, what is all of this about? What is going
on here?
[Silence.]
Can anybody tell me?
[Silence.]
Before we enter the No Man's Land between the seminar
and the lecture?
[Silence.]
Shall we end it there?
[Silence.]
Shall we go on?
[Silence.]

(NOTE: The title of this piece is deliberately misleading.)

Concplags and Totplag:
Lanark Exposed

Hos ego versiculos feci, tulit alter honores.
— Virgil

Ficta voluptatis causa sint proxima veris.
— Horace

On 2 March 1757, Damiens the plagiarist was condemned "to make the *amende honorable* before the main door of the Church of Paris", where he was to be "taken and conveyed in a cart, wearing nothing but a shirt, holding a torch of burning wax weighing two pounds"; then,

> in the said cart, to the Place de Grève, where, on a scaffold that will be erected there, the flesh will be torn from his breasts, arms, thighs and calves with red-hot pincers, his right hand, holding the pen with which he committed the said plagiarism, burnt with sulphur, and, on those places where the flesh will be torn away, poured molten lead, boiling oil, burning resin, wax and sulphur melted together and then his body drawn and quartered by four horses and his limbs and body consumed by fire, reduced to ashes and his ashes thrown to the winds.[1]

For its abolition of this degree of punishment for this species of crime, Alasdair Gray, "author" of *Lanark*, stands as a direct beneficiary of the French Revolution.

I

The "Epilogue" to Alasdair Gray's *Lanark*, a black hole of a chapter in which the narrative laws of conventional realism are gaily annihilated (the "Epilogue" itself, paradoxically, appearing, so far as the sequential numbering of pages can be taken as a measure, several chapters "before" the "end" of the novel), alarmingly announces, at the head of an "Index of

---

[1] *Pièces Originales et Procédures du Procès Fait à Robert-François Damiens*, III (Paris, 1757), pp. 372-4.

Plagiarisms" which materialises, seemingly *sui generis*, in a columnar marginality which squeezes the main body of the text into only two thirds of each page for its duration, thus generating considerable visual anxiety, that a great deal of the novel is, with varying degrees of concealment, thieved:

> There are three kinds of literary theft in this book:
> BLOCK PLAGIARISM, where someone else's work is printed as a distinct typographical unit, IMBEDDED PLAGIARISM, where stolen words are concealed within the body of the narrative, and DIFFUSE PLAGIARISM, where scenery, characters, actions or novel ideas have been stolen without the original words describing them. To save space these will be referred to hereafter as Blockplag, Implag, and Difplag. (*Lanark* 485)[2]

The "Epilogue", according to the novel's "Table of Contents", is "annotated by Sidney Workman", his commentary comprising, as well as the "Index of Plagiarisms", thirteen pedantic and distracting footnotes which signal, as well as their own gratuitousness, their equal derivation, along with the rest of the novel, from the previous textual practices of more distinguished forebears. Footnote 6 informs us that "from T.S.Eliot, Nabokov and Flann O'Brien" is stolen the idea of "a parade of irrelevant erudition through grotesquely inflated footnotes" (*Lanark* 490).

The bewildering effect of the entire "Epilogue" is achieved but also contained by indications that "Sidney Workman" is to be read as an *alter ego* of *Lanark*'s author, a persona adopted by Gray which enables him to debunk and undermine himself as part of a typically postmodernist enterprise of textual deconstruction and iconoclasm. Sidney Workman thus bears a similar relationship to Gray as does Lanark the character to his author (a.k.a. the king and the conjuror) in their verbal confabulation in the

---

[2] All quotations from *Lanark: A Life in Four Books* (Edinburgh, Canongate, 1981) are followed throughout by the novel's short title and appropriate page number in parentheses.

main body of the text of the "Epilogue".[3] Thus, in footnotes 6, 7, 8 and 11, Workman is supremely contemptuous of the grandiloquence and Gongorism of Gray's *magnum opus* (*Lanark* 489-90, 492, 493, 496).[4] But

---

[3] This relationship itself is an inversion of the grumbling dependence of Dan Milligan on his author, Spike Milligan, in Milligan's novel *Puckoon* (1963). The fact that this literary larceny is not recorded in the "Index of Plagiarisms" betrays what we shall come to see as Gray's major diversionary tactic in *Lanark*, the hitherto undetected ploy of secreting major crimes by confessing to a multitude of minor ones. The critic must, therefore, not take the "Index" at its word, and should bear in mind always that the triad of plagiarisms acknowledged in the "Index" is not comprehensive. There is also a great deal of CONCEALED PLAGIARISM, or Concplag. The degree of systematic Concplagging in *Lanark* will emerge in the course of analysis.

For the moment, however, quotation of one passage should be enough to demonstrate the lineage of *Lanark* from *Puckoon*. The following exchange is to be found on p. 9 of the Penguin edition of the latter (Harmondsworth, 1965):

[Milligan] rolled his trousers kneewards revealing the like of two thin white hairy affairs of the leg variety. He eyed them with obvious dissatisfaction. After examining them he spoke out aloud. 'Holy God! Wot are dese den? Eh?' He looked around for an answer. 'Wot are dey?' he repeated angrily.

　　'Legs.'
　　'Legs? LEGS? Whose legs?'
　　'Yours.'
　　'Mine? And who are you?'
　　'The Author.'
　　'Author? Author? Did you write these legs?'
　　'Yes.'
　　'Well, I don't like dem. I don't like 'em at all at all. I could ha' writted better legs meself. Did you write your legs?'
　　'No.'
　　'Ahhh. *Sooo*! You got someone else to write your legs, someone who's a good leg writer and den you write dis pair of crappy old legs fer me, well mister, it's not good enough.'
　　'I'll try and develop them with the plot.'

Compare Lanark's discovery of his author (*Lanark* 481). Lanark's ability to bemuse his author by demonstrating his knowledge of matters unknown to the latter contrasts with Milligan, who always has to bow to Milligan's superior understanding.

[4] Workman is thus presented as performing literally the function which Macherey ascribes to all critics in the thrall of the "normative fallacy": "Because it is powerless to examine the work on its own terms, unable to exert an influence on it, criticism resorts to a corroding resentment. In this sense, all criticism can be summed up as a value judgment in the margin of the book: 'could do better'." Pierre Macherey, *A Theory of Literary Production*, tr. by Geoffrey Wall (London, Routledge and Kegan Paul, 1978), p. 16.

in footnote 13 Workman divulges details about the novel's production in
the form of courteous acknowledgments to secretaries and friends which
make it clear that he is to be seen merely as Gray in disguise (*Lanark* 499).

The reader's sense of the manageability of this profoundly paradoxical
text rests, then, on a bedrock sense that a real author (Gray) is amusing us
by ridiculing himself in a super-sophisticated and contradictory manner by
means of a recognisably fictional *alter ego*, Workman. If it could be
demonstrated that there actually were a real person called Sidney Workman
whose work did appear within the pages of *Lanark*, we would be unable
to sustain our present understanding of the "Epilogue" and its function in
the novel as a whole. To take just one example, it would be difficult for
us to accept that Alasdair Gray or his publisher would have permitted such
satirical devastation to jeopardise the commercial prospects of his *début*
novel. Any misunderstanding as to Workman's fictive *doppelgänger* status
would bring down the entire pack of textual cards. (One interprets the
remark "The emperor has no clothes" differently, if it is spoken by the
Emperor himself, than if it is uttered by a boy in the watching crowd.)

What, then, are we to do with *Lanark* (or do *to* Alasdair Gray — after
such knowledge, what forgiveness?) when it can be demonstrated that
Sidney Workman was, indeed, an historically real person? What if,
moreover, it can be shown that the same Sidney Workman did not, in fact,
write the "Index of Plagiarisms" and accompanying footnotes, but that
these were, indeed, written by Alasdair Gray *as annotations to a
manuscript called Lanark*, written by Sidney Workman, which Gray
ruthlessly appropriated and, in the most monumental act of literary forgery
since the Ossian affair of the eighteenth century, passed off on an
unsuspecting public as his own, giving Sidney Workman an ironically
subsidiary rôle as mere glossographer?[5] What if, in other words, the entire
body of *Lanark*, with the exception of the "Epilogue", the "Prologue",
some minor episodes and revisions and a few pretentious drawings, is not
simply a composite of confessed Blockplags, Implags and Difplags, and
unacknowledged Concplags, but the embodiment of that much more
profound scandal, **TOTAL PLAGIARISM, Totplag**? The implications for
our reading would, surely, be momentous and disturbing were it to be
established beyond doubt that *Lanark* is indeed, in all essentials, a work of
a Workman.

But this is not a matter for mere speculation. In the pages that follow
I intend to offer evidence which renders this fact incontrovertible.

---

[5] It is perhaps a prolonged troubled conscience which has made Gray assign
precisely this rôle to himself in a recent work, *Poor Things: Episodes from the Early
Life of Archibald McCandless, M.D., Scottish Public Health Officer* (London,
Bloomsbury, 1992), of which he is in fact the genuine author.

Antoine Ouvrier (1865-1939) in the 1930s

II

Sidney Workman was my maternal grandfather.

His own father, Antoine Ouvrier, was born into an Alsatian family of potash miners resident just north of Mulhouse since at least the fifteenth century. In 1871, when Antoine was just six years old, Germany annexed Alsace and Lorraine. Many Alsatians fled to Belfort, the only part of the region preserved from Prussian imperial rule, and others who could do so took flight across the Vosges to find sanctuary in France. Later in life Antoine would recall how his uncle, a cobbler named Cicatrix, having deserted the French imperial army at Metz in September 1870, paid a fleeting visit home that month before enlisting in one of the workers' battalions that stormed the *Hôtel de Ville* in Paris on hallowe'en of the same year. Cicatrix also reportedly took part in the demolition of Napoleon's victory column on the *Place Vendôme* the following May, and died in full glory on a barricade a week before the collapse of the Commune. The day after the fall of Paris to Bismarck on 28 January 1871, by contrast, Antoine and his family woke up in Motherwell.

In the unpublished first volume of his unfinished autobiography, *From Mulhouse to Motherwell*,[6] Antoine explains that his mother's cousin had eloped with and later married a Scottish mining engineer, Sidney Buff, whom she had met in Strasbourg while on holiday in the summer of 1866. It was by means of this connection that the Ouvriers found refuge and a livelihood in Lanarkshire. For a few years Antoine's father worked in local mines, but then moved into textiles in Lesmahagow and, around 1890, advanced to the position of under-manager in a mill in Lanark. It was here that Antoine, now at the rather advanced bachelor age of twenty five and with no settled ambition in life other than to be a poet (a vocation which caused his father endless expense and anxiety), met and fell in love with the daughter of a local widow, Oliphant Gouge. Antoine and Oliphant were married in 1893. Their first and only son was born on 28 June of the following year, and they named him Sidney, in honour of the man who had given shelter to the Ouvriers in the dark and early refugee days of Antoine's youth. Acknowledging at last his family commitments, Antoine accepted a job in the mill procured for him by his father. Although he had no talent for manufacturing and was unable to advance himself in it in any significant way, he was, by all accounts, perfectly happy in his domestic life, having few private interests beyond the well being of his wife, the rearing of his son, and a passion for reading.

It is hardly surprising that Sidney Ouvrier should have come, in later

---

[6] MS in my possession.

life, to write a novel in which the same character appears with two different names. From his earliest lesson in French at school, when the Francophile dominie tortured him by translating his surname for the rest of the boys, Sidney endured the schizophrenic experience of being registered as one person on official documents and constantly addressed by the much more disrespectful English equivalent in everyday blether.[7] He suffered a perpetual sense of social exposure before those who insisted on hailing him by the English version of his surname alone, and records in one early diary the advent of a terrible, cold hatred for his mother, when she, for the first time, used this appellation: "i wish i woz neer deep water i wid waid in and she wid watch me drown and she wid greet and id bee glad!"[8] Soon his father took to using the familiar term as well, but Sidney continued to blame his mother exclusively for the extinction of his French and lofty-sounding identity, and harboured an intensifying bitterness and apathy towards Oliphant Ouvrier, which was not mellowed even by her painful illness early in 1911, when he wrote, "This afternoon Mum was operated on for something to do with her liver. It seems that for the past year or two old Doctor Lake has been treating her for the wrong illness. I'm ashamed to notice that yesterday I forgot to record that she'd been taken into hospital. I must be a very cold selfish kind of person. If Mum died I honestly don't think I'd feel much about it."[9]

This is not the place to embark on a detailed biography of Ouvrier. That requirement may become a real one when his actual literary achievement is acknowledged, and it is the case for such recognition which

---

[7] As with many passages in the novel, the detail of the evacuee Thaw telling his schoolmates "that 'wee' was French for 'yes'" (*Lanark* 132) takes on an added significance when the national descent of the real author is known: the notion of a psychological reconciliation between his French and Scottish identities is here inscribed. There is, consequently, a poignancy in Thaw's spirited defence of the learning of the French language and his subsequent forced abandonment of it under maternal and peer pressure in favour of "dead" Latin (*Lanark* 148-50), which the reader who believes Gray to be the author cannot begin to perceive.

[8] Sidney Ouvrier, "My Daily Diary", primary school jotter, 28 August 1902 (in my possession). It is no coincidence that exactly the same date is found on the stone discovered by Duncan Thaw shortly before he attempts to, or does, drown himself (*Lanark* 353), or that the young Thaw envisages killing himself shortly after an altercation with his mother (*Lanark* 123).

[9] Sidney Ouvrier, *Journal 1911*, 13 January 1911 (written in a Lanarkshire school science notebook, in my possession). The passage appears *verbatim*, with the name of the doctor being the one alteration, in Duncan Thaw's diary (*Lanark* 191), written similarly during his last year of schooling.

this essay aims to present. Suffice to say that, having performed with
distinction in his final examinations, Ouvrier was able to proceed to the
University of Glasgow, to read French and English Literature, largely
thanks to the financial bounty which descended on the family following the
untimely death of Oliphant Ouvrier in April 1911. Antoine Ouvrier had
been most diligent in his life assurance arrangements.

From his point of view the most memorable, and from ours the most
significant enrolment made by the young Ouvrier at Glasgow, was in his
first year, when he attended a course of lectures given by John Hepburn
Millar. Millar was Professor of Constitutional Law and Constitutional
History in the University of Edinburgh, but gave this particular series as
a visiting lecturer in Scottish Literature at Glasgow in the academic year
1911-12.[10] It was thanks to this course that Ouvrier's abiding passion for
Scottish writing of this period was ignited and, as we shall see, knowledge
of its content is essential to an understanding of the sources behind major
sections of the novel later to be published as *Lanark*.

Millar's lectures took the form, by and large, of an evaluative survey
of the main prose writers of the two centuries: Drummond, Urquhart,
Mackenzie, Kames, Blair, and so on. But the most material inclusion, so
far as we are concerned, is his discussion of James Burnett, Lord
Monboddo (1714-1799). This writer is recorded, of course, in the "Index
of Plagiarisms" of *Lanark*, where he is treated in scornful terms. For
instance:

> He was a court of session judge,
> friend of King George and an erudite
> metaphysician with a faith in satyrs
> and mermaids, but has only been
> saved from oblivion by the animad-
> versions against his theory of human
> descent from the apes in Boswell's
> *Life of Johnson*. (*Lanark* 494)

No objective reader of Millar's discussion of Monboddo would come away
with that impression of his abilities, and it is therefore doubtful that Sidney
Ouvrier wrote these words. Millar does deal with the disagreement between
Johnson and Monboddo, but in much less summary and partial terms than

---

[10] The lectures were published almost immediately in John Hepburn Millar,
Scottish Prose of the Seventeenth and Eighteenth Centuries (Glasgow, James Maclehose
and Sons, 1912).

these, and has at least the grace to consider Monboddo's writings instead of relying on Johnson's contemptuous and reflexive dismissal of them. "It is beyond question," Millar tells us, "that Monboddo was a man of deep and extensive learning" whose knowledge of ancient tongues was remarkable and whose defence of Greek "is most refreshing and salutary doctrine for our own age, which has witnessed an insolent attack upon the cause of Greek at the English Universities, and its shameful betrayal in our own".[11] Praising Monboddo's principled refusal "to embellish his writing with meretricious ornament" (a resistance not so remarkable, one might add, in the inferior draughtsman whose Concplags form the various titlefaces to the published version of *Lanark*), Millar discusses his two major works, each of which appeared over a number of years: *Of the Origin and Progress of Language* (6 vols., 1773-1792) and *Antient Metaphysics, or the Science of Universals* (6 vols., 1779-1799). Of perhaps most moment for a consideration of the rôle played by Monboddo in *Lanark* are the following remarks:

> The *Metaphysics* winds up with a most interesting chapter on the condition of Scotland, in which Monboddo deplores rural depopulation and the swallowing up of small lairds by great. Though a zealot for the improvement of agriculture (and it is recorded that one night he went out with a lighted candle to take a look at a field of turnips), he insists that it ought not to be carried out at the expense of the farmers and cottars. "There are many in Scotland," he says, "who call themselves improvers, but who I think are rather *desolators* of the country. Their method is to take into possession several farms, which no doubt they improve by cultivation. But after they have done so they set them off all to one tenant, instead of perhaps five or six who possessed them before."[12]

It is manifest from this that the historical Monboddo's humane view of the society of his own time is virtually diametrically opposed to the fictional Monboddo's rapacious social policy in his own world, a consequence of pathological hostility towards "desperadoes" and "irresponsible intellectuals" who "seem anxious to break the world down into tiny republics of the prehistoric kind, where the voice of the dull and cranky would sound as loud as the wise and skilful" (*Lanark* 545-6). The fictional Monboddo

---

[11] Millar, p. 220-2.

[12] Millar, pp. 227-28, quoting from Monboddo's *Antient Metaphysics*.

is therefore a product of artifice, a construct, a distortion, but is not recognised as such by the author of the "Index of Plagiarisms", who seems to believe that the historical Monboddo was actually as eccentric and dangerous as this representation. The "Index of Plagiarisms" and the novel thus appear to be at cross purposes, an indication that they were not composed by the same individual.

The individual who wrote the "Index of Plagiarisms" was certainly not Sidney Ouvrier. To begin with, there is the evidence of Ouvrier's own editions of the works of Monboddo cited by Millar. These were bequeathed to the present writer on the death of his grandfather in March 1967. If the extensive marginalia in Ouvrier's hand are anything to go by, all of the volumes were read with a thoroughness which few undergraduates of today could muster, and their rarity and expense suggest an interest in the author which a low evaluation would seem to preclude. Moreover, all of these marginal comments show either interest or approval on the part of the reader — none are negative. Ouvrier reading Monboddo is the opposite of Blake reading Sir Joshua Reynolds. On these grounds, it is impossible to see the annotator of Monboddo and the annotator of *Lanark* as one and the same man.

But a curious and accidental piece of evidence clinches the case. This is a holograph letter inserted inside the front cover of volume three of Ouvrier's copy of Monboddo's *Antient Metaphysics*. For over twenty years after the bequest of this letter the present writer was unable to identify its author. Here is the text of the letter in full:

Dublin, 14 February 1940

Dear Sid,

Herewith I return the Monboddo volume with warmest thanks for the loan of it. An extraordinary character, to be sure. I hope you haven't minded me holding on to it for so long. It's just that it provided me with some terrific notions for a book I've just finished. The only good thing about it is the plot and I've been wondering whether I could make a crazy play out of it. When you get to the end of this book you realize that my hero or main character (he's a heel and a killer) has been dead throughout the book and that all the queer ghastly things which have been happening to him are happening in a sort of hell which he earned for the killing. Towards the end of the book (before you know he's dead) he manages to get back to his own house where he used to live with another man who helped in the original murder. Although he's been away three days, this other fellow is twenty years older and dies of fright when he sees the other lad standing in the door.

Then the two of them walk back along the road to the hell place
and start thro' all the same terrible adventures again, the first
fellow being surprised and frightened at everything just as he was
the first time and as if he'd never been through it before. It is made
clear that this sort of thing goes on for ever — and there you are.
It is supposed to be very funny but I don't know about that either.
I think the idea of a man being dead all the time is pretty new.
When you are writing about the world of the dead — and the
damned — where none of the rules and laws (not even the law of
gravity) holds good, there is any amount of scope for back-chat and
funny cracks.

B. O'N.

It was not until 1988, when the present author, in the course of tracking
Gray's fabrications to their lair, was pursuing the trivialising allusions
which litter the "Epilogue", that the identity of "B. O'N." became clear.
Footnote 6 of the "Epilogue" wishes to persuade us that the novel is a
monumental and multiple Difplag: "The index proves that *Lanark* is erected
upon an infantile foundation of Victorian nursery tales, though the final
shape derives from English language fiction printed between the 40's and
60's of the present century. The hero's biography after death occurs in
Wyndham-Lewis's trilogy *The Human Age*, Flann O'Brien's *The Third
Policeman* and Golding's *Pincher Martin*" (*Lanark* 489). On looking into
the O'Brien novel, first published posthumously in September 1967, I
discovered a "Publisher's Note" appended to the book, which states, "On
St Valentine's day, 1940, the author wrote to William Saroyan about this
novel, as follows", and proceeds to reproduce, *verbatim*, the entirety of the
above quoted letter, with the exception of its first four sentences, which are
replaced with the single sentence, "I've just finished another book."[13]
Thus I discovered that "B. O'N." was, of course, Brian O'Nolan, the
Irishman who wrote under the pseudonym of "Flann O'Brien". It became
clear that O'Nolan, writing to Saroyan and Ouvrier on the same day about
the same matter, did what many busy correspondents do for the sake of
temporal economy, and wrote substantially the same letter to two
unacquainted recipients, modifying the opening of his letter to Ouvrier only
on account of the Monboddo volume he was returning therewith.

We need not dwell on the personal relationship between O'Nolan and
Ouvrier. There is in any case very little detail. According to Ouvrier's
diaries they met only twice, on consecutive evenings (22 and 23 May

---

[13] "Publisher's Note" to Flann O'Brien, *The Third Policeman* (Picador, 1974), p.
173.

1933), in the same bar in Köln, Germany, where Ouvrier had gone to examine the cathedral as early research for the novel which was to become *Lanark*. (He almost instantly abandoned Köln as the model for his cathedral because it was "too big".[14]) Ouvrier records that O'Nolan, then only just more than half Ouvrier's age, introduced himself by claiming to be studying at Köln University. Ouvrier doubted this, but was impressed by O'Nolan's ostensible erudition to the extent that he loaned him the Monboddo volume which he had been reading when O'Nolan accosted him. They exchanged addresses and agreed to meet the next evening, at which time O'Nolan would return the volume. When Ouvrier returned to the bar on the following night O'Nolan was drunk, had failed to bring the book, and almost immediately launched into what Ouvrier took to be a pro-German tirade. Ouvrier, whose personal family history had been so shadowed by German military aggression, lost patience with the young Irishman, threw a glass of beer over him, and left. Only later did he remember that he had not recovered the Monboddo volume. When he returned to Scotland in June, he wrote to O'Nolan's Dublin address, but received no reply.[15] In his diaries he records writing to the same address on at least eight occasions in the next twelve months, each time to no avail, at the end of which he gave up, never expecting to retrieve the prized Monboddo. His astonishment at receiving the book out of the blue six years later was acute.[16] But understandably, he never replied to O'Nolan's letter.

As it stands, this is the kind of literary *minutiae* which deserves a half column in *Notes and Queries*. Why is it important? Crucially, the evidence establishes that *Lanark* was not and could not have been in any way indebted to *The Third Policeman*. Indeed, to understand the relationship,

---

[14] Sidney Ouvrier, *Journal 1933*, 24 May 1933 (quarto notebook, in my possession).

[15] It seems, in fact, that O'Nolan remained in Germany until June 1934, and thus may not have received any of Ouvrier's letters. But his "German interlude", rather like his ambiguous feelings for the Nazis, remains essentially unelucidated. The obscurity is only deepened in Peter Costello and Peter van de Kamp, *Flann O'Brien: An Illustrated Biography* (London, Bloomsbury, 1987), pp. 45-50, whose attempts to discover more about this period than O'Nolan himself later recorded run into a brick wall: they too can find no objective evidence of any enrolment at Köln University, and even June 1934 as the termination date of his sojourn, they tell us, is uncertain. They are forgivably unaware, also, of the meeting of these two nascent literary giants, and of O'Nolan's consequent debt to Ouvrier.

[16] The diary entry for 16 February 1940 is a contrary verbal explosion of bliss and fury.

one is required really to reverse its terms: that is to say, *The Third Policeman*, in its portrayal of the mad experimentalist de Selby, presents by means of bogus scholarship a caricature of Monboddo, which would have been impossible without the learnedness and aid of the real author of *Lanark*. This can be quite specifically established. The first extended passage on de Selby in *The Third Policeman* announces the influence patently enough to any Monboddoist:

> De Selby has some interesting things to say on the subject of houses. A row of houses he regards as a row of necessary evils. The softening and degeneration of the human race he attributes to its progressive predilection for interiors and waning interest in the art of going out and staying there. This in turn he sees as the result of the rise of such pursuits as reading, chess-playing, drinking, marriage and the like, few of which can be satisfactorily conducted in the open. Elsewhere he defines a house as "a large coffin", "a warren", and "a box". Evidently his main objection was to the confinement of a roof and four walls.[17]

Anyone who knows Monboddo's *Antient Metaphysics*, and particularly the third volume which O'Nolan held onto for almost seven years, will deduce from this that he studied it rather carefully. Millar's summary of *Antient Metaphysics* makes this clear enough:

> The chapters on Man are probably the most interesting in the book. It is there that we get the author's most characteristic views. He is a great advocate of the open air. So are we all nowadays, but we do not carry our enthusiasms to his lengths, and object to houses and clothes altogether. As for the use of fire, it "only serves to aggravate the mischief of houses and clothes".[18]

Readers of *The Third Policeman* will not fail to notice here, additionally, the provenance of de Selby's regret at "industrial activities involving coal-tar by-products".[19] De Selby's doctrine of "hydraulic elysium" ("'water is rarely absent from any wholly satisfactory situation'") is, furthermore,

---

[17] O'Brien, p. 19.

[18] Millar, p. 226, referring to Monboddo's *Antient Metaphysics*, vol. III, pp. 80, 92.

[19] O'Brien, p. 101.

positively Monboddoesque: as Millar tells us, "Monboddo is a great believer in water for external as well as internal use. He would like to see public baths erected in the Highlands for the benefit of the inhabitants, who never change their shirts, once they put them on, till they are reduced to rags."[20]

We know that, after a rejection of *The Third Policeman* by Longman in 1940, O'Nolan was so stung that he "made up tales of losing it at a pub, on a drive through Donegal ... The great lost novel was a secret, something that remained unknown to all save his closest friends."[21] There is no question, then, of Ouvrier having ever read it. It was not published until September 1967. Ouvrier had already died in March of the same year. It may be objected that there is enough in O'Nolan's letter to Ouvrier to give him the idea of incorporating the "hero's biography after death" notion into *Lanark*, as well as borrowing the "hero, ignorant of his past, in a subfuse [*sic*] modern Hell, also from Flann O'Brien" (*Lanark* 490). This may be a tenable argument, but it does not address the issue at hand, namely the authorship of the "Index of Plagiarisms" and associated footnotes. The "Index of Plagiarisms" (*Lanark* 495) and the footnotes mention "Flann O'Brien" and "*The Third Policeman*", but it would have been impossible for Ouvrier to have done so. Ouvrier had never heard of either. He knew Brian O'Nolan only under that name. O'Nolan's letter to him, although giving an outline of the plot of his novel, did not inform him of the title. Ouvrier died before *The Third Policeman* saw the light of day. Nothing more is required to demonstrate the impossibility of the "Index of Plagiarisms" and footnotes being the products of Ouvrier's endeavour.

In the face of its internally contradictory evidence, it is impossible to resist the conclusion which the "Epilogue" insists that we partly deny: namely, that the "Index of Plagiarisms" and footnotes were in fact written by Alasdair Gray. Their purpose is to reveal that *Lanark* is a patina of forgivable (forgivable because confessed) plagiarisms. Such a confession is intended, no doubt, to lead the ordinary reader to admire the spectacle of a literary artist at last "coming clean" about his own vast pretension; even, perhaps, to wonder at the consummate artistry and irony of "employing" a fictional "real" worker (Workman) to this end. But, for anyone in possession of the evidence withheld from "the ordinary reader", Gray's *Lanark* has, as Walter Benjamin might have said, an origin which

---

[20] Cf. O'Brien, pp. 126-8, and Millar, p. 227.

[21] Costello and van de Kamp, p. 64.

s/he cannot contemplate without horror.[22] The proper reaction to Gray's admission of widescale textual pilfering ought to be the same as that with which we greet a politician's disclosure of an error of judgment: we should search for the greater evil eclipsed by the divulged lesser. Blockplags, Implags and Difplags are purloinments of a trifling, juvenile, ultimately tolerable character. But to admit them as part of a strategy to conceal the graver atrocities of Concplag and Totplag is hardly vindicable. It is the duty of literary scholarship to tear asunder the veil that prevents recognition of such duplicity. And after such knowledge, what forgiveness?

III

Before detailing the evidence which will unmask *Lanark* as a Totplag, some qualifying divarication as to the nature of Concplag may be in order. Some modern theorists would deny the validity of the system of intellectual property rights on which the concept of plagiarism depends, but this is not a debate in which we need to become embroiled, as Gray himself, in the "Epilogue", is prepared both to invoke the concept and to indulge in the customary moralising associated with it ("A property is not always valuable because it is stolen from a rich man" [*Lanark* 490] — how true!). It may be objected, however, that not all Concplags — a term which can be applied to any verbal item "thieved (without acknowledgement)" (*Lanark* 490)[23] — are Concplags. Some may simply be masquerading as Conc-

---

[22] On re-reading, I see that this sentence in itself is nothing more than a politically corrected Implag. There is no "might" about it. Benjamin actually did say this. See his "Theses on the Philosophy of History", in *Illuminations*, ed. by Hannah Arendt, tr. by Harry Zohn (Glasgow, Fontana, 1973), p. 258, where he is describing the cultural consequences of the domination of the working by the ruling class — by way of a Bellonic metaphor — in words that equally well depict the usurpation of Ouvrier which Gray exultantly enacts: "Whoever has emerged victorious participates to this day in the triumphal procession in which the present rulers step over those who are lying prostrate. According to traditional practice, the spoils are carried along in the procession. They are called cultural treasures, and a historical materialist views them with cautious detachment. For without exception the cultural treasures he surveys have an origin which he cannot contemplate without horror. They owe their existence not only to the efforts of those who have created them, but also to the anonymous toil of their contemporaries. There is no document of civilization which is not at the same time a document of barbarism."

[23] Ironically, this remark describes the author/king/conjuror's theft of a device from Milton. But it was Milton who defined plagiarism as copying without improving. Gray's one laudable achievement is the resurrection of this traditional understanding of

plags, transparent to the weakest intellectual vision. And indeed, it has to be admitted that a certain kind of textual banditry is so manifestly impossible to conceal that one must have recourse to a more refined notion to explain it. Plagiarisms of this sort are obvious because they are promiscuous borrowings from documents with which sufficient members of an interpretive community will be familiar for it to be impossible for their debentured status to be misunderstood. This device may therefore be classified as OBVIOUS PLAGIARISM, or Obvplag.

The titleface to Book Four of *Lanark* is a useful example of Obvplag. It Obvplags the title page of Hobbes's classic of political philosophy, *Leviathan* (1651), in a manner that requires no illustration. The obviousness of the Obvplag does not rest in the evident similarity of the contents of the illustrations, but in the widespread cultural recognition, the fame, of the Hobbesian icon. There would be little likelihood of Gray succeeding in passing this image off as his own. Technically speaking, he does not actually register the borrowing in the "Index of Plagiarisms". Under the entry for Hobbes he simply notes, "In a famous title page this state is shown threatening a whole earth with the symbols of warfare and religion" (*Lanark* 490). This should surely count as implicit acknowledgment.

The matter of undecidability between Concplag and Obvplag can be theoretically resolved, I am persuaded, by the introduction of a duplex system of categorisation of plagiarism consisting of ACKNOWLEDGED PLAGIARISM, or Ackplag, and UNACKNOWLEDGED PLAGIARISM, or Unackplag. By means of a diagram (opposite),[24] it is a simple matter to show how these two categories subsume all previously discussed forms of plagiarism, with the exception of the universal Totplag. In this representation two general forms of plagiarism, Ackplag and Unackplag, are shown, each consisting of the subsets Blockplag, Difplag and Implag. Obvplag is the grey area shared between Ackplag and Unackplag, and there may be categorical overlaps between Obvplag and Blockplag/Implag/Difplag. Concplag is a subset specific to the larger set Unackplag, and, for the purposes of this study, is not considered to overlap with Obvplag. The universal set, represented by the border of this diagram, may be taken to be Totplag.[25]

---

plagiarism in contradistinction to the unsophisticated modern definition which sees plagiarism as merely a borrowing to which one does not admit.

[24] Hereby Ackplagged from the English logician, John Venn (1834-1923).

[25] Why, the reader may ask, are unacknowledged Blockplags, Implags and Difplags not subsumed within unacknowledged Concplags? Such a reader's extraordinary attention to detail may be commended, but is more properly to be suspected.

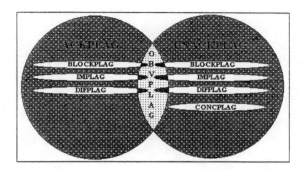

It should, theoretically speaking, be possible to assign each plagiarism in *Lanark* to a point on this diagram. Thus the titleface to Book Four, arguably, would be situated in either of the doubly shaded areas in which Implag, Obvplag, Ackplag and Unackplag meet. Where, however, would we place, for example, the titlefaces to Books One, Two and Three? These are not Obvplags. If one were to present the titleface to Book Four to a cross-section of moderately well-educated persons, it is likely that the frequency of identifications of its relation to Hobbes's *Leviathan* would be pretty high. This is not the case, however (taking the titlefaces in the order in which the reader encounters them), with that to Book Three (which is modelled on that to Sir Walter Ralegh's *History of the World* [1614]), to Book One (Sir Francis Bacon's *Instauratio Magna* [1620]) or to Book Two (Andreas Vesalius' *De Humani Corporis Fabrica* [1543]). I have placed these pictorial reworkings before various distinguished Renaissance specialists without a glimmer of specific recognition. I did not even recognise them myself.[26] Unlike Hobbes, none of this trio of polymaths appears in the "Index of Plagiarisms". No one, then, could seriously make a case for these titlefaces being Ackplags. They are undoubtedly Concplags.[27]

---

[26] For the identification of each I must acknowledge the endeavours of Valerie Durow, a postgraduate student under whose supervision I am currently working. I trust that she will offer corresponding acknowledgment of my brilliant intuition as to the rôle played by quantum theory in the narrative structure of *Lanark* in the thesis on which she is currently engaged. Impressive as its early drafts are, Durow's thesis is unlikely to be the last word on *Lanark*, as she prefers to labour under the illusion shared by most naïve readers, namely that the novel is the imaginative product of Alasdair Gray.

[27] It is true that the first (Canongate) edition of the novel bears on the frontispiece the slogan "WITH ALLEGORICAL TITLEFACES IMITATING THE BEST

Sidney Ouvrier (1893-1967) with his mother, Oliphant Ouvrier, née
Gouge (1868-1911), in 1910. The child has not been identified.

PRECEDENTS". This was removed in subsequent editions. It may therefore be
desirable to make the case for the titlefaces being acknowledged Implags, or Obvplags,
in the Canongate edition, and Concplags in subsequent editions. But it is possible that
many readers will come to find this method of categorisation unwieldy if it is employed
with quite this degree of nicety.

A measure of the intensity of Gray's Concplagging can be gauged by analysing the "Prologue", which he first published in the *Glasgow University Magazine* in 1974, "the so-called 'Prologue' being no prologue at all, but a separate short story", as a footnote in the "Epilogue" informs us (*Lanark* 499). The "Prologue", according to the novel's "Table of Contents", tells "how a nonentity was made oracular", and is narrated by the oracle, a wholly disembodied voice, "sexless and eager", which speaks "on an odd unemphatic note, as if its words could never be printed between quotation marks" (*Lanark* 104). Accordingly, the oracle's words are not rendered with the punctuational conventions used in writing to signal speech. Gray proceeds, in the "Prologue", to take this as a licence to use the work of other writers without accreditation — in short, to Concplag mercilessly. It is possible to distinguish at least five major authors who are Concplagged in the "Prologue".

(1) *Karl Marx.* Much of the "Prologue" is an extended rewriting of classic passages from the great historical materialist's work. The oracle's story, in which a bleak accountant *cum* stockbroker tells how he came to lose his bodily existence, may be taken as a cautionary Marxist tale revealing the perils of attempting to put idealist philosophy into practice: "I have already mentioned my distrust of physical things. They are too remote from the mind. I chose to live by those numbers which are most purely a product of the mind and therefore influence it most strongly: in a word, money" (*Lanark* 108). In particular, although the oracle is hardly a Marxist, it has a quasi-Marxist understanding of the contradictions within what Marx called the universal equivalent form of value, namely money. Compare the following words of the oracle with Marx's thesis, in *Capital*, that "historically speaking, capital invariably first confronts landed property in the form of money":[28]

It puzzles me that people who live by owning or managing big sums of money are commonly called materialistic, for finance is the most purely intellectual, the most sheerly spiritual of activities, being concerned less with material objects than with values. Of course finance needs objects, since money is the value of objects and could no more exist without them than mind can exist without body, but the objects come second. If you doubt this, think which you would rather own: fifty thousand pounds or a piece of land valued at fifty thousand pounds. The only people likely to prefer

---

[28] Karl Marx, *Capital: A Critique of Political Economy*, vol. 1, tr. by Ben Fowkes (Harmondsworth, Penguin, 1976), p. 247.

the land are financiers who know how to increase its value by renting or reselling, so either answer proves that money is preferable to things. (*Lanark* 108-9)[29]

Consider the above, to take just one additional germane example, with what Marx himself has to say in *Capital* about "the fetishism of the commodity" (the commodity in the case of the oracle being money):

> The commodity-form, and the value-relation of the products of labour within which it appears, have absolutely no connection with the physical nature of the commodity and the material relations arising out of this. It is nothing but the definite social relation between men themselves which assumes here, for them, the fantastic form of a relation between things ... To the producers, therefore, the social relations between their private labours appears as what they are, i.e. they do not appear as direct social relations between persons in their work, but rather as material relations between persons and social relations between things.[30]

The oracle's disappearance, or increasing abstraction as a consciousness from the physical world, is a narrative of the reified alienation which is the consequence of extreme commodity fetishism. To risk a paradox, it may be said that the oracle embodies this abstraction. Whether or not the oracle's progress can be said also to symbolise the process, at one time believed by socialists to be inevitable, of capitalism eventually disintegrating under the pressure of its own internal contradictions, is an open question.

(2) *Albert Einstein*. The oracle's apparent reversion to infancy, subsequent to adulthood, signified by his waking to find himself in a nursery uttering baby talk (*Lanark* 112), is a Concplag of Einstein's theory

---

[29] Lanark himself puts his finger on one of the contradictions in this: "'You said money can no more exist without objects than mind without body. Yet you exist without a body.'" The oracle replies, "That puzzles me too" (*Lanark* 117).

[30] Marx, pp. 165-6. Cf. also Marx's extensive comments about money and alienation in "Economic and Philosophical Manuscripts (1844)", in Karl Marx, *Early Writings*, tr. by Rodney Livingstone and Gregor Benton (Harmondsworth, Penguin, 1975), pp. 279-400, which are also Concplagged by the oracle. It is worth noting one other prophetic remark made by Marx in this regard, given that the oracle is in effect a man who becomes a commodity: "If commodities could speak, they would say this: our use-value may interest men, but it does not belong to us as objects. What does belong to us as objects, however, is our value" (*Capital*, vol. 1, p. 176).

that a person travelling faster than the speed of light will get younger. It may owe a more immediate debt to an astronaut's encounter with a "Star-Child" on passing through a "Star-Gate" in a much-hyped contemporaneous science fiction feature film,[31] but this itself was just an earlier Concplag of Einstein.

(3) *T.S.Eliot*. The oracle is, in a sense, a literary artist. He tells a story. As such, the experience he recounts is obscurely related to Eliot's doctrine of artistic depersonalisation in his (in)famous essay of 1919, "Tradition and the Individual Talent": "the progress of an artist is a continual self-sacrifice, a continual extinction of personality".[32] Eliot goes on to liken the mind of the artist to a catalyst which remains inert and neutral in the chemical reaction which it effects: "the more perfect the artist, the more completely separate in him will be the man who suffers and the mind which creates".[33] Like Eliot's shred of platinum, the oracle has no sense of identity or relatedness to its environment: "I had become bodiless in a bodiless world. I existed as a series of thoughts amidst infinite greyness" (*Lanark* 111). It is not surprising to witness a writer whose primary talent resides in his failure to resist such easy puns on his own name being persuaded by the pernicious Eliotic description of the artist's mind as a kind of compost bin, "a receptacle for seizing and storing up numberless feelings, phrases, images, which remain there until all the particles which can unite to form a new compound are present together".[34] The regrettable feature of Gray's function in *Lanark*, however, is that only an infinitesimal number of the feelings, phrases and images the novel launches on the world are actually his own.

(4) *Roland Barthes*. "Writing is that neutral, composite, oblique space where our subject slips away, the negative where all identity is lost, starting with the very identity of the body writing."[35] The impact of Barthes' iconoclastic squib of 1968 on the "Prologue" is incontestable: "Later I sat on a swivel chair above fathoms of emptiness, grey emptiness

---

[31] For the book of the movie, see Arthur C. Clarke, *2001: A Space Odyssey* (London, Hutchinson, 1968).

[32] T.S.Eliot, "Tradition and the Individual Talent", in *T.S.Eliot: Selected Prose*, ed. by John Hayward (London, Penguin, 1953), p. 26.

[33] Eliot, p. 27.

[34] Eliot, p. 27.

[35] Roland Barthes, "The Death of the Author", in *Image-Music-Text*, tr. by Stephen Heath (Glasgow, Fontana, 1977), p. 142.

all around except where, six feet to the right, a pencil moving on its point across an angled notepad showed where my secretary was taking down the words I dictated to her" (*Lanark* 111). It comes as no shock that Gray should wish to collaborate in the "removal of the Author"[36] in a novel whose real author he had already effaced in a manner we are soon to learn more about. One can understand perfectly his agreement with Barthes' pseudo-consensual pronouncement that "we know that a text is not a line of words releasing a single 'theological' meaning (the 'message' of the Author-God) but a multi-dimensional space in which a variety of writings, *none of them original*, blend and clash".[37] However, to have acknowledged a textual theft from a *French* writer would have been to come too close to reality for comfort. Hence Barthes is Concplagged and omitted from the "Index of Plagiarisms". It provokes no wonder that only one French writer (and that the most predictable) appears in the "Index" (*Lanark* 496).

(5) *H.G.Wells*. It could be claimed that the relation of the "Prologue" to Wells's *The Invisible Man* (1897) is an Obvplag, particularly since the protagonist repeatedly manifests himself in that novel as *vox et praeterea nihil*.[38] But, as with Marx and Eliot, Wells appears in the "Index of Plagiarisms" precisely to divert the reader's attention from this source by focusing it on texts or passages where the relationship is actually much more tenuous (*Lanark* 498, 494, 488 respectively). One cannot help but note, in this connection, the ironic perception in footnote 5 of the "Epilogue" to the effect that "the author's amazing virulence against Goethe is perhaps a smokescreen to distract attention from what he owes him" (*Lanark* 488).

IV

We must proceed to the sorry uncovering of the Totplag.

Any brief account of Ouvrier's adult life runs the risk of giving the

---

[36] Barthes, p. 147.

[37] Barthes, p. 146. Emphasis added.

[38] True also of the Good Fairy in O'Brien's *At Swim-Two-Birds* (Harmondsworth, Penguin, 1967), a book too many of whose ideas are seconded into *Lanark* to be briefly enumerated. Cf., for example, the recommendation made to modern novelists by O'Brien's hero (p. 25): "The entire corpus of existing literature should be regarded as a limbo from which discerning authors could draw their characters as required, creating only when they failed to find a suitable puppet."

impression of a character out of Georges Perec.[39] The following brief account is based on the copious, although not chronologically comprehensive, journals which he left after his death.

He did not succeed in graduating from the University of Glasgow. The Great War opened just as he was preparing to enter his final year, and he signed up almost instantly. He was understandably caught by the double tidal wave of *entente* patriotism. The German occupation of Belgium, we should remember, would have struck many French observers as a repetition of the Prussian imperialism of 1871, and unsurprisingly he went with full paternal approval as well as, no doubt, the military example of his great uncle Cicatrix. He did not, however, see any real action, as his linguistic abilities meant that he was detained behind the front line as a liaison and translation officer servicing the British and French high commands. In this capacity he was present at the conclusion of the Versailles treaty on 28 June 1919 (incidentally his twenty-fifth birthday), which returned Alsace and Lorraine to French hands. He was then demobilised. He claims not to have returned to Scotland mainly on account of a disaffection with his father, now turned a socialist and follower of John MacLean, over Antoine's participation in the famous "riot of George Square" of 31 January 1919. While the son translated, liaised and jubilated at Versailles, the father, after the fashion of his political mentor, and also citing the Republican family precedent of Cicatrix, was serving a six months' prison sentence for kicking a police constable in the testicles on the very spot where, ironically, the Glasgow municipal authorities were later to erect the War cenotaph. Sidney felt that his father's conduct was seditious and refused to communicate with him for more than a decade.

Exactly how Sidney Ouvrier got through the following thirteen years remains obscure. His extant correspondence from this time is sparse. He kept no journal throughout the twenties, and did not resume it until 1931. In his memoirs he is elusive and discreet about the entire period. It does, however, emerge that almost exactly at the moment when (as Orwell was to record in 1940) "Paris was invaded by such a swarm of artists, writers, students, dilettanti, sight-seers, debauchees and plain idlers as the world has probably never seen",[40] Ouvrier typically left to retrace his origins to Mulhouse, where he seems to have remained, settled, married in 1923, and spawned a daughter (Martine Daly, née Ouvrier, the present writer's

---

[39] I am thinking particularly of Rorschach in that hotchpotch of Implags, *Life: A User's Manual*, tr. by David Bellos (London, Collins Harvill, 1987).

[40] George Orwell, "Inside the Whale", in *Inside the Whale and Other Essays* (Harmondsworth, Penguin, 1962), p. 9.

mother) in 1929. His wife, Ouvrière, absconded with the doctor who officiated at the delivery. He never managed to trace her thereafter, but how concerted an effort he made is a matter for speculation. Precisely what Ouvrier did to maintain himself and his wife in the twenties is uncertain. The answer is perhaps very little, if his only child's recollections of coming to consciousness amid squalor, hunger, confusion, penury and misery are anything to go by. Ouvrier's domestic hopelessness was certainly grave if, as Martine attests, she was cooking, cleaning and sewing for him long before she attended infant school. But this may be unreliable testimony, given the vagaries of childhood recollection, or the possibility that Ouvrier may temporarily have gone to pieces after his wife's desertion.

Thanks to the resumption of his journals we do know that in the early 1930s he wrote a novel, largely based on his War experiences. The novel appeared in 1932, under the imaginative title *La Guerre d'un Ouvrier* and the pseudonym Robert Walker.[41] According to Ouvrier, the one critic who reviewed it compared it to *Le Grand Meaulnes*, but this review has not been located. The novel was not much read, but it allowed Ouvrier to get into literary society. A few months later he founded a quarterly review which he entitled, rather bizarrely, *Les Préjudices*, thereby wishing no doubt to signify that the review had none. It appeared twice and then folded. None of the authors published in it subsequently established themselves, and where Ouvrier got the money for the enterprise is a mystery. Martine recalls being dragooned as a three-year-old into stuffing envelopes with complimentary copies, which were then despatched to prospective subscribers. Though Ouvrier is very close with precise details on this point, it seems probable that it was a vanity-publishing enterprise. In any case, of all his pre-war projects it is the only one he does not describe as a total failure.

In late 1932 Ouvrier suddenly returned to Glasgow, reconciled overnight to his father. This event coincided with Ouvrier's discovery that his father was now a rather affluent man, having in 1925, unknown to Sidney, and improbably given his lifelong lack of initiative, patented a non-toxic screw-bolt for children's wooden toys, which were harmless if licked or sucked. The plasticisation of the toy industry in the 1950s has rendered this device obsolete, but between the registration of the patent and his death at the age of seventy-four in 1939, this screw-bolt earned Antoine Ouvrier

---

[41] Robert Walker, *La Guerre d'un Ouvrier* (Paris, Les Editions du Tonneau, 1932). It was, of course, under the same pseudonym that Chapter 12 of *Lanark* first saw the light of day, as runner-up in the 1958 *Observer* short story competition. Ouvrier chose the surname because, apparently, it approximated to Mulhouse pronunciation of the English word "worker". No one seems to have noticed this felicitous irony.

Ouvrière Ouvrier, née Touslejours (1901-?),
Sidney Ouvrier's absentee wife.

over thirty thousand pounds. He continued with his mill work in Lanark as usual until his retirement in 1930, by which time sufficient revenues from the screw-bolt had amassed to allow him to purchase a spacious and splendid domicile in the Shawlands district of Glasgow. His confrontation with a granddaughter, in his closing years, was as unexpected and as welcome as his son's discovery of a possible inheritance.

Relieved of the necessity of daily toil, as Antoine Ouvrier became committed to supporting financially his son's quest for the literary acclaim to which as a youth he had himself aspired, Sidney soon conceived a fiction on an epic scale. The primordial idea was a narrative whose movement, symbolically or otherwise, would encapsulate the massive difference between the pre-war and post-war worlds. The pre-war order would be figured in "a narrative of dissolution", embodied even at the level of the hero's surname: "Thaw: a melting from a solid, frozen, crystalline state; a descent from ice-perfect condition to fluid, swamping, anarchic *mélange*".[42] As the switch from English to French diction perhaps indicates, the result of the "descent" was deeply bound up with Ouvrier's personal experience of that dark, unrecorded post-war decade in Mulhouse. He made the decision early on to symbolise the central epochal contrast in a clash of narrative forms, the pre-war being represented in a realist and the post-war by a surrealist style. But shortly after his return from Germany in June 1933 the project became split into two separate novels. He began to write the first of these in earnest in that same year.

In its early development, this epic was one of long drawn-out composition rather than prodigious verbal substance. It is difficult to imagine that the 250-page fiction which resulted should take an entire fifteen years to finish. Even for a man of leisure the average rate of completion of one page every twenty-two days is stunning. But the next we know of the novel is the following cataclysmic rejection of it by the first publisher Ouvrier sent it to, the Glasgow firm of William McLennan and Co.:

11 November 1948

Dear Mr Walker,
I write with reference to your recently submitted manuscript novel, *Duncan Thaw*. I am sorry to say that we are unable to proceed with publication. Last year we published a novel on a very similar theme, Mr J.F.Hendry's *Fernie Brae: A Scottish Childhood*. Indeed, I hope you will not take it amiss if I say that this is a far superior novel to your own with which, I am almost certain from

[42] Sidney Ouvrier, *Journal 1933*, 24 February 1933 (in my possession).

the evidence of your own MS, you are familiar. (I note in passing that your place of residence is rather close to that in which Mr Hendry's novel opens.) I would venture so far, in fact, as to say that your own novel gives the impression of being a somewhat cursorily dashed off, at times even directly plagiarising, imitation of Mr Hendry's. On these grounds my advice is not to circulate it to other publishers, as we should certainly be forced to take legal action if any were so foolish or so undiscriminating as to be persuaded to bring it into the light of day.

Yours faithfully
W. McLennan
Proprietor and Managing Director[43]

It was no doubt on receipt of this that Ouvrier decided to rethink the entire enterprise. He seems to have returned to his earlier conception of a bi-partite epic. It took him another eight and a half years to complete it.

It is not amazing, by the way, that Gray, when he came to expose in the "Index of Plagiarisms" the seemingly myriad local and global influences behind Ouvrier's *Lanark*, should miss the most decisive impact of all. To be sure, D.H.Lawrence makes a fleeting appearance in the "Index" (*Lanark* 492), but the actual Lawrencean influences at work in *Lanark* are not in the slightest apprehended. Lawrence and Ouvrier were near contemporaries. Both were provincials who earned their social mobility by hard scholarly graft. Both were of mining stock. Ouvrier read all of Lawrence's works as they came out. He was leafing through *Sons and Lovers* at a western front British area HQ while the Battle of Loos raged a handful of miles away. Is it merely coincidence that, in this autobiographical novel, Lawrence, whose education and natural talents were almost entirely literary, should render his hero's artistic gifts as painterly ones, as Ouvrier was to do with Thaw? Or that the *Bildungsroman* half of Ouvrier's epic should, like Lawrence's, be saturated with familial dynamics and a developing youth's sexual yearnings and disappointments? Again, Ouvrier bought *The Rainbow* when it was first published in 1915. He first read it during the Somme offensive and re-read it at the time of Passchendaele. Lawrence's idiosyncratic melding of

---

[43] The MS version of the novel to which this was a response has not survived. Ouvrier inserted the letter into his journal without comment, other than the question, "Who is J.F.Hendry?", which he pencilled at the bottom of the page. Although, as this proves, McLennan's terrible accusations were wholly unjust, Ouvrier seems to have taken his advice. There is certainly no trace of any further correspondence relating to *Duncan Thaw*.

sensuality and religion, particularly his aesthetically expressed views on the
sexual possibilities of cathedrals, find themselves replicated in *Lanark*.
More generally, Lawrence was prophetic about the world-shattering nature
of the War, a master of the kind of apocalyptic rant and an exemplar of the
insidious paranoia which suffuse Ouvrier's epic.

In his final years, of course, Ouvrier had plenty to be paranoiac about.
He finished *Lanark* in November 1957. He had taken so long to do so that,
for the sake of preserving a sense of contemporaneity, he had been forced
to reframe the timescale of the novel, which now related to the Second
rather than the First World War. He left it to be typed by Martine and took
a holiday, journeying through Switzerland to Frankfurt, then travelling on
to Athens, Constantinople, Odessa and Alexandria. In early January 1958
he sailed to Gibraltar, where he had taken a house for three months,
intending to visit an old army friend, Jock Brown. Brown had been in the
Highland Light Infantry in Flanders, but was now working as a Toc H
representative in Gibraltar, running an armed forces leave hostel there.[44]
The typescript arrived from Martine on 14 January 1958. A week later,
Ouvrier wrote back to her, requesting that she enter a fresh typed copy of
Chapter 12 of the novel in the *Observer* short story competition, which he
had just seen advertised.[45]

A fortnight later he met Alasdair Gray.

V

The scene, if not the crime, is almost accurately described in Gray's
own essay, "A Report to the Trustees of the Bellahouston Travelling
Scholarship". This is a glum, prolix, exculpatory ramble, written in April
1959, in which Gray tries to satisfy the patient and aggrieved trustees as
to why, their having offered him a Trust award to

---

[44] The Toc H developed in France during the First World War, among British
soldiers who wanted spiritual communion and found the official army priests too
sectarian and not always near when things got tough. After the war it developed into
a charitable organisation providing food, clothing and shelter to the needy, fighting
loneliness and hate and encouraging Christian comradeship. The name derives from the
obsolete telegraph code for T.H., initials of Talbot House, Poperinge, Belgium, the
original headquarters of the society.

[45] Postcard from Sidney Ouvrier to Martine Ouvrier, 21 January 1958 (in my
possession).

find a cheap place to live in southern Spain, paint there for as long
as the money would allow, then travel home through Granada,
Málaga, Madrid, Toledo, Barcelona and Paris, viewing on the way
Moorish mosques, baroque cathedrals, plateresque palaces, the
works of El Greco, Velázquez and Goya, with Bosch's *Garden of
Earthly Delights*, Brueghel's *Triumph of Death*, and several other
grand gaudy things which are supposed to compensate for the
crimes of our civilization ... I eventually spent two days in Spain
and saw nothing of interest.[46]

In the course of this laboured exercise in layabout apologetics, Gray
recounts how he landed, ill, in Gibraltar, then met, befriended, admired
and was helped by Jock Brown. What he omits to record is that Jock
Brown, ever solicitous for the social welfare of those in his charge,
introduced him to Sidney Ouvrier. Ouvrier visited Gray in Jock Brown's
hostel on several occasions, mainly to see how he was progressing with a
mural, the *Triumph of Neptune*, with which, Gray proudly tells us, he spent
some time decorating the walls of the hostel common room. When it
emerged in conversation that Ouvrier had completed a novel, whose final
draft he had just finished correcting, Gray managed to persuade him to
lend it to him to read.

One day in early March 1958, Ouvrier received a distressing telegram
from Martine, to the effect that there had been a fire in the study at the
Shawlands house which had destroyed many of his papers, including the
manuscript copy of *Lanark*. (His diaries were saved because he always kept
them in a safe he had had installed in the drawing room.) In a state of
some agitation, Ouvrier made prompt arrangements to return to Glasgow
and then went to the hostel. There he was told by Jock Brown, who knew
nothing of the novel, that he, Brown, had paid for a plane ticket to London
for Gray and that he, Gray, had flown out the previous evening. Ouvrier,
now in a condition of apoplectic anxiety (and, we should remember, in his
sixty-fourth year), suffered an immediate mental and physical collapse
when he realised that Gray had taken the typescript of the novel with him.

It is just possible that Gray departed with the novel purely as a
consequence of hasty packing. If so, his report to the Bellahouston trustees,
written just over a year later, reveals an early determination to capitalise
on his mistake. He carefully inserts in the report descriptions of authorial
activity designed to give the impression that he was at work on a novel

---

[46] Alasdair Gray, "A Report to the Trustees of the Bellahouston Travelling
Scholarship", in James Kelman, Agnes Owens and Alasdair Gray, *Lean Tales* (London,
Abacus, 1987), p. 181.

before and during his foreign trip. But on careful reading these appear
vague and decidedly ambiguous. Take the following account of how he
apparently passed the time in a Gibraltar hospital before moving on to Jock
Brown's hostel (i.e. before being introduced to Ouvrier, whose existence
he at no point acknowledges):

> A few years ago I had begun work on a tragicomical novel
> and meant to write some more of it in Spain. In my luggage was a
> Cantablue Expanding Wallet, a portable cardboard filing cabinet
> shaped like an accordion and holding two complete chapters and the
> notebooks and diaries from which I meant to make the rest. I put
> this on my bedside locker and began working. I was slightly
> ashamed of this activity, which struck me as presumptuous because,
> like Scott Fitzgerald, I believed the novel was the strongest and
> supplest medium for conveying thought and emotion from one
> human being to another, which meant that a novelist needed to
> understand great states of feeling, and although twenty-three years
> old I had never known carnal love and feared I never would; banal
> because one or two friends had also started writing a novel, and the
> rest had thought of writing one. So when the nurses asked what I
> was doing I lied and told them I was writing this report.[47]

In his time at Jock Brown's hostel, he later asseverates, "I wrote five
chapters of my book".[48] Much more recently, with typically reinvigorated
mendacity, he has stated that "I began to write the *Thaw* section of *Lanark*"
in Summer 1953.[49]

Ouvrier never fully recovered from the blow of losing the corrected
original of the typescript. He was three months in Gibraltar's King George
V hospital before he regained enough strength to return to Glasgow.
Martine, when she went to Gibraltar to be with him, found him in a
monomaniac mental state over the disappearance of the novel whose
tortuous composition had consumed the previous twenty-five years of his
life (an overall rate of 16.3 days per page). She could not fully understand
his concern, because the two carbon copies had not been touched by the
fire and her telegram hadn't said that they had. Despite her reassurances,

---

[47] Gray, "A Report to the Trustees ... ", p. 194.

[48] Gray, "A Report to the Trustees ... ", p. 204.

[49] See Bruce Charlton, "Checklists and Unpublished Materials by Alasdair Gray",
in *The Arts of Alasdair Gray*, ed. by Robert Crawford and Thom Nairn (Edinburgh,
Edinburgh University Press, 1991), p. 199.

even after their return to Shawlands, Ouvrier languished in a condition of mortal woundedness and inconsolable apathy. When Chapter 12 of the novel appeared in the *Observer* later that year, at just the moment when, had he exploited this initial success, he may have managed to find a publisher for the entire work, he was apparently so aggrieved at being only the competition runner-up that he interred the two carbons in the safe and never mentioned them again.

Martine Ouvrier left her father's home to marry Dalton Daly, a fibre glass factory machine operative, in 1959. The present writer, their only son, was born in 1963. Sidney Ouvrier died, aged seventy-two, on 2 March 1967.

VI

The received wisdom about the compositional history of *Lanark* is nothing more than a product of the calculating imagination of Alasdair Gray, foisted by him onto a gullible public and a critical establishment enslaved to the authority of authorhood, even where the latter is assumed rather than actual.[50] His account of the prolonged hold-ups in getting it published under his own name we have no cause to doubt.[51] Delay was in any case inevitable. Gray saw Chapter 12 of the novel published in the *Observer* in 1958, as the note on prior publication on the flyleaf of the published novel establishes. He entertained a properly high estimate of the novel's worth, but would clearly have to bide his time and not risk circulating the manuscript while the real author might possibly be doing the same. It is not too fanciful, then, to picture Gray, throughout the 1960s, keeping one eye warily roving through publisher's catalogues while the other hopefully scanned the obituary columns.

In the meantime, he revised and embellished the expropriated typescript. Comparison of the published novel with Ouvrier's surviving

---

[50] The hapless Bruce Charlton, for instance, is quite content to act as a conduit for such obvious unlikelihoods as the following: "*Lanark*'s most remote ancestor is the improbably [!! - M.D.] titled *Obbly Pobbly* from 1951, featuring as its semi-autobiographical protagonist 'a potato-headed intellectual schoolboy ... [who would] go on a pilgrimage which would lead him out of the everyday drabness of post-war respectable working class Glasgow, through a fantasy pilgrimage, ending in an era of untrammelled artistic production'". Bruce Charlton, "The Story So Far", in Crawford and Nairn, pp. 12-13.

[51] Transmitted by Gray through the slavishly faithful medium of Charlton. See the two preceding footnotes.

carbons reveals that, in the main, Gray's textual fiddling was directed almost entirely to giving the impression that Duncan Thaw was based on himself. This was not so very difficult, as it turned out, because Thaw was not a self-portrait of Ouvrier. Indeed, even in the original, Duncan Thaw, by sheer chance, was much more like Alasdair Gray than the urbane Sidney. Gray was forced, of course, to change small particulars. In the early sections of the Thaw narrative he rewrote the details of Duncan's schooling to parallel his own, so that, for example, the educational establishment he attends is in Dennistoun, Glasgow, whereas Ouvrier's Thaw goes to school in Lanark. The "Prologue", a wholly extraneous short story of Gray's invention which he no doubt had lying about, was simply bunged in with no regard to its entirely distracting effect. Most cruelly, of course, Gray composed an "Epilogue" in which the hero meets the author and outwits him by telling him things about his own verbal creation which the author does not know. Furthermore the real author, Sidney "Workman", is diminished to the scale of a peripheral functionary in the same "Epilogue", which is brazen enough, at one point, obscurely to confess the novel's wholly piratical status, its condition of being a Totplag:

> "Your survival as a character and mine as an author depend on us seducing a living soul into our printed world and trapping it here long enough for us to steal the imaginative energy which gives us life." (*Lanark* 485)

The origins of this sentence lie in the treachery at Gibraltar, as anyone acquainted with the history will recognise.

The most comic interference performed by Gray, however, lay in his attempts to "complete" what he saw as an unfinished masterpiece. He did this by writing six additional chapters, numbered forty-five to fifty, which, to the puzzlement of many readers, are referred to in the "Index of Plagiarisms" without appearing in the published volume. Alison Lee, in an appendix to her book *Realism and Power*, has arranged these references in a meaningful order, but her explanation of their importance is so crazily and credulously inaccurate that it needs to be countermanded:

> The Index of Plagiarisms points to the ultimate open ending. References are made to plagiarisms in Chapters forty-five to fifty, which is only remarkable once the reader discovers that the novel ends at Chapter forty-four. In order to figure this out, however, the reader has to read in precisely the way which is undermined by the discovery of these absent chapters. He or she has to read for correspondence as he or she is encouraged to do by the illustrated

The present author (1963-) with his mother,
Martine Daly, née Ouvrier (1929-), in 1964.

title pages. In the plags to these missing chapters, real authors and texts are combined with fantastic events in chapters which are themselves, of course, fictions. When they are put in order by chapter and paragraph, the plags seem to depict the story of a cosmic battle which continues past the end of *Lanark*.[52]

Could one hope to find a specimen of contemporary literary criticism in which sense and nonsense are more inseparably lashed together? Why this reflex in the critical brain — a Pavlovian phenomenon indicating that the putative theorylubber is in fact intoxicated by the rarefied air of authorial infallibility — asserting that these "Index" references are cunning deployments borne out of Gray's ineffable genius? Why not even a speculative contemplation of the most transparently commonsensical explanation of the matter? Is it not possible that they refer to actual chapters which Gray eventually, on advice, omitted, and that he quite simply *forgot* to cross out the corresponding "Index" entries? Why no mention of this as even a remote hypothesis?

I shall offer the necessary explanations in due course, but it does, indeed, turn out to be the case that Gray, believing the conclusion to Ouvrier's text ("Goodbye" [*Lanark* 561]) to effect an inadequate sense of closure, wrote a further ninety-two typescript pages in which, briefly, the following events are narrated:

Chapter 45:	Grant's fart sets a group of monkeys fighting (see *Lanark* 496, 490);
Chapter 46:	A Red Sea-type wave engulfs everybody, including Grant and the monkeys, from which only Sergeant Alexander and his peace force emerge alive. They reach dry land, only to be blocked suddenly by God (see *Lanark* 497, 496);
Chapter 47:	God apologises, but explains that he drowned Grant and the monkeys out of mercy because they were going to die soon anyway. He promotes Alexander to Major and gives him a blank map. Alexander thanks him and replies, "Inadequate maps are better than no maps; at least they show that the land exists" (see *Lanark* 491, 493);
Chapter 48:	A Martian Headmaster approaches (actually a Concplag from Wittgenstein's *On Certainty*), on a

---

[52] Alison Lee, *Realism and Power: Postmodern British Fiction* (London, Routledge, 1990), p. 113. For the helpful appendix, see pp. 126-7.

motorised bed, accompanied by a cricketer and his singing wife, and an attendant android, who is cleaning the bed. The android finds an adder in the engine of the bed and throws it to God. God reacts in the manner of a woman receiving roses on St Valentine's day. He turns into a Goddess and kisses the android (see *Lanark* 493, 497, 496, 492);

Chapter 49: The Goddess' kiss-of-death transforms the android into Rima's corpse. General Alexander and the peace force hold a requiem mass for her, after a disagreement as to her religion. They then make a "mock-military excursion" (marching for forty-five paragraphs) to the top of Mount Vesuvius, down the crater of which they kamikaze in a waiting tramcar (see *Lanark* 492, 498);

Chapter 50: All of the characters in the novel assemble on a ledge under the volcano (Malcolm Lowry Concplag) to recite a valedictory poem ("In a wee while, dearie" etc.) before leaping in unison, mass suttee style, into Vesuvius' molten heart. Immolating corpses, from a speculative aerial view, spell the words "HYPER-UTOPIAN EUPHORIA" (see *Lanark* 492, 498-9).

The reality of these ludicrous supplements to Ouvrier's epic can be established only by following the operation of a network of unlikely coincidences, whose supervention I shall conclude my investigation by explaining.

Speaking concisely, illumination on this score came to the present writer as follows. It is common knowledge that, after failing, like Ouvrier, to publish the Thaw half of *Lanark* on its own, Gray managed in 1973 to secure an option on *Lanark* from the publishing firm Quartet. When he eventually submitted the manuscript in 1976, it was rejected and returned to him, the reason given being that it was too long.[53] It is, of course, customary practice in the publishing trade, although technically a copyright violation, to retain photocopies of rejected manuscripts on which the firm has previously bought the right of first refusal. (The legal loophole is that such documents can be copied if treated as "enclosures" with authors' or agents' letters in correspondence files.) In the normal run of things, of course, and for obvious legal reasons, access to these copies would be

---

[53] Charlton, "The Story So Far", p. 15.

denied to anyone outside the organisation. Quartet's dealings with *Lanark* did not depart in any particular from this tradition.

It so happened, in the late 1980s, that the present writer had submitted a publishing proposal for a monograph on literary detection to Quartet, and was invited by the appropriate commissioning editor to visit the firm's London office to discuss the matter. When I arrived, the Quartet premises were a scene of some confusion. I saw dozens of black plastic bags, and many heaps of old fashioned box files, on the edge of the pavement, obviously placed there for the sanitation department to collect and destroy. Looking into a few of them I was aghast and astonished to discover a chunk of tea-stained typescript beginning with the familiar words "Lanark opened his eyes and looked thoughtfully round the ward" (cf. *Lanark* 357). I seized the manuscript, my heart drumming in the realisation that I was holding a photocopy of the original typescript, recognisably hammered out on my mother's old Olivetti, of Book Four of my grandfather's epic novel! In the few minutes remaining before my appointment I took the opportunity to search the adjacent files for the remainder, but with no success.

I proceeded, in a state of not inconsiderable excitation, through corridors of supreme chaos and bustle, to my commissioning editor's office. In particular I remember, passing door after door, paper shredders being operated at a rate and with a throughput not incomparable with the pulping which apparently occurred at the White House in the closing weeks of President Bush's administration. Upon my arrival my editor informed me that a rumour had broken just that morning that the firm had been a victim of either a merger or a takeover (I forget which), a commercial fashion sweeping the industry at that time, and that the melée surrounding us was the instant consequence of an as yet unfathomed proprietorial change of hands. All potential publishing projects were up in the air as of now, he informed me, apologised, and said he hoped we could do business if he managed to find another editorial incarnation once the whirlwind had passed.[54]

"Never mind about that!" I said, brandishing the typescript. "What I'm interested in is this!" I explained how I had found it and asked his permission to keep it, given that it was about to be rubbished. His first reaction was to tell me that the permissions office was on the floor above. Then, realising the idiocy of this remark, he corrected himself and, without so much as examining the typescript, denied me such permission. He told me that to remove the typescript would be a criminal act since it was not

---

[54] The rumour seems to have been entirely spurious, for Quartet is still owned today, as it has been since 1976, by Naim Atallah. They never published my book, all the same.

my property and intended for the municipal incinerator. The question of property I could have disputed. Sidney Ouvrier had not signed the copyright of his novel over to anyone, and as his legal heir I was now in control of his estate. In that respect, the typescript already belonged to me. But, turning these thoughts over in my mind, I realised that argument was entirely unnecessary. Laughing, and wishing him farewell, I left the permissionless publisher with a quarter of my grandfather's *opus* under my arm.

This was how I came to know of the actual composition of chapters forty-five to fifty as referred to in the "Index of Plagiarisms". For the part of the copy of the typescript I now possessed, as well as containing what looked like a misplaced "Epilogue", did not end at chapter forty-four. The familiar concluding lines in my grandfather's carbons ("I STARTED MAKING MAPS WHEN I WAS SMALL" etc.; cf. *Lanark* 560-1) had been excised, and in their place, in a similar but slightly smaller typeface, were ninety-two additional typed sheets whose bizarre contents I have already summarised.[55]

VII

To conclude. I have described this as a succession of unlikely coincidences. Indeed, it may seem that matters have so worked out that one could envisage only a Divine Plan as having framed them. True, it is hard to believe that I now possess a typescript of Alasdair Gray's, just as he possesses one which is, by rights, mine. But these illicit appropriations are hardly equal in weight or in value, if one reflects on the unpublishable nature of the item I hold in comparison to the literary fame with which his textual brigandage has furnished him. It is also, I must reflect, a staggering irony that I, the living person who has most reason to detest the trivial *divertissements* with which Gray has sullied my grandfather's labour of love of two and a half decades, should be, by virtue of my own familial proximity to the victim of the atrocity, the only individual besides the miscreant himself who understands their full, haughty, pedantic import.

In quieter moments, when my spleen gives way to a more philosophical disposition — often following the consumption of a medicinal draught, mind-expanding substance or realist novel — I find my whirling thoughts coming to a centre in the question of what the words would be, were he by

---

[55] Actual quotation from them has, on legal advice, been resisted. Gray's litigiousness, as his much-publicised action over the staging of one of his plays in the 1980s showed, is not worth provoking.

my side, that my admirable old *grand-père* would utter in summation of the unhappy history it has been my sorry and profitless duty here to recount. The words that I hear are not any of his own, but those of a great poet and contemporary, who was also incidentally a notorious practitioner of plagiarism, and whose lines I shall therefore reproduce without accreditation, as they may not even be his own:

> After such knowledge, what forgiveness? Think now
> History has many cunning passages, contrived corridors
> And issues, deceives with whispering ambitions,
> Guides us by vanities. Think now
> She gives when our attention is distracted
> And what she gives, gives with such supple confusions
> That the giving famishes the craving. Gives too late
> What's not believed in, or if still believed,
> In memory only, reconsidered passion. Gives too soon
> Into weak hands, what's thought can be dispensed with
> Till the refusal propagates a fear. Think
> Neither fear nor courage saves us. Unnatural vices
> Are fathered by our heroism. Virtues
> Are forced upon us by our impudent crimes.
> These tears are shaken from the wrath-bearing tree.

"It's" Misspelled: History of an Error in *The Waste Land* [1]

You find not the apostrophas, and so miss the accent.
— *Love's Labour's Lost*, iv.ii.12

Printers have persecuted me without a cause.
— *Psalms* 119:161, as misread by the compositor of the so-called "Printer's Bible"

---

[1] Written with Alexander George and first published in the *Bulletin of the Bibliographical Society of Australia and New Zealand* XI, 4 (1987), pp. 169-70. If either of us had had foreknowledge of the inordinate recalcitrance of editors of, and the extreme pickiness of readers for (not to mention the sheer bad manners regulating) the majority of the small number of international bibliographic journals, we would probably never have written this brief but pioneering article in the textual archaeology of Eliot's great poem. As it was, having written the piece (and, what's more, having the conviction with regard to our researches that we did), we showed a perseverance in seeking a sufficiently enlightened publisher which, under the adverse circumstances, appeared absurd to many of our acquaintances and colleagues. The fact that the paper actually bounced to and fro across five continents before eventually securing a home only made our eventual satisfaction that much more thorough. As well as its intrinsic merits, then, the piece should provide encouragement to all writers despondent on account of recurring rejection from publishers who fail to understand the originality and profundity of many of the submissions they see: it certainly stands as evidence that what in time proves to be widely celebrated and highly influential intellectual work is regularly snubbed and disparaged by the rampant conservatism of much of the academic publishing industry. With these supplementary ends in mind, I have taken the opportunity to reproduce it here in a "variorum" version. That is to say, I have included alongside the text the detractions, sneers, undervaluations, and spasmodic glimmers of insight, of the several misguided editors and readers who rejected the piece when it was offered to them. Parenthetical references denote the following journals, personal correspondence with which is in every case the source of the comments attached: *Library* = *The Library: Transactions of the Bibliographical Society* (London, England); *Papers* = *Papers of the Bibliographical Society of America* (Williamsburg, Massachusetts); *Bibliotheca* = *Bibliotheca Asiana* (Tashkent, Uzbekistan); *Digs* = *Textual Digs in Africa* (Cairo, Egypt); *Excremento* = *Excremento Bibliográfico* (San Miguel de Tucumán, Argentina). These were by no means the only publications to which we made submission — merely the handful that took the trouble even to reply.

Although published simultaneously (mid-October 1922),
the first English and American
printings of T.S.Eliot's *The
Waste Land* show several dis-
crepancies (*The Criterion* 1, 1
[October 1922] and *The Dial*
73, 5 [November 1922] respectively). One such discre-
pancy recurs five times in the
refrain of the bartender in ll.
141, 152, 165, 168 and 169 of
the poem, which occur in section II, "A Game of Chess":
The Criterion prints "HURRY
UP PLEASE IT'S TIME",
whereas *The Dial* has
"HURRY UP PLEASE ITS
TIME". There is no doubt as
to Eliot's intentions here: his
typescripts consistently read
"IT'S".[2] The American text is
therefore in error.

The error, nonetheless, was
retained in the first American
book edition of *The Waste
Land* (New York, Boni and
Liveright, 1922), while the
first English book edition (Ric-
mond, The Hogarth Press,
1923) is correct in this regard.
The next two English book
publications, however, raise a
problem: both *Poems 1909-25*
(London, Faber, 1925) and
Collected Poems 1909-35 (Faber, 1936) print "ITS". What

"The subject of attention is of course
one of great interest, and your particular observations should be of interest
to our readership. I am not aware that
this variant has attracted comment elsewhere" (*Library*).

"'There hath bene euer a discrepance in
vesture of youthe and age ELYOT'
(*OED*)" (*Bibliotheca*).

"As with its author, a mistake was
made in allowing the poem to cross the
Atlantic" (*Excremento*).

"Boy oh boy!" (*Digs*).

"An error in a game of chess typically
leads to defeat" (*Excremento*).

"Neither Woodward nor Beare comments specifically on this problem
(though Woodward observes somewhat
disarmingly on the way 'a report on all
the changes in punctuation as the poem
was reprinted is an undertaking too
large for this paper')" (*Library*).

"First — there *is* a point worth making
— ITS or IT'S will not change the
world" (*Library*).

"The relationship between the Hogarth
Press and Boni and Liveright editions
needs further investigation to establish
whether other differences might give
some clue to the descent of texts.
Beare (*SB*, 9, 1957) and Woodward
(*PBSA*, 58, 1964) between them probably cover this ground, but if no clue is
offered, this needs to be made plain"
(*Library*)."

'On the punctuation of this ... verse ...
a great controversy has arisen FARRAR'
(*OED*)" (*Bibliotheca*).

"Transcontinental   transcribbling!"
(*Digs*).

"'So much on punctual niceties they
stand 1795' (*OED*)" (*Bibliotheca*)."

has to be explained here is why the misspellings, hitherto occurring only in American editions, crept into the English texts. The interest of this is that many subsequent English collections, unlike the original English periodical and book editions, wrongly print "ITS": this is true, for instance, of *The Waste Land and Other Poems* (Faber, 1940), *Collected Poems 1909-62* (Faber, 1963) and *The Complete Poems and Plays of T.S. Eliot* (Faber, 1969). Our hypothesis is that, because of the greater number of errors in the Hogarth Press edition as compared to Boni and Liveright's, the latter may have been adopted as the printer's copy for *Poems 1909-25*.[3]

Interestingly, the error in question is found neither in Faber's limited edition of *The Waste Land*, three hundred copies of which were published in December 1961, nor in the second impression of *The Waste Land and Other Poems* (Faber, 1971). In the latter, the mistake is silently corrected. Despite these changes, the error has not been remedied in any of the other Faber collections, in which the

" ... as presented the hypothesis looks a little exposed ... it would appear to need a great deal more support beyond what is here offered: certainly the relative scarcity of [*sic*] the Hogarth Press edition does not seem an especially promising line of arguement [*sic*] ... the attribution of 'awareness' to the publishers is conceivably over-generous? — one needs to know, perhaps, rather more about the circumstances and the techniques of production which applied in the editions here considered. If we are talking about re-setting of the text (by whatever method) the variant or error have [*sic*] been introduced and/or emended in that process" (*Library*).

"Varicose, variolitic, vaticanical, vaticinal, verbally verrucated, verbigerating versicle! Mere meretricious metromania, deserving vapulation, a good Pounding!" (*Excremento*).

"Even for so small a detail far more comprehensive and thoroughgoing analysis of the texts seems called for. Hypotheses need the support of closer investigation of all available resources in an effort to substantiate them, and to limit the occasion for further speculation as narrowly as may be. (If as Beare says the Hogarth 1923 printing took its text from *Criterion* and the notes from B & L, then someone at Faber must have had access to a copy of the latter, and may simply have adopted it, as the 'authoritative' first complete (poem + notes) edition, as copy text for the 1925 and subsequent reprints ...)" (*Library*).

IT + -*s* of the possessive or genitive case, and at first commonly written *it's*. ...] From translation all Science had it's-of-spring FLORIO' (*OED*)" (*Bibliotheca*).

"Uh-huh." (*Digs*)

poem is reprinted. Indeed, though the first edition of *Selected Poems* (Harmondsworth, Penguin, 1948) and several subsequent Faber reprintings do not contain the error, it was re-introduced in one of the paperback impressions published between 1966 and 1972.[4]

Finally, we might highlight one more error, especially confusing because it involves an emendation for which there is no justification. In an appendix to the facsimile of *The Waste Land*, Valerie Eliot reprints the text of the first (American) book edition of the poem. Her version reads "HURRY UP PLEASE IT'S TIME" (see pp.138-9). Yet, as we have noted, the Boni and Liveright edition of 1922 omits the apostrophe.

"On this basis, I am afraid I am unable ..." (*Library*).

"'The text Deut. 6 hath the negative, Thou shalt serue no strange gods 1581' (*OED*)" (*Bibliotheca*).

"Nope." (*Digs*).

"Never, never, never, never, never!" (*Excremento*).

"Dear Mr. Daly: We regret that we cannot accept the note, '"It's" Misspelled: History of an Error in *The Waste Land*,' by you and Mr. George, for publication and return it herewith. As it stands, the paper is simply an enumeration of incomplete data, from which no firm conclusions can be drawn. Even the one tentative hypothesis you advance is not explored in any way (a careful analysis of the texts in question should go a long way toward determining whether or not the Boni and Liveright edition was used as a copy text for Faber's 1925 edition). Sincerely" (*Papers*).

'I have seen a Grammarian toure, and plume himselfe over a single line in Horace Sir T. Browne' (*OED*)" (*Bibliotheca*).

---

[2] See Valerie Eliot, ed., *The Waste Land: A Facsimile and Transcript of the Original Drafts* (London, Faber, 1971), pp. 12, 14, 18, 20.

[3] For comparative textual evaluation of the various editions and general discussion of the textual history of the poem, see Daniel H. Woodward, "Notes on the Publishing History and Text of *The Waste Land*", *Papers of the Bibliographical Society of America* 58 (July/September 1964), pp. 252-69.

[4] The 1965 impression prints "IT'S", the 1973 impression "ITS". Unfortunately, none of the intervening impressions is available in the Faber archive, so it is at present impossible to state precisely in which the error was re-introduced. The authors would be grateful for further information on this point.

Crackpot Texts, or Nonsense Plumb'd, Explor'd, & Sustain'd

The title of this essay provokes the objection that its author must either be guilty of a mere pretence to ignorance, or should not write about what he does not understand. Yet while there is much in Kafka that I do not understand, I believe that I do understand some things in Kafka by understanding my not understanding Kafka. At least the situation is somewhat kafkaesque. On the eve of a visit to his beloved fiancée which led to the first — inconclusive — breakup of the engagement, Kafka wrote: "I write differently from the way I speak, speak differently from the way I think, think differently from the way I ought to think, and so on down into the deepest darkness." What is perhaps appropriate is the sense of being a talking onion: voices, layer upon layer, each contradicting the next.[1]

---

[1] Peter Heller, "On Not Understanding Kafka", *The Kafka Debate: New Perspectives for Our Time*, ed. Angel Flores (New York, Gordian Press, 1977), p. 24. This is the only footnote, although not the only reference, which will appear in this essay. Given the absurd subject matter of the piece, the amphigorious frame into which the essay is placed (or between the spars of which it recedes), it would be an act of bad faith, at variance with the argument laid before the reader herein, to foster the illusion that clarity or enlightenment is to be found by his or her consulting the precise passages which would otherwise be signified by a spray of annotation flying, like grit from the sole of a goosestepping boot, at the base of each page. The reader wishing to experience such marginalial hallucinations may do so by consuming another item in this volume, "Concplags and Totplag" etc. Where passages are quoted they are quoted with accuracy (none are invented, at least not by me, although I cannot answer for my *alter ego*); the names of actual authors, I grant, are sometimes, but not always, omitted or replaced by fictive ones for mainly, but not totally, economic reasons (things are thus made more difficult for publishers on the lookout for permissions fees: they will actually have to have read and remembered their authors as well as put them into print to earn their crust by this method); specification of page numbers is neglected with a consistency bordering on the professional; and if certain citations possess a somewhat elliptical aura, this is usually, although there are exceptions, in imitation of the literary style of the original thus cited. My cavalier attitude to roundhead footnotes is furthermore a compositional application of the practical insight that bits of trash one would normally assign to the dustbin can just as easily be spread all over the living room, a tactic which ensures that visitors are unable very readily to make themselves comfortable. My reason for footnoting Heller is sheer politeness — akin to the *hello* I would offer as you arrive at my door but before I present you with the rubbish-strewn lounge — rather than recommendation. His article is an interesting pioneer piece on the merits of incomprehensibility, but it gets dafter the longer it grinds on (the paragraph quoted is its first) by invoking all manner of bogus dichotomies (e.g. "life itself"/"interpretation"). It was written in the days before critical theory gave all our unintelligible lives a meaning, something to live and die for, as is obvious from Heller's mid-essay crisis when he wistfully pines, "if only there were some master-discipline that would enable us to ascend or descend from, say, the physio-psychological to the sociological, the philosophical, the theological interpretations and to relate them to one another so as to assign each its place". Indeed. One can imagine Kafka smirking.

I

Above ground, in every metropolitan and civic centre, suitably dressed authors and readers intermingle meaningfully in the translucent rays of common sense and linear narrative, which, when they wane, as they must towards the end of each day, never fail to do so without a satisfying sense of closure. Beneath these urbane boulevards, squares, avenues and terraces, however, in a semantic sewer-void, and usually round the clock, much smaller bands of authorats and readerodents splash, squelch and fraternise nakedly in saturnalian debauches of textual rigmarolery and flapdoodle delirium. The rôle of the critic in such circumstances, conventionally, is to stand sentinel at the grille which separates city from sough (a drain-gate known, in the Scottish dialect of the present writer, and for obvious reasons, as *the stank*), thus preventing the citizens of the upper world from slipping inadvertently into the nether and, simultaneously, deodorising any whiffs or waifs which manage to ascend from the effluvial to the perfumed region.

Again, in most private houses the breadth and depth, circumference and radius of the land, fictionists are frequently permitted to thrust their organs of meaning into booklovers rendered prone by the rigid realism and logical plenitude which what appeared to be a mere floppy paperback can assume after half an hour of dedicated and patient foreplay. Yet, in the should-be contentful moments following such amicable intercourse, conquistador and seduced are often disconcerted by the muted ululations, snortings and ejaculations of much more monstrous copulations being conducted in the unexplored attic above the roof above their heads. In such a situation the critic arrives like a Rentokil officer who, for a modest fee, pokes a head and an arm above the trap door of the loft to thunder liberal jets of intellectual pesticide into every corner before descending to seal the portal with a semi-permanent surrealist repellant.

Or, if you like, most readers and authors spend most of their time on the grim mainland hacking at a hard sematological coalface or soberly engaged on an onomastic assembly line where component words drift past on conveyor belts of text. Meanwhile a vicious minority, parasitic on this virtuous majority, live lives of permanent linguistic crapulence, discoursing in an absurdist polyglot medley on the jamboree islands of Choreophrasia, a small archipelago periodically engulfed by tidal waves of bilge and tornadoes of tommyrot. Critics are usually either cartographers who leave these islands off their maps, or tourism copywriters who omit them from their brochures.

Such are the tasks of the critical enterprise as commonly understood. (We ought perhaps, at this point, although not necessarily in this connection, to make some trenchant enquiries about certain less orthodox critical schools. Is it any coincidence, for example, that two of the most prominent cultural materialists in this country — Terence Hawkes and Terry Eagleton — both have surnames, and perhaps noses, suggestive of rapacious birds of prey? Or that, furthermore, although atheists, they possess Christian names of wildly improbable similarity? One has a right to wonder if the chances of having an article accepted by *Feminist Review* would be increased by submitting it under the *nom de plume* of Teri Kestreldome, and, whether or not, what conservative critics such as Roger Scrotum or Sir Frank Commode would have to say about the matter. For an actually existing critique of British Marxism from an America-Italian perspective, however, see Umberto Eco and Noam Chomsky's celebrated *Eco-Noamic and Philosophical Manuscripts*.) The present writer, on the other hand, was trained in the Orphean/Dantesque/Marlovian/Briefing-For-A-Descent-Into-Hell school of intellectual endeavour, and consequently has the advantage over his peers of a much more amphibious disposition. I am the Captain Nemo of the literary critical world. So grab your rubber suit and hop on board, explore the half-charted depths in my enchanted submarine.

(Again, are you really trying to tell me that Tony Bennett, author of *Formalism and Marxism* [London, Methuen, 1979] and Tony Benn, author of *Arguments for Socialism* [London, Jonathan Cape, 1979] are two separate people? Pull the other one.)

Definitions, definitely, are where we ought to begin. What is a *crackpot text* anyway? Typical reviewer's cant — " — a *tour de force* which breaks the mould of — " — offers a splendid synonym: to *crackpot* (verb) is to *mould-break* (verb). An author who breaks textual moulds is thus technically a *crackpotter* (noun), but the English language, conscious as ever that its whimsicality sustains domestic employment among those who elect to expound its mysteries to bewildered non-natives, bamboozlingly calls such an author a simple *crackpot* (noun) instead. Some of the problematics of this terminology become obvious if one contemplates the crackpotting process in terms of a concrete, or porcelain, image. Picture a toilet bowl (which is a kind of pot, conveniently enough). To *crackpot* (verb) here is to exert a pressure or force (e.g. time, too many bums) which will cause such a number of cracks to appear in the smooth wall of the bowl that it finally shatters and collapses, with all the attendant indignity, olfactory punishment and plumber's fees. But if the exerter of the pressure or force is *also* designated a *crackpot* (rather than a *crackpotter*) we confusingly tend to think of *him* or *her* as the *cracked pot*, the pot which is cracked, in this case as a fetid depository of human evacuations. Little can be done to obviate this endemic terminological inexactitude short of using words which are decidedly un-English in their specificity. I do not intend to alienate my readers by this pedantic device, and so I will simply state here that, in what follows, where I use the term *crackpot* as a noun, I would wish to be understood as meaning *crackpotter*.

The practice of writing a text which breaks a mould (the mould is usually *meaning*, incidentally, and the result of the breakage *nonsense*) is known as *crackpottery*. Some literary theorists have made crackpottery into a profession, but this study is concerned primarily with those writers who have raised it to the status of an art.

Crackpots have been the subject of recent experimental investigations designed to ascertain whether or not their artistic faculties are the products of genetics or environment. One particular thesis — that crackpots are characterised by an abnormal swelling in the lower left region of the *cerebellum*, usually reaching the size and shape of an egg, but often disguised by the scalp — has recently gained currency. The evidence is presented in two related papers by the distinguished brain specialist Colin Blakebore, "Crackups in Dali's Cranium" (*Physiological Aesthetics*, vol. 65 [Summer 1992]) and "Inner Skull Deformations in Three Dadaists" (*Text and Cortex*, vol. 19 [Fall 1993]). Blakebore argues that the growth, which appears as a small knob at puberty in both men and women and enlarges slowly but steadily thereafter, causes rearrangements of the grey matter mainly of the *cerebellum* but also of the *cerebrum* which, although unpredictable in their effects, are most commonly associated with linguistic misperformances (antiphrasis, solecism, lapsus calami, catachresis, dipsobabble), failures to sustain logical sequencing and progression (paralogism, semantic heterostrophy), confusion of metaphor and reality (tropic psychosis), a generally disordered state of mind (cacothymia), and mild periodic (lunar) paranoia. The swelling eventually effects a fatal fissuring of the skull behind the left ear (hence its popular appellation, *crackpot's vesuvius*). Blakebore emphasises, however, that the aetiology of the condition is obscure, and hopes to investigate its possibly hereditary nature by means of projected progeny and predecessor studies. One so far inexplicable discovery is that few victims of the illness tend to write about themselves, but that those who do are always male. (The interstices between autobiography and masculinity have, of course, been visited on several occasions, although not under pathological influence, by Umberto Eco — most concertedly in *Eco Homo*.) There we must leave *crackpot's vesuvius* to the scientists — for we are concerned with its implications for literature rather than headaches — but not before noting that, as usual, the artists got there ahead of them. Adrian Mitchell, in his superb poem of the early sixties, "Veteran with a Head Wound", describes how "Shapes lounged around his mind chatting of murder,/Telling interminable jokes,/Watching like tourists for Vesuvius to burst." Another sufferer, the poet Hugh MacDiarmid, who wrote an entire book about historical crackpots entitled *Scottish Eccentrics*, seems to have had an intuitive understanding of the disorder when he said of himself, "My job, as I see it, has never been to lay a tit's egg, but to erupt like a volcano, emitting not only flame but a lot of rubbish." MacDiarmid's favourite word, "antisyzygy", seems also to express consummately the mental condition precipitated by the illness.

II

To go on as we meant to begin, let us consider the case of Franz Kafka, a man whose occiput has not yet been exhumed, but which might prove of interest to science if it were. (Why is it, by the way, that most of the epoch-making writers of German have surnames which seem to be onomatopoëises of human respiratory functions? Thus "Nietzsche" is more of a sneeze than a name, "Schopenhauer" more a yawn than a philosopher; "Marx" is a belch and "Hegel" a hiccup; while "Goethe" is a splutter and "Kafka" a dry cough. Makes you wonder.) It's not that crackpottery begins with Kafka, I ought to say, but you can only go so far down in a submarine before things start to get much too gloomy to allow you to distinguish anything at all, and few would disagree that Kafka is pretty murky. Walter Benjamin said that Kafka's novels "are set in a swamp world", and he was right, which is why I'll be using more than just that quotation from the essay he wrote on the tenth anniversary of Kafka's death. There are plenty more adventurers than Benjamin in this swamp as well. As far back as 1974 Bert Nagel pointed out that the secondary literature on Kafka (whose complete works, if we discount his personal writings, can be bought in two medium size paperbacks) had already exceeded ten thousand items. Everybody agrees that none of these optimistic commentators has pierced the murk in the slightest: they have simply analysed the quality of the murk itself. Trying to locate and grasp definite meaning in Kafka has proved as difficult as trying to substantiate the presence of a plesiosaur in Loch Ness. It just can't be done.

Take the famous cathedral chapter in *The Trial*, in which we read a parable about a man from the country who comes to the door of the Law but is prevented from entering by a guard. This section of the novel and its consequence is sufficiently familiar to you, I trust, not to require my wasting valuable space and permissions money reproducing the translated text. (There is a slim, grim collection of essays on *The Trial* in which the editor, Harold Bloom, in an introduction, reproduces the entire text of the

parable despite the fact that it appears, again *in toto*, in one of the pieces
he has included in the same volume, only forty-four pages later.
Outrageous!) The gist of it, if you haven't, is that the man waits all his life
and is never admitted. With his dying breath he asks why no one else has
ever come to the door, since everyone strives to attain the Law. The guard
tells him that the door was intended for him, the man, alone, and that he,
the guard, is now going to close it. End of parable. Now, this had actually
appeared on its own as "Vor dem Gesetz" ("Before the Law") in Kafka's
The Country Doctor, but what Kafka does with it in *The Trial* is place it
in a context in which it is addressed to K. by a priest as a means, the priest
hints, of curing K. of what the priest calls a delusion. (The relevant
preceding part of the exchange, beginning with K., is: "'But you are an
exception among those who belong to the Court. I have more trust in you
than in any of the others, though I know many of them. With you I can
speak openly.' 'Don't be deluded,' said the priest. 'How am I being
deluded?' asked K. 'You are deluding yourself about the Court,' said the
priest. 'In the writings which preface the Law that particular delusion is
described thus: before the Law stands a door-keeper ... '" etc. etc.) Kafka
also adds over two thousand words of exegetical argument between K. and
the priest over the import of the parable, on which they cannot agree.
Benjamin asks rhetorically if the parable as it appeared in *The Country
Doctor* would have led the reader

> to the never-ending series of reflections traceable to this parable at
> the place where Kafka undertakes to interpret it? This is done by
> the priest in *The Trial*, and at such a significant moment that it
> looks as if the novel were nothing but the unfolding of the parable.
> The word "unfolding" has a double meaning. A bud unfolds into
> blossom, but the boat which one teaches children to make by
> folding paper unfolds into a flat sheet of paper. This second kind
> of "unfolding" is really appropriate to the parable; it is the reader's
> pleasure to smooth it out so that he has the meaning on the palm of
> his hand. Kafka's parables, however, unfold in the first sense, the
> way a bud turns into a blossom.

These remarks are almost as superbly opaque as the parable they are
commenting on, while possessing the same apparently innocent limpidity
of meaning. What exactly *is* the difference between the way a bud and a
sheet of paper unfold/are unfolded? That the bud isn't flat? Is that it? And
what if you've never taught children to make paper boats because your own
parents, like mine, never took the trouble to teach you, because their
parents, etc. etc. — doesn't that make a difference? This is truly inspired

criticism, written after the example of its original, and indebted to it even in the detail of its imagery. Slyly, Benjamin here alludes to the passage in which, circumvented by the Deputy Manager and the manufacturer, "it seemed to K. as though two giants of enormous size were bargaining above his head for himself. Slowly, lifting his eyes as far as he dared, he peered up to see what they were about, and then picked up one of the documents from the desk at random, *laid it flat on his open palm*, and gradually raised it, rising himself with it, to their level. In doing so he had no definite purpose" etc. etc. (Chapter VII, emphasis added). This very precise, calculated laying flat of the paper on the palm is said by the narrator to have no definite purpose. Benjamin's text, acting as a mirror to Kafka's, casts back this image, a little wrinkled, a little reversed, but no more clearly. To intervene between the country man and the guard with a "meaning" to their exchange on the palm of your hand would be as pointless and only likely to lead to the same rebuff as K., the Assessor, receives from his Deputy Manager, who "merely glanced at the paper without even reading what was on it, for anything that seemed important to the Assessor was unimportant to him, took it from K.'s hand, said: 'Thanks, I know all that already,' and quietly laid it back on the desk again." You see what I mean?

With Kafka, fiction as assurance, as certitude of communication, as a thing which securely begins, middles and ends, is no more. *The Trial* subjects it to such enigmatic internal pressure that the toilet pan of the novel lies sundered, capsized, inelegant and fascinating to look at on the floor of the reader's privy. Benjamin the plumber is called in, but neither his tools nor his attitude are the expected ones: he spends a long time marvelling at the fracture lines, explains how some of them occurred, moves the fragments around with his thumb, and invites the reader to share his sense of enthralled bafflement that each should be just the shape it is and no other. The reader disagrees that each *is* just the shape that he says it is and no other, and also has doubts about exactly what caused those fracture lines, after the articulation of which, and some dispute, Benjamin shrugs his shoulders and leaves, with no agreement having been reached about his bill. Benjamin sees, naturally, that Kafka has wryly foreshadowed those ten thousand plus critical engagements with which intellectuals will attempt the literary equivalent of biting candy floss once it has been placed on the tongue. In the "fiction", the parable of the Law ("Before the law …") is explicated by a professional agent (the priest) to a disadvantaged but sceptical subject (K.); in the "real world", the meaning of an author's work is explained by a critic to a reader who would be crazy to be credulous. The second process is pre-emptively rendered absurd by the first, because the first is a fable about the inaccessibility of meaning, the futility of attempting to get across the threshold of the text to the semantic security which is desired and envisaged as lying beyond it. (It needs to be observed, however, that it can remain absurd only in an impossible world in which readers experience no intestinal emergencies. As soon as those start to make themselves felt the wrecker of the thunderbox and the unworldly plumber will probably appear in a different light — even, perhaps, on a legal summons.)

Some of this has been said already, with less economy and more abstruseness than I can muster, by Jacques Derider. "Devant la Loi" can be found in Alan Udoff's edited anthology, *Kafka and the Contemporary Critical Performance* (Indiana University Press, 1987), and what a performance it is! Apparently the transcript of a Derider lecture — fourteen thousand polysyllables of tantalising postponement, labyrinthine syntax and leisurely circumbendibus — it must have gone on for about two and a half hours. (My favourite joke in it is the baroque, self-defeating transition, "So as not to deplete the temporal economy of which I have to take account, I shall say without further delay ... "; and what he goes on to say is "that I cannot give nor am I withholding a response" to a question he has just asked. He then guesses that the audience's reaction to this incapacity, this non-denial — there still seem to have been people in the room, but then this was only fifteen minutes in — might be to "suppose that I am leading you toward a purely aporetic conclusion or in any case toward a problematic overstatement" and, after heaping some more qualificatory onions on top of this beefburger, concedes, "You may be right." All of this in one paragraph. The man's a genius.) We cannot say, indeed, how long it lasted, because it defeated even the translator, Avital Ronell, who seems to have taken to heart a remark Derider quotes from the priest in *The Trial* — "the script is immutable and the commentaries often merely express the despair this causes" — for there she breaks off entirely with a "translator's note" which says, "Derider's text continues; but, blind and weary, I shut the text-door here." Not even the translator, presumably some kind of Derider votary, could stay awake till the end! There can be few comparable contemporary exhibitions of the exhaustive power of imperspicuity.

Derider's main aim seems to be to establish his *différance* from Walter Benjamin, evidently not convinced that the facts of the latter's deceased status are sufficient to put this beyond any doubt. Thus "Devant la Loi" does what Benjamin suggests is unlikely by taking *The Country Doctor* version of the parable and demonstrating that it *can* lead the reader (well, *this* reader) to a never-ending series of reflections. That said, a lot of what Derider says is what Benjamin would have said had he been more loquacious, or French: that "'Before the Law' does not tell or describe anything but itself as text"; that it "is the narration of ... inaccessibility to the narration"; that "reading a text might indeed reveal that it is untouchable, properly intangible *precisely because it can be read*, and for the same reason unreadable to the extent to which the presence within it of a clear and graspable sense remains as hidden as its origin"; that it "from the outset produces a *mise en abîme*" of virtually anything that can be said about it. And yet, engulfed as he is, Derider proves that a drowning man can continue to provide entertainment for the watchers on shore. One of the most diverting yet profound asides of his lecture concerns the disregard within the western intellectual tradition for the "incredible story of noses" and their relation to the female genitals: "perhaps one has not been overly attentive to the hairs within nostrils which are sometimes indecently exposed — to the point, indeed, that they sometimes have to be trimmed". Would the importance of that to Kafka have occurred to Benjamin?

(It is worth noting here, for it will cost us nothing to do so, that Christopher Norris changes trains in chapter one of his Fontana Modern Masters book on Derider [1987] by pointing out that the latter was arrested "on a trumped-up charge of possessing drugs" while in Prague in 1982, where he took part in an "unofficial" seminar, visited Kafka's grave without, as I've said, digging it up, and worked on "Devant la Loi". Now the possession of illicit substances by French cultural theorists in foreign countries is not, if we are to believe the confessions of Derider's deceased contemporary, Michel Fuckall, so very unknown. Yet, regardless of this detail, we ought perhaps to give the Czech authorities their due for putting Derider through a more genuinely Kafkaesque experience than he seemed to be seeking, the benefit of which, probably, is that "Devant la Loi" is three and a half times more impenetrable than it would have been otherwise. It might also be worth advising Christopher ["Chuck"] Norris, for it involves a comparison which he may take as a terrific compliment, that, given his own uncanny physiognomic and phrenological resemblance to Vladimir ["Ilyich"] Lenin, he himself ought to be careful in these changed days about accepting similar invitations to St Petersburg.)

III

It is an obvious step from Franz Kafka to Frank Kuppner, not just because "Frank Kuppner" is so reminiscent of "Franz Kafka" that one finds it difficult to accept that it is a real name (its proprietor gives away its assumed nature when he tells us, in his "novel, of sorts" entitled *A Very Quiet Street* [Polygon, 1989], that his mother was also called "Kuppner", for this, we know, is not the name she was born with), but also because

Kuppner's creative territory is the Prague of the West, Reykjavic of the South, Bogota of the East, and Kinshasa of the North — I mean, of course, that still centre of this geographical crucifer in which I, too, have my origins — that one-time Cancer of Empire, now Empire of Cancer, the city of Glasgow. I vaguely remember (I don't have the text in front of me) Max Brod putting on record a conversation, the sociable opening gambit of which, on Kafka's part, was, "We are nihilistic thoughts, suicidal thoughts that come into God's head." Brod pleasantly interpreted this as an expression of the Gnostic view of life, in which God is an evil demiurge and the world the result of his Fall. "Oh no," Kafka said, winking no doubt, "our world is only a bad mood of God, a bad day of his," at which Brod giggled back a deduction to the effect that there was, then, hope outside the manifestation of the world that we know. Kafka cackled in seeming agreement, "Oh, plenty of hope, an infinite amount of hope — " and then dissolved in a fit of laughter that eventually had him on his back, kicking his legs in the air like a man who has been transformed into an insect, before he managed to regain enough composure to shriek, " — but not for us!" and then sank once more into the mire of his glee. Anybody who has read, tried to read, or acknowledged after a couple of pages the impossibility of reading Frank Kuppner's "Lost Work", may recognise its origin in this spirited witticism of the earlier F.K. Whether or not Kuppner knows Kafka said this is hardly material. It's the sort of thing you can overhear in Glasgow every Friday night.

"Lost Work" is a thirty thousand word web of prose, the first of three totally unrelated sections in Kuppner's *Ridiculous! Absurd! Disgusting!* (Carcanet, 1989). Its narrator knows everything that Kafka said, because its narrator is God (for the most part — which is to say, other voices intervene; the narrator describes himself — that is, occasional sexual metamorphoses aside, it does seem to be male — as, somewhat enigmatically, "at least half-responsible for the creation of the universe", and in "Lost Work" hails — this is an appropriate verb, for what he does speak is on the whole a shower of abuse — his creation at large, which, at one discourteous moment, he addresses collectively as "you peculiar extrapolations of potassium"). It is a God, however, who seems to be living in a Kafkaesque universe (towards the end — although this temporal/spatial indication is obviously problematical as a referent to a discourse which is taking place in eternity/infinity, "eternity" itself being merely a convenience, according to the narrator, who says of it, "of course I would not use that word if I had not forgotten the expression which indicates the longer time-scale within which I habitually operate" — there is even a giant insect). A large amount of this will become obscurer as we proceed. For the moment, the sense of delight at opening a book and *finding* a "Lost Work" ought to be registered. However, one's pleasure in a discovery can only be maintained by a perception that it possesses a worth, and this is a property (even at the level of exchange-value as opposed to use-value, the latter clearly being negative) which "Lost Work" immediately shows little claim to deserving. (I bought the remaindered book which contains it for 25p in a Nottingham store, a price which gives it a value, as a mere commodity, of 8.33 recurring pence. With hindsight, this seems expensive.)

On the other hand, the title may not *be* "Lost Work". The God of this text has reached such a full understanding of his enormously fed-up condition that he has decided to end it all, to extinguish himself and everything ("What is causing me to die is the knowledge that I am immortal"). Therefore the title may be a slip of the pen for "Last Work" which the narrator either failed to notice, noticed but refused to correct, or deliberately crafted (if the last can be said of a parapraxis); certainly at one point he does make "a disgraceful slip of the pen which I shall not bother myself to correct" (i.e. "shitting" for "sitting") and, at another, we are given a preposterous date to locate his reading of a newspaper — 1086 was before the invention of printing — and he remarks, in square brackets, that it is "a charming misprint of mine which I chose to retain". If "Last Work" is/was/will be the intended title, however, one may legitimately ask why it is the *first* work in *Ridiculous! Absurd! Disgusting!*, although this would be no more paradoxical than the narrator's own self-undermining remarks about having come to the end of what he has to say, but still saying it (e.g.: "At this point, I destroyed this work", or "We have now gone beyond, for reasons that are obvious, the end of this work. It is therefore necessary that, merely to signal the further passage of unnecessary time, I simulate another fragmentary universe, whether of discourse or of life, or of the one symbolizing the other, and continue to talk, in a non-existent voice, of unimportant, incoherent things"). There are other titular possibilities which it may be wiser not to explore. We shall stick to the idea of it being a "Lost Work" in what follows, and wish that it had stayed that way.

I prefer, in fact, to think of "Lost Work" as referring, not to the text itself, but to the act of reading it. One sign of Kuppner's consummate artistry is that most of his writing truly deserves grand aesthetic assessments which are normally invoked only hyperbolically — "instantly forgettable", for example, is a judgment which genuinely does apply to "Lost Work". I've read it five times and I can't remember anything definite about it, and the reason I keep bunging in quotations from it is to remind myself that I actually did so rather than (in my profession this is sometimes necessary) pretended I did so. When you get to the "end" of "Lost Work" (the last line, by the way, is "I forget the original ending"), you can recall only very dimmest, fuzziest, most shadowy, impalpable things contained within its boundaries, wherever they are. It runs through the understanding like an express train through a country station, leaving you discomposed and trembling a little on the platform. It is like a disagreeable curry which, at the moment the last portion of it hits the maw, is comprehensively vomited forth again, only a hint of it remaining as a slight taste in the gullet. This last is a more serviceable analogy, since the "work" performed in consuming it (never mind the expense of buying etc. etc.) is "lost" by the failure to digest. But, to be more precise, "Lost Work" is really like a dream from which you wake up ("Actually, a lot of your history is, literally, a yawn") and strain to recall. But you might as well try to sit on a cloud, embrace your own reflection in a pond, or attempt to get the welfare benefits you are entitled to.

A standard piece of surrealism, then. A slice of night life, full of Freudian omissions (if a thing can *be full of* omissions, e.g.: "[a word is missed out here]"; [expletive deleted]"; "[name removed here]"), denials and reversals ("That is not true, but it is how I choose to lie to you at the moment"; "Had I thought of saying this earlier, I would have said the opposite"); and that classic form of repression, refusal to own up to having the intellectual equipment to make sense of it all ("I think, he often said thoughtfully, that I am never quite going to be able to explain all this fully"; "I confess that in thinking this over I do not completely understand it, or fathom the coherence which it no doubt possesses. I suppose I was not paying as much attention as I should have been doing under the circumstances"). But as well as this ("It is the detailed knowledge of trivia that most reveals the God") there are many of those sublime hypnagogic insights and intuitions of the sort which the Viennese totalitarian of the psyche was always insisting had a meaning if the patient would only stop stalling (e.g.: "Things get better. Things get worse. Things stay the same. And all at once"; "Every sunrise was fashionable once"; "what would a photograph of something be if it were a photograph of something else?"; "it is perhaps because we can look through women's pockets that we assume that we can never die"; "It makes as much sense to think of a heaven made for earrings as one made for the people that wear them"; "You should try to develop enough skill to be able to write literature, and then write something else" etc. etc.).

Now there are so many fundamental problems with Freud's methodology that it's astonishing (although not as astonishing as the comparable longevity of surrealism, the Freudian aesthetic) that it is still found useful. Let me describe one of its flaws that I have noticed (this will save me looking up textbooks so that I can recycle those that others have noticed). This is to do with the idea that dreams are wish-fulfilments of thwarted desires experienced during the immediately preceding period of wakefulness. The problem with this theory is that it is endlessly self-fulfilling, to prove which, I ask the reader to imagine the following scenario, which surely must have been repeated many times. Freud, at Berggasse 19, Vienna, on any day that his biographers will not quarrel with, is trying, as he often valiantly did, late into the night, to decode the manifest content of his own previous night's dream, to uncover its latent content. But, as must have happened on countless occasions, he finds himself unable to do so. He retires in a state of some intellectual dissatisfaction, his desire to decode the dream thwarted. He wakes up next morning from a dream in which his thwarted desire is satisfied, in which his wish to understand the dream of the *preceding* night's sleep is fulfilled — that is, he has dreamed about discovering the latent content of the *other* dream which had eluded him during his waking hours. Now, I ask you, is this a solid foundation on which to build a science? For it suggests that, to work out the most profound problems, thinking is an inefficient analytic tool which one may as well discard. The best thing to do is have a kip.

Here I feel under an obligation to confess something, and, as I'm a Catholic, and the words "obligation" and "confess" have a significance within Catholicism which they do not have in the language of certain religions with a shorter and less ornamented history, please understand that the following statement is a considered, calculated, and reverent one. (Incidentally, the only literary critic of comparable stature who is a Catholic, to my knowledge, is David Lodge, despite the scurrilous allegations to the contrary made by Calvin Knox in "Orange Lodge", *The Lozenge*, 1 April 1994.) Frank Kuppner often makes such confessions too, although not in "Lost Work", and I have already, earlier in this essay, praised a critic for imitating his crackpot original (the more precise among my readers may reflect that "to imitate" need not mean "to do the same as" but "to represent oneself as doing the same as", but this is an ambiguity of no importance in the present situation). In short, between writing the last word of the previous paragraph and the first word of this, I went to bed. There was a more serious intention in mind in taking this step than simply ensuring that "Lost Work" did not lead to lost sleep. In short, I wished to discover whether or not the Freudian technique might actually work. Would my desire to understand Frank Kuppner, continually denied by Frank Kuppner himself, be satisfied by Morpheus? The outcome was most curious. *I dreamed that I was reading paragraphs of continuous prose which were not held together by any logical glue.*

(If this seems harsh on Freud, it is perhaps in reaction to his irritating habit of establishing connections between the obviously unconnected.

There were some occasions, of course, when he was happy to live with rather than conjure away contradictions. His comment on the following anecdote from *Jokes and Their Relation to the Unconscious* is a good example:

> "A. borrowed a copper kettle from B. and after he had returned it was sued by B. because the kettle now had a big hole in it which made it unusable. His defence was: 'First, I never borrowed a kettle from B. at all; secondly, the kettle had a hole in it already when I got it from him; and thirdly, I gave him back the kettle undamaged.'" Each one of these defences is valid in itself, but taken together they exclude one another. A. was treating in isolation what had to be regarded as a connected whole ... We might also say: "A. has put an 'and' where only an 'either-or' is possible."

This "mutual cancelling-out by several thoughts" is habitual in Kuppner. The statement, "Even though I long ago finished uttering my last words ... I nonetheless still continue to do so" is a straightforward example: one can continue the work of finishing something, but one cannot continue to do something one has finished.)

If perspicacity was not occasioned by this method, nonetheless certain thoughts occurred to me after its execution, although not necessarily consequent upon it, which I had not divined by any prior means. These insights do not dispel in any far-reaching respect the monstrous incubus of imbecility squatting above "Lost Work" which, like Euclid's *pons asinorum*, has to be passed over before any true enlightenment can be attained. But it does allow enhanced appreciation of some of the local colour. There is a formidably nonplussing passage, for instance, in which Kuppner allows a group of toes belonging to two feet to engage in the following banter, or what the narrator bemusingly calls "a widespread discussion ... among the eager litigants, a word more normally used to invoke a process at law":

> Death is only a metaphor for literature, asserted one. (It was probably thinking of English literature, but neglected to particularize.) ...
>
> A uniform is an attempt to render independent judgement irrelevant, soberly suggested a fourth, or perhaps a fifth.
>
> Everyone over 50 years of age is a person over 50 years of age, added a fifth who had once had a reputation as a sage. The opposite is true of those who are under 50 years of age, it

continued.

But why oppress people, cried a sixth, seventh or eighth passionately, in the name of some questionable distant abstraction, when you can oppress them in their own name?

Age is age, reflected one, and wisdom is wisdom. (Some of them glanced at each other a little uneasily.)

We can remember nearly everything — except what it is we talked about almost all the time, blurted out perhaps the smallest member of that assembly.

Now one has to remind oneself that this entire business is narrated by a Divine Being who will by definition have read Nietzsche and, shall we say, been none to pleased, to put it mildly, by that German philosopher's, shall we call them, anti-Tetragrammatonical tendencies. Certain deities, we need no reminding, are vengeful, and these anti-aphorisms are presumably to be taken as a witty theophanic negation of — or thunderous oracular rebuff to — Nietzsche's favoured form of satirical jousting (if we have worries over their pronouncement by a bunch of traditionally speechless digits we need only remind ourselves that in Nietzsche's maxims there are anvils talking to hammers, or the complete reverse of this, and numerous other comparable idiocies). Similarly, the portrayal of the All-wise and Almighty as suffering from a host of neuroses and paranoias — the most distinctly articulated of which is connected with a prejudice that the whole of humanity is paying him far too much attention ("I wish you would all stop following me around"), as if he were or could be prey to the psychological weaknesses described by that other arch atheist, whose Berggasse *chaise-longue* may comically be assumed to be the context in which the outpouring of this supramundane monologue is couched — is a relatively transparent lampoon of the same order. Prefer, if you will, a reading in which thirty thousand words are expended for the purposes of a mere postmodern allegory of the decline of authorial omniscience. I make my own predilection for apocalyptic conclusions explicit here and now.

In the end, then (although there is no end), it is possible to argue that, for all its metafictional coprostasis, metaphysical hypostasis, and metadictional homeostasis, "Lost Work" is that thoroughly traditional (though frequently stylistically metagrobolically metastatic) project, a textual trial of faith, a *Pilgrim's Progress* as seen from the other end of the cosmic telescope. It may be, in other words, that, with a remarkable moral courage uncommon to this day and age, Kuppner has composed a narrative which, by means of its own looped, circumvoluted and meandering logic, its penchant, as the French would say, to make *un voyage de zig-zag*, emerges as a militant warning against the corruptions and comforts of metajargonistic apostasis:

> Needless to say, the God capable of underpinning a world in which people can die by being struck on the head by a block of frozen excrement dropped from a passing, invisible, inaudible plane — which is, alas, what I am — is perfectly capable of designing an afterlife which will be seen and enjoyed only by those who did not believe in it. True believers, if they are very lucky, just die, disappear, are forgotten about. I tell you here and now, and I know that as true believers you will not doubt me, that only true believers are extinguished at death. Unbelievers live on, joyously.

But I don't, personally speaking, believe this.

IV

(Umberto Eco and David Lodge have recently explored the anxieties of European house swapping, each in his characteristically self-aggrandising manner, in *The Eco-Lodgy Movement*, most revealingly in the latter's diatribe against the acoustics of the former's bedroom in the chapter entitled "Eco Chamber".)

V

We ought to move on. One of the pleasures of a submarine is that, defended from the element in which one is immersed, it is possible to witness a bewildering variety of species at close range with little risk of personal harm. There are, I need to remind you, sharks in these waters, as well as the whales and dolphins which we have so far been admiring, and numerous creatures which one can name but which are yet to be classified precisely: Samuel Beckett, Christine Brooke-Rose, John Cage, Lewis Carroll, e.e.cummings, Maxim Decharné, Theresa Falcon, Pierre Guyotat, B.S.Johnson, James Joyce, Jacques Lacan, Flann O'Brien, Ezra Pound, Raymond Queneau, Peter Reading, Alain Robbe-Grillet, Ellis Sharp, Gilbert Sorrentino, Laurence Sterne, Sir Thomas Urquhart ... But I note that you appear unhappy. Indeed, you have been looking unseaworthy for quite some time and I see, from that volume of Barthes which you are leafing through, what the cause of it might be. Let me save you the bother and quote the passage you are hunting from that admirable but slightly overlong essay, "Introduction to the Structuralist Analysis of Narratives":

> Is everything in a narrative functional? Does everything, down to the slightest detail, have a meaning? Can narrative be divided up entirely into functional units? We shall see in a moment that there are several kinds of functions, there being several kinds of correlations, but this does not alter the fact that a narrative is never made up of anything other than functions: in differing degrees, everything in it signifies. This is not a matter of art (on the part of the narrator), but of structure; in the realm of discourse, what is noted is by definition notable. Even were a detail to appear irretrievably insignificant, resistant to all functionality, it would nonetheless end up with precisely the meaning of absurdity or uselessness: everything has a meaning, or nothing has.

The immediate question this poses is, did Barthes, during his life, ever consult a psychoanalyst? For, as Bernard Sharratt has indicated, in one of his incarnations in that imaginary periodical of real reviews by fictional critics of unwritten texts, *The Literary Labyrinth* (Harvester, 1984), "the paranoid sees significance in *everything*". One might additionally object that Barthes' definition of nonsense is a tad tautologous: it amounts to saying that "apparent" meaninglessness is not "really" meaningless because meaninglessness signifies (i.e. "means") the meaningless, or itself. Barthes' phrase, "the meaning of absurdity", is itself absurd, meaningless, if we read those words with their proper meaning. Only by introducing definitional absurdities could we allow it to be meaningful. (And by the way, if you look at Barthes' *The Pleasure of the Text* you will find him talking generically about what he calls "a text with no shadow ... with no fertility, with no productivity, a sterile text" which is meaningless, gives rise to nothing — and it is clear that he does not consider such texts impossible to write, even if they are impossible to read. "The text needs its shadow," he adds of a text that is to be in the slightest way readable, "some ideology, some mimesis, some subject".)

However, I begin to feel the drift of your discontent. Having seen my advertisement for this little tour as "Nonsense Plumb'd, Explor'd, & Sustain'd" you have clearly understood "Explor'd" to mean (ha!) more than "having a look around", "parting the weeds and gasping" etc. etc. What you want, in short, I think, is some kind of generalised waffle about nonsense as well — a statement as to the conditions of its existence, or, should I say, more exactly, an explanation of the environmental factors which lead to the extinction of sense. You suspect, no doubt, that my powers don't extend that far. I believe, on the other hand, that you want more than you've paid for — either that, or you have a rather gullible view of advertising. But I don't wish you to depart feeling that I haven't meditated on these matters. They don't call me Nemo for nothing.

Barthes provides us with some fuel, whatever his shortcomings (here! drop him in the furnace!), not least in his insistence that a prerequisite for the understanding of narratives is recognition of the need to go "beyond the sentence" — the largest unit with which linguistics deals — into discourse analysis. This is as true of nonsensical as it is of meaningful diegeses (forgetting, for the moment, Barthes' idiosyncratic commitment to the idea, demolished above, that all diegesis is meaningful). Take the following from Kuppner's "Lost Work", an example of what Barthes calls a "micro-sequence", or small group of sentences:

> First, and I hope you are listening, although really it is a matter of complete indifference to me, it can be painful to have to understand that other individuals are just as autonomous as oneself. Even if they are. They are just as much the centre of the universe as oneself is. That is to say, probably not at all. All I am saying here is: you just have to accept this. That is what emotional maturity is, and it is not what constitutes a valid excuse for absence from an important lecture. Of course, we can discuss this later, but not so much as certain other topics.

By and large, taken in isolation, each of these seven sentences makes fairly workable sense (although the aside in the first sentence, which equates "hope" with "complete indifference" is imbecilic, admittedly, and the words after the conjunctives in the last two sentences do, it is true, render each something of an enigma). It is possible to imagine — we would be able to construct — a discourse in which each "flowed" coherently, without being reworded, with other sentences in the micro-sequence. However, this is what Kuppner (or God) has failed (or deliberately refused) to do. The second of the two fundamental processes of language proper which Barthes identifies — "articulation, or segmentation, which produces units (this being what Benveniste calls *form*) and integration, which gathers these units into units of a higher rank (this being *meaning*)" — seems not to be being enacted here. Many key micro-sequences of "Lost Work" are made up of sentences which do not stick together in this way, although their spatial collocation gives the illusion, or promotes the expectation, of coherence. (It has not escaped my attention that the micro-sequence above, in its failure to cohere, is a demonstration in its form of what its content [discontent?] says: "other individuals are just as autonomous as oneself", is its burden, and accordingly the sentences which make up the micro-sequence are "just as autonomous" as one another — "that is to say, probably not at all". Painful as such a style may be to readers, they are being advised that they "just have to accept" it.) Considered as a whole, "Lost Work" comprises a series of such micro-sequences which regularly, like the sentences of which each is composed, have contradictory or inscrutable relations to one another. Continuity in "Lost Work" is, by and large, a flow of *grammar* and *voice* rather than meaning: with a few unfathomable exceptions, all of the micro-sequences consist of grammatically conventional sentences seemingly spoken/written/thought by a consciousness which pronounces itself that of a Supreme Being.

Let us go further and ponder the range of discourses clustered around nonsense (for convenience I will use surrealism as a source of examples of nonsense). One must distinguish at least the following:

(a)   celebrations of nonsense (historical, polemical, inciting), which usually call upon its presumed liberatory, anarchic or spectacular potential, etc. etc. (these are plentiful);

(b)   taxonomies of nonsense, which aim to provide a list of the various classes of nonsense, the known practitioners in each class, etc. etc. (this is a science in its infancy);

(c)   theories of nonsense, which consider the discursive possibilities exploited by nonsense, the political, social, economic and cultural features which determine it, etc. etc. (there are few of these, although there is a plethora of theories of meaning which can serviceably be adapted to read as theories of nonsense by the simple insertion, where appropriate, of negatives and antonyms).

Each of these, for the sake of analysis, is usually assumed not to employ the techniques of nonsense itself, but in practice this is rarely the case. In the way that doctors contract the diseases of the patients they treat, each of these discourses *about* nonsense regularly becomes infected *by* nonsense. "Les 5 Commandemants" of René Magritte and E.L.T.Mesens, for example, is a good example of a celebration of nonsense which, although it is a manifesto for surrealist painting, betrays many of the attributes of the literary fanfaronades which are its cousins:

1.   In politics we will practise auto-destruction with all our might, and trust in human virtues.

2.   All our collaborators must be handsome so we can publish their portraits.

3.   We will energetically protest all erudite decadence, *The
      Charterhouse of Parma*, dadaism and its substitutes, morality,
      union of north and south, syphilis in its various stages,
      cocaine, scratchy hairs, compulsory education, polyrhythm,
      polytone,   polynesia,   carnal   vices,   and   particularly
      homosexuality in all forms.
4.   Our freshness will submit neither to second-hand tubes nor to
      our friends' wives.
5.   Under all circumstances we will refuse to explain precisely
      what will not be understood.

This is followed by an ostensibly explanatory afterword which reads, "Our
enterprise is as mad as our hopes. Having taken the greatest precautions
with things of the least importance, we will claim nothing; love of the most
superior girls is more important. 'Hop-la, Hop-la,' that is our motto."
(This was published in 1925. The translation is Margaret I. Lippard's, in
Lucy R. Lippard [ed.], *Surrealists on Art* [Prentice-Hall, 1970].) Now,
unless the composition of these commandments is viewed as a non-political
act (and how could it be?), there should have been no more commandments
after the first. Indeed, once written, the first could only remain consistent
with itself by being destroyed. It is thus precisely absurd. However, to
point this out may be to contradict the fifth commandment, and so one
might argue that the series has in that regard a certain consistency. I think.
Have I read it properly? (One of the features of surrealist rationales
[irrationales?] — from Breton to Duchamp to Ernst to Picabia — is their
general refusal to entertain the kind of self-doubt I have just displayed.
This openness and appeal for reassurance is one of the charming features
of postmodernism which distinguishes it from the brashness of modernism
— isn't it?)

The most commonly frequented taxonomies of nonsense are library
classification systems. What is nonsensical is that none of these systems
group crackpot texts, for all their subdivisions, together under one heading,
but scatter them all over the place under entries for various schools and
names (dada, T.S.Eliot, new criticism, conservative thinkers etc. etc.), thus
failing to notice that these are all species of the same genus. This habit
creates the impression that the most prevalent form of discourse in our
culture is merely an intermittent phenomenon.

The only aesthetic investigations I know which have seriously grappled
with nonsense are those which invoke frame theory. Frame theory as
applied to art is essentially the old Russian formalist idea of *ostranenie*
(estrangement) given a bit of renovatory whizz-bang by cognitive
psychology. It is rather popular among reader-response theorists. Frame

theory aims to describe the methods whereby knowledge is stored and, when required, activated (Husserl, by the by, was talking about the "reactivation" of models of intelligibility long before frame theory, but frame theorists seldom acknowledge their reactivation of his model). Essentially, as any bluffer's guide to frame theory will tell you, it proposes that, exposed to any phenomenon, a witness will normally, however subliminally, attempt to interpret/identify/categorise the phenomenon according to a "frame" which originates in the witness's previous experience. "Phenomenon" here is a term denoting a vast range of possibilities, from actual physical artefacts to linguistic formulations to emotional states. For instance, vast dull crusty daubs of paint on a wall might be interpreted by the frame "vandal" or "abstract expressionist" (the context will usually, though not always, allow one to decide between the two); the sudden appearance of the phrase "*Qu'est-ce-que ça veut dire?*" in an English text will be referred to different frames by a reader who understands French and a reader who doesn't but recognises it when s/he sees it (the former will switch to a frame which might be called reading-in-French while the latter will call on an oh-dear-that's-French frame; rather confusingly, however, the result for both will be to think "What does that mean?"); an individual who is feeling depressed will invoke the frame "capitalist economics", etc. etc. Some of these examples are very misleading, of course, because frames are not really concepts but ways of organising concepts. All the same, I think you probably get the idea. If you don't, well, that's just fine, because it often happens in "real life" too (an interesting frame in itself, that one) that you come up against something that just doesn't seem to make immediate sense, or, in other words, doesn't fit into any particular frame you are able to invoke. In these situations, frame theorists tell us, what individuals do is valiantly attempt to build a frame which will make sense of the phenomenon.

To cut a long story short, and avoid some of the ins-and-outs and shake-it-all-abouts which frame theorists glory in, I'm sure you're intelligent enough to see how this can be applied to literary texts. Where it links up with the formalists' notion of *ostranenie* is in the idea that the literariness of a text is a function of its capacity to confront the reader as, at least initially, and in some if not all respects, strange and bewildering. Literary language, it is argued, *estranges* readers from the frames which they habitually employ either in their reading or their experience, and challenges them to build a new frame or frames for the interpretation of the text. Now this theory of literariness is so open to the most patent objections (it was, to risk a neologism, spreadeagletoned long ago) that it is needless to list them. The reason a great many aestheticians have not abandoned it is purely strategic, for, as well as permitting the claim that the training in frame-building which the consumption of art precipitates is intrinsically pleasurable (we all enjoy a challenge), it implies a much more extraordinary utilitarian value for aesthetic study. The following, from Morse Peckham's *Man's Rage for Chaos: Biology, Behaviour and the Arts* (Schocken Books, 1967), is about as extreme a formulation of this position as you will get:

> Art, as an adaptive mechanism, is reinforcement of the ability to be aware of the disparity between behavioural patterns and the demands consequent upon interaction with the environment. Art is rehearsal for those real situations in which it is vital for our survival to endure cognitive tension, to refuse the comforts of validation by affective congruence when such validation is inappropriate because too vital interests are at stake.

Got that? In other words, *art is a major player in the game of evolution.* It equips us for that Darwinian flashpoint in which we are threatened with extinction from a hostile environment by *simulating such an environment in aesthetic terms* [e.g. a crackpot text] *and provoking the development of cognitive "survival strategies"* [e.g. struggling to make sense of it] *which would not otherwise emerge* [e.g. from reading realist novels]. Now, this is an amazing inflation of surrealist apologetics, a Defence of Nonsense on the Grand Scale. The only pity is that it is such nonsense itself.

For a start, it mostly doesn't work in practice. Leave an average crackpot text in your average hotel room, register your average guest at reception, go to your average spyhole and watch said guest perusing said text, and the likelihood is that you will witness it hurled against the furthest wall, with various scatological expletives catapulted after it, on average, within fifteen minutes. From Peckham's argument it follows that such an average guest has little chance when the next ice-age comes or, pursuing the Hitchcockian scenario I see I have accidentally replicated, when you step into her shower cubicle five minutes later with a butcher's knife. ("*Psycho* as Evolutionary Allegory": now there's a title for a paper.) (This may also be why only bibles tend to get left in hotel rooms. Although many people, interestingly enough, will tell you that the bible is nonsense from beginning to end.)

Of course, it could be countered that the objection I have just raised applies only to casual, consumerist readers rather than those chosen ones subjected to an actual *course of study* in literature ("there is a literature which doesn't reach voracious masses" — Tristan Tzara). These readers aren't allowed to throw books against the wall, are actually forced to talk about them to one another, and made to write essays on them for their teachers. It is arguably these obligations, rather than the set texts, which impose the hostile environment Peckham welcomes so heartily. But the concern I have about viewing an undergraduate degree in arts as a dry run for evolutionary catastrophe isn't that it doesn't feel like the real thing (it does), but that everybody conducts themselves just as nonsensically as they would if it *were* the real thing. Simple "estrangement" experiments confirm this. The following example is one I myself conducted recently as part of a film studies course.

Two groups of six students watched separately the same twenty minute segment of a Hollywood feature film which was entirely unfamiliar to all of them. To prevent any undue influence on the responses of the groups I absented myself on each occasion, recording the group's reactions to the viewing by means of a covert video camera. The first group was asked to watch the film with the volume on, the second with the volume off. The collective demeanour of the first group might be called "consumerist" (i.e. they remained glued to the screen and paid absolutely nil attention to one another throughout). The results of a questionnaire completed afterwards by this group demonstrated a considerable consensus as to what the film was "about" and a remarkable degree of certitude among all the individuals that the film "communicated" its content relatively unambiguously to each of them. Students in the second group, by contrast, displayed a multitude of behavioural signs suggestive of extreme uncertainty. After five minutes or so their puzzlement became increasingly vocal, as members of the group began to ask questions of the what's-happening-here, who-is-he, what's-over-there, do-you-think-this, do-you-think-that, is-she-going-to, what-the-bloody-hell sort, to such an extent that the collective behaviour might best be described as intensely, and intensifyingly, interactional. It seems safe to assume that the lack of soundtrack, the radically estranging feature in the second group's experience of the film, is what prompted these interrogative strategies, which were quite absent in the first group.

One additionally remarkable difference between the two groups, however, was their behaviour during minutes sixteen and seventeen of the film. *During these two minutes the soundtrack is utterly silent.* (The choice of film was no accident on my part.) In other words, groups one and two were experiencing exposure to precisely identical stimuli in this part of the experiment: a totally soundless long shot of the hero, viewed through a telescope by the heroine, walking into the distance with his back to the camera. Perhaps surprisingly, however, the established behaviour pattern was altered in neither group during this short period. In other words, group one maintained an observatory silence (thus behaving identically to the heroine in the film at this point, incidentally), while group two continued to become increasingly fractious and irritable at the escalating divisions among its members as to what was "going on". This result appears, at first glance, to be a remarkable vindication of frame theory. Offered an acceptable frame (the soundtrack), group one unanimously accepted it and used it as an interpretative tool in their "reading" of the film; deprived of this frame, group two, like Pirandello's six characters, seemingly went in search of one by adopting a classically heuristic *modus operandi*. For advocates of the "adaptive mechanism" school of Peckham, the enquiring nature of its reaction to "the demands consequent upon interaction with the environment" is the important feature of the second group's behaviour. Whether or not they reached the agreement or consensus shown by group one, it is the "cognitive tension" exhibited by this group which Peckham would see as a "rehearsal for those real situations" in which such tension is "vital for our survival". What throws Peckham's theory into crisis, however, is the startling discontinuity (or continuity?) of behaviour manifested by members of group two in the final three minutes of the film. In this brief duration the discord in the group reached such a pitch that words were abandoned in favour of fists, nails, and kneecaps aimed at groins, the outcome of which was that three of the students had to be hospitalised and one put under police arrest. The results of the experiment remain perforce inconclusive (and, alas, unpublished) because of the impracticability, under the circumstances, of administering the intended questionnaire to this group. But there is enough evidence here, one suspects, to cast fairly radical doubt on the notion that aesthetic estrangement activates modes of thinking which enhance the possibilities of survival. Human kind cannot bear too much cognitive tension, it would appear.

The usual legacy of prolonged engagement with crackpot texts by don't-throw-it-at-the-wall readers is a corollary of the internal strife and breakdown suffered by this second group of students. The methodical and purposive mental routine described by Inez Hedges in *Languages of Revolt* (Duke University Press, 1983) —

In frame theory, the reading or perception of a work is viewed as an inductive process in which the reader/perceiver tries to "match" perceived conceptual structures with conceptual frames stored in memory. In the matching process he or she employs a "search" technique, calling up one frame after another until a match is made. If no frame to which the conceptual structure can be matched exists in memory, then he or she will attempt to learn a new frame whose characteristics will be hypothetically deduced from the context of the material being evaluated.

— is hopelessly utopian when compared to the bleak existential struggle to which, in actuality, this refers. It would be less romantic to envisage the reader of crackpottery as a young lover, unforeseeably and ruthlessly dumped by her paramour, calling up one friend after another, until she twigs that all must be abroad with their own gallants, that she is the one Troilusless Cressida under the moon, bereft, disconsolate, that no imaginable one can replace he whom fate has sundered her from, that life is henceforth without meaning, and that permanent oblivion is one, just one, paracetamol bottle away.

It is perhaps the pain of confronting this pain which makes Hedges slide unwittingly from her description of frame-making as *an active process internal to and controlled by the reader* (a thesis towards which I am sceptical) to one in which frame-making appears as *a series of primary cues internal to the text which trigger, in a quasi-Pavlovian manner, secondary frame-building mechanisms latent within the reader* (a model of which I am incredulous). Thus "the effect of new genres is to force the reader or perceiver to modify his or her cognitive strategies of perception" (note how the reader here has become the object, rather than the agent, of the process: the face-up-to-reality-honey-he-isn't-coming-back argument); thus, as the scattered incidents and fragments of Breton's *Nadja* are all presented as "surrealist" experiences by the narrator, "it is up to the reader to integrate them into a picture of what would constitute such an experience" (baby-you-just-gotta-make-the-best-of-what-you've-got); indeed, this can even be seen as "a form of training for the effort demanded of him or her in the second part of *Nadja*" (you'll-never-get-another-man-if-you-go-on-moping-like-this); "the effect of the fragmentary form of the text, however, is to force the reader to 'reprocess' the experience so that he or she retraces the steps in the act of construction" (when-this-nightmare-is-over-you'll-feel-stronger-for-it-having-happened); and "the reader's experience of the book will help him or her learn the surrealist mode of thought" (it's-good-you're-starting-to-see-the-world's-a-real-cruel-and-crazy-place); etc. etc.

The problem with Hedges is that her crackpot texts are Hieronymus Bosches which she treats as if they were join-the-dots drawings, and the images of them which she constructs are resultantly infantile, neutered, vacuous: Dali and Bunuel's *Un Chien Andalou*, under her structuralist third degree, confesses to being little more than a cinematic series of variations on an oedipal theme. As Stephen Heath points out in *The Nouveau Roman* (Elek, 1972), certain texts hit rock-bottom banality when recuperated in this fashion. The translation of crackpottery into everyday common sense is like planting a triffid in a geranium tub. The protest of Hedges' victims, hearing her judgment, is likely to be that of the innocent convict, following a court's: "I've been framed!"

VI

Taller to-day, we remember similar evenings,
Walking together in the windless orchard
Where the brook runs over the gravel, far from the glacier.

Again in the room with the sofa hiding the grate,
Look down to the river when the rain is over,
See him turn to the window, hearing our last
Of Captain Ferguson.

It is seen how excellent hands have turned to commonness.
One staring too long, went blind in a tower,
One sold all his manors to fight, broke through, and faltered.

Nights come bringing the snow, and the dead howl
Under the headlands in their windy dwelling
Because the Adversary put too easy questions
On lonely roads.

But happy now, though no nearer each other,
We see the farms lighted all along the valley;
Down at the mill-shed the hammering stops
And men go home.

Noises at dawn will bring
Freedom for some, but not this peace
No bird can contradict: passing, but is sufficient now
For something fulfilled this hour, loved or endured.

The above notoriety appeared as "XXVI" in W.H.Auden's *Poems* (Faber
and Faber, 1930). Auden retained it as "Taller To-day" in his *Collected
Shorter Poems 1927-1957* (Faber and Faber, 1966), but did not reprint the
second and third stanzas. (The gross anonymity of "Captain Ferguson" had
proved the most considerable irritant to readers of the original. It is a pity
that Auden bowed to such pressure to vaporize him, since in the poem we
fittingly do "hear our last/Of Captain Ferguson", the fact that it also
happens to be the first we hear of him being neither here nor there. The
joke is that the irate critics, missing this felicity, went on to ensure in their
long-winded speculations that this was, on the contrary, *far from* the last
that was heard of the Captain.) As he did while revising all of his earlier
work, Auden also dropped definite articles wherever he found this
metrically viable (damage to "sense" was not, for obvious reasons,

something that needed to be weighed up). Thus in the revised text the "the" of line two became "a", and the first "the" of line sixteen (now line nine), like the second "the" of line seventeen (now line ten), was omitted. In a "Foreword" to the 1966 volume, written on the pretext of explaining why he had left so much out and changed so much that he had left in (but the irony of Auden pleading ever to have felt that "I did not wish critics to waste their time, and mislead readers, making guesses ... which would almost certainly turn out to be wrong" is too breathtaking to be overlooked), he asserts that "some poems which I wrote and, unfortunately, published, I have thrown out because they were dishonest, or bad-mannered, or boring". While none of these epithets is inapplicable to much of what he left in, it is notable that impermeable obscurity was not an operative criterion in this deselection process. A dishonest poem Auden defines as "one which expresses, no matter how well, feelings or beliefs which its author never felt or entertained"; the fact that such a poem might concur with the views of its reader he doesn't even consider, which throws a contradictory light on his notion of bad manners, "the consequence of an over-concern with one's own ego and a lack of consideration for (and knowledge of) others"; an insight once again flouted in the expressed opinion that boredom "is a subjective reaction but, if a poem makes its author yawn, he can hardly expect a less partial reader to wade through it". The *insouciance* with regard to obscurity is perhaps reassuring, for it implies at least that, whatever else it is, Auden doesn't see it as dishonest, boring or bad-mannered. But those readers who sense that Auden's "Foreword" itself displays all three of these characteristics are likely, I fear, to come to the same conclusions about *Collected Shorter Poems* as I have.

It would be an opportunity lost, nonetheless, not to attempt to learn something about the workings of nonsense from one of its chief mechanics. Take the first stanza of this much lamented text:

Taller to-day, we remember similar evenings,
Walking together in the windless orchard
Where the brook runs over the gravel, far from the glacier.

Firstly, nobody knows who "we" denotes other than evidently perambulating beings ("walking" is the only word in the poem which makes improbable the charming possibility of the speaker being a tree; the royal "we" is discounted on account of "together"). Secondly, what is "similar" about the evenings is deeply ambiguous (were they previous evenings in which they felt "taller to-day"? were they evenings in the same orchard? were they evenings spent walking together but not in the windless orchard? were they simply windless evenings? were they other evenings also spent far from the glacier? or were they evenings similar in some unstated respect whose similarity just happens to occur to the speaker during a stroll with at least one other through the orchard?). Thirdly, how "far from the glacier" are they? Fourthly, is the glacier a metaphor as well as a topographical feature? If so, fifthly, can you be "far from" a metaphor or, sixthly, is "far from" a metaphor as well?

Now it may be that these are the frame-building questions which conscientious readers ask when Auden fails to provide them with the frame of interpretation they expect. It's more likely that an inconclusive struggle with a neurotic upshot takes place which Sharratt, in another context and yet another persona, has empathetically described: "in attempting to 'understand' these … images the reader is brought to an awareness of the weirdness, the slippery difficulty, the peculiar oddness of that very process we call 'understanding': are we *sure* that we have 'understood' even one of these phrases fully, adequately, appropriately? Even more, do we know (and if so *how* do we know?) that we have 'understood' what is constituted by this total combination of compact images?" It is not the twists and turns in the Empsonian maze readers have to struggle through which many say frustrates them, however, but their realisation that, with Auden, the maze has not exploited the unique possibilities of its material. The thing about Auden's maze is that it might as well be made of stucco as hedge. Substituting some of these words for metrically suitable others would not alter, *mutatis mutandis*, the questions asked above:

> Tanned well to-day, we remember comparable scorchers,
> Talking together in the swelt'ring fishbar
> Where the chips cost less than the chicken, far from the motorway.

Here, "we" are unidentified and unnumbered, apart from their stated capacity for speech. What is "comparable" about the scorchers is just as uncertain (were they previous scorchers on which they felt "tanned well today"? were they scorchers contemplated from the same fishbar? were they scorchers spent talking together but not in the swelt'ring fishbar? were they simply swelt'ring scorchers? were they other scorchers also spent far from the motorway? or were they scorchers comparable in some unstated respect whose comparability just happens to occur to the speaker during a conversation with at least one other in the fishbar?). Etc. etc. One can contemplate rewriting the entire poem after this fashion:

> Once more in the room with the pork chops hiding the plate,
> Glance down at the peatbog which the drain is over,
> Watch him spit at the scarecrow, fearing a blast
> From Field-marshal Mandible etc. etc.

Such (usually better) parodies are commonplace. But would this exercise not demonstrate precisely the singularity of Auden's nonsense? If questions of the same structure can be asked of such a rewrite, would any reader, nonetheless, be interested enough in it to wish to ask them? Taller is different from tanned well, scorchers are not the same as evenings, orchards suggest possibilities which fishbars don't, chips and chicken belong to a different conceptual order than brooks and gravel, and a motorway lacks a great deal of the potential figurative resonance of a glacier etc. etc. One set of terms has associations which clearly do not belong to the other. The elements of Auden's vocabulary, unlike my own, are saturated in a poetic solution *which is a product of their own combination* (they are not poetic in isolation) and previous discursive practices. All nonsense is equal but some nonsenses are more equal than others. It is not (*pace* Barthes) that Auden's poem signifies, in the failure to cohere of its images, its own absurdity. On the contrary, what it signifies precisely is its own linguistic status as poetry. "This is poetry," it says. "You are in the presence of the poetic." How philosophically sagacious, culturally enriching or socially indispensable such a signification may be (it is statements of the obvious, arguably, which most require continual utterance) are issues which I leave to the determination of those more qualified than me to ponder them. But this much is clear (here we reach towards our closureless close): meaningful coherence may be an adjunct to, but is not a precondition for, such a signification.

VII

Two years after writing all of this, bought Jean-Jacques Lecercle's *Philosophy of Nonsense: The Intuitions of Victorian Nonsense* (London, Routledge, 1994) in a second hand bookshop in Woodstock, Oxfordshire. A year later, read it. Now, a year after that, have to admit it's better than this. So don't read me, read Lecercle. Sorry.

VIII

My head's killing me.

Gray Eminence and Kelman Ataxy: a Reply to H. Baum

John Buchan wrote some of the best thrillers ever published in English and some of the best popular historical biographies. Some of his books sold by the hundred thousand, but, like some greater men, he always hankered after success in spheres not suited to his talents. Just as Cicero wanted to write poetry, so John Buchan wanted to be a statesman. He was obsessed with the idea of greatness. Those who knew him will tell that he had no political gifts of any kind.[1]

— From an obituary of Lord Tweedsmuir (John Buchan), quoted by Hugh MacDiarmid in "Scottish Arts and Letters" (1942), in Alan Riach (ed.), *Hugh MacDiarmid: Selected Prose* (Manchester, Carcanet, 1992), pp. 157-8

I am not usually given to replying to replies in academic publications. It is well known that more readers read replies than the original articles to which they are replying, just as many readers read reviews of books rather than the books, but I assume that subscribers to a journal such as this are sufficiently conscientious not to judge me solely by the description proffered by a detractor, and will, if interested enough in the matter, be in a position to consult the well-intentioned review of mine which occasioned Harry Baum's sulphuric assault in the last issue of *CaleDon*, and weigh the two up in their personal scales of reason and justice. Being doused in vitriol is something I measure by a utilitarian calculus. Like most terrorist manoeuvres, it may injure one personally but (assuming survival) can only otherwise enhance one's public notability. Unfortunately, Baum sprayed his acid in such a typically all-points-of-the-compass fashion that he seemed to miss me altogether, in ways that, on balance, I consider worth putting on record. The one remaining moral baulk to publishing a *tu quoque* is news

---

[1] This article was commissioned and then suppressed (on the grounds of objection to its "poor taste" - an explanation which disguised evidently political second thoughts) by the editor of *CaleDon: An Oxbridge Review of Scottish Affairs*, who has also refused permission to reprint in this volume my original review and Harry Baum's reply. Much of the flavour of our disagreement can be gathered from this piece itself, but those readers interested in pursuing the dispute are referred to my "Scotland the Gray with Kelman's Mayonnaise", *CaleDon* IV, 4 (Autumn 1992), pp. 443-52, and Baum's "Stopping the Daly Express: a Defence of Kelman and Gray", *CaleDon* V, 1 (Winter 1993), pp. 99-106.

of the sad (and, one can't help reflecting, wholly avoidable) departure from life of Harry Baum himself, between the publication of his rejoinder and my composition of this one.[2] Although he is thus no longer in a position to reply to this reply to his reply, or to make claims as to libel and the like, I cannot imagine that Harry Baum, were the positions reversed, would have permitted such narrowly personal considerations to restrict the free-flow of intellectual exchange.

Baum's basic hostility to my treatment of "Scotland's two premier fictionists" (a phrase redolent of London newspapers, but let that pass) is double-barrelled. Firstly, he claims that "Daly's public and ill-tempered condemnations of the work of James Kelman and Alasdair Gray are well-known", a judgment based on his misreading of two earlier pieces of mine, which he seems to assume imply that my view of anything either writer produces is entirely prejudicial.[3] Secondly, and peculiarly for a Marxist, he subscribes to the rather Romantic credo that political propaganda produced by *littérateurs* enjoys something akin to papal status (though that is not a phrase of his) in that (these *are* his words) "artists are the finer conscience of their society" (replace "society" with "race" and this sounds just like a formulation of either of those famous socialists, T.S.Eliot or F.R.Leavis). Now, I very much doubt whether Kelman or Gray would agree with this — the latter, certainly, refers to "poets and novelists, people as unnecessary to the good of a country as its journalists and restaurateurs"[4] — though each would likewise dissent, presumably, from my own stated position, namely "that when creative artists resort to direct

---

[2] Harry Baum died in Oxford, aged fifty-two, on 8 February 1993. He had just returned from Dundee after four wet and bitterly icy days of activism in support of the sacked Timex factory workers. He was carried, cold and unconscious, on Sunday 7 February, from the Edinburgh-Poole inter-city train at Oxford, where he was returning to resume a lecture course on philosophical deconstruction and literary hermeneutics. His regrettably fatal condition was later diagnosed as pneumonia. Predictably, the revolutionary newspaper for which he had written for over a decade used the opportunity, not to issue an obituary tribute to his tireless (if somewhat eccentric) commitment to its pet causes, but to carp about the economic imperatives within late capitalism which led to the discontinuation of heating on Sunday long-haul trains, and to lay down a fourteen-point policy for a rejuvenated and comprehensively nationalised public transport system.

[3] See "Your Average Working Kelman" and "Concplags and Totplag: *Lanark* Exposed", elsewhere in this volume.

[4] Alasdair Gray, *Why Scots Should Rule Scotland* (Edinburgh, Canongate Press, 1992), p. 56. This is the pamphlet (hereafter referred to parenthetically as *G*) I initially reviewed along with James Kelman, *Some Recent Attacks: Essays Cultural and Political* (Stirling, AK Press, 1992) (hereafter referred to parenthetically as *K*).

political pronouncements they seldom do more than reveal themselves to
be footlers and fools". Baum explains his notion with a tedious and
demonstrably bogus theoretical digression which argues that artists have a
"tangential (but not wholly external) relationship to the material processes
by which the consciousness of most other citizens is thoroughly
determined" and that they therefore have a "quasi-objective perspective"
on social and political issues not accessible to the latter. This distressingly
pre-Gramscian formulation is hardly worth the negligible expenditure of
time it would take to rebut it. Few readers, I believe, will prefer it to my
own commonsensical view that you ought to persist in doing what you can
do well and leave things you can't do well to those who can, regardless of
how many fireworks Baum lets off about my "uncritical acceptance and
promotion of the capitalist division of intellectual labour".

My animosity to Gray's 1992 election pamphlet (effectively though not
explicitly a piece of propaganda on behalf of the Scottish National Party)
Baum explains as originating in little more than personal irritation on my
part at not being included, on account of my living south of the border, in
Gray's definition of the Scots: "by Scots I mean everyone in Scotland who
is able to vote. Many folk who feel thoroughly Scottish live and vote in
England, America or Hong Kong: but this book is about Scottish
government so lumps them with Scots below the age of eighteen" (*G* 5).
I did not, in fact, discuss this definition in my review, and Baum's
conclusion is therefore mere malicious imputation. Nonetheless, the
absurdity of Gray's definition becomes patent when put beside his later
statement on the origins of nationality: "different kinds of land produce
different kinds of people" (*G* 11). Here, Scottishness is an index of *coming
to consciousness* within the boundaries of a certain territory, not simply a
result of depositing yourself there at any particular time for whatever
reasons you happen to have. Moreover, most of Gray's pamphlet is
historical (rambling and tendentious too, but more of that later) in a fashion
that absolutely excludes the "many who think themselves English but work
here as hoteliers, farmers, administrators and directors of Scottish
institutions" which, he contrarily claims, "my definition cheerfully
includes" (*G* 5). Take his account of "The Protestant Scottish Conscience
(or Soul)", which he suspects was "created" between the reigns of James
V and James VI, and resembles the Swiss, Danish and Dutch Protestant
Consciences, except that

> the absence of a firm government, law-abiding landlords and a
> comfortable clergy made the Scottish soul a bleaker, less social
> thing. It is as if we had a small god in our brain who may
> sometimes sound like John Knox or a local schoolteacher ... (*G* 26)

Let us leave on one side the wayward generality of this (does Gray really consider the Swiss, Danish and Dutch the reverse of bleak and anti-social?). The point is that "we" here cannot "cheerfully include" anyone other than those who have been formed directly by this Protestant Conscience (that is, Scottish Protestants), or indirectly by the putative cultural pervasiveness of it (for example, Scottish Catholics). In other words, it *cannot* include those who were *not* brought up in the dark shadow of the Scottish Protestant tradition. The extremely thin political case put forward in *Why Scots Should Rule Scotland* rests on a narrative of the historical experience which has formed "the Scots" into an identifiable nation, but the "Scots" of the pamphlet's title additionally includes a cluster of groups of diverse ethnic origins — Irish, English, Asian, Chinese, etc. — which have a merely residential, not historical, qualification. Now, neither of these definitions of "the Scots" is objectionable in itself. One might want to distinguish "ethnic" Scottishness from "political" Scottishness, and say that to possess full democratic rights in a self-governing Scotland an individual must demonstrate only the latter (for instance, by residing in the country). What *is* objectionable, however, is to argue for a social system to regulate the lives of "political" Scots from the historical experience of "ethnic" Scots, since the two groups are not co-extensive (for example, many "ethnic" Scots have emigrated from Scotland, while many "political" Scots are immigrants to the country). Yet this is Gray's naïve procedure in *Why Scots Should Rule Scotland*. My criticism, then, is hardly that I feel personally left out of Gray's scheme of things, but that I wouldn't want to be included in a self-governing polity conjured out of such illogical thin air in the first place.

Indeed, systematic reasoning is not really ever on Gray's agenda: as I pointed out in my initial review, it is the very lack of this quality in Gray's fiction which has ensured its tremendous success. Being unreasonable — or depicting worlds in which unreason reigns — is Alasdair Gray's forte. It is also a talent singularly inappropriate in the devising of political programmes. One of the unfortunate features of our culture, however, is that accomplishment in one field can sometimes be made into a licence to issue proclamations of the most bizarre and outrageous nature in another. Nowhere is this more evident than the general permissiveness of publishers and public alike in allowing imaginative writers to pose as political savants. Harry Baum takes me to task for daring to suggest that the example of Hugh MacDiarmid has perhaps had an unfortunate influence on the conduct of Scottish letters in this regard, thus missing entirely my point that MacDiarmid, as an actual founder of a political party, an electoral candidate, and someone whose creative work was itself part and parcel of an explicit political programme, had a prerogative in this matter to which few of his aftercomers have a claim (the blurb to Gray's pamphlet assures us, for instance, that he "belongs to no political party"). It is their own estrangement from practical politics *other than in the privileged capacity of "writer"* which makes the imitation of MacDiarmid by some of our contemporaries so baneful.

Gray, in fact, is perfectly aware that reasonableness is low on his list of priorities in *Why Scots Should Rule Scotland*. He admits that the pamphlet is propaganda, although the rather innocent definition of "propaganda" he employs is that of the *Chambers Twentieth Century Dictionary* ("any activity for the spread of opinions and principles, especially to effect change or reform"), with a few riders:

> Yet even honest propaganda of the non-Goebbels sort tends to use clichés and rhetorical exaggerations. These can simplify an argument and make it more exciting for a while, but in the long run I agree with what Talleyrand said — anything exaggerated is irrelevant. In my effort to avoid rhetoric and give a broad-minded instead of single-minded argument I may sometimes sound too dry and factual. However, my publisher has promised to look over my shoulder and make suggestions if she thinks I am in danger of losing your interest. (*G* 9-10)

This appeal to plainness and honesty is itself utterly disingenuous. The intervention of the publisher, who throughout the pamphlet has sporadic "conversations" with Gray in playscript format, is a technique Gray relies upon to "naturalise" the ramblingly oral nature of his historical monologue, and thus legitimise its eccentricities, excesses, and irrelevancies. It is not, in fact, when he is being "dry and factual" that Gray's "publisher" intervenes, but when he is talking off the point (*G* 15), becoming emotive (*G* 48), exaggerating (*G* 50), or indulging in prolixity (*G* 62). It is itself a wholly rhetorical device of the sort he claims to eschew. The effect would be similar if I were, in the midst of this article, to digress as follows.

Zoilus Editor: You don't seriously expect readers to believe that there is a periodical called *CaleDon*, do you?

Author: No, but if there ever is an Oxbridge Review of Scottish Affairs, I expect this is what it will be called.

Zoilus Editor: What about Harry Baum, then? Is he an invention as well?

Author: I'm afraid so. I liked the pun on "H.Baum" too much to be able to resist it. I also had other associated puns in mind. I could accuse him of being "baumbastic", for example.

Zoilus Editor: If that managed to raise a laugh it would not be a very resounding one.

Author: Perhaps you underestimate the *inward laughter* with which weak puns

	are relished by some people.
Zoilus Editor:	Perhaps you overestimate it! But tell me, what's the *point* of inventing
	an opponent, or of referring to bogus publications which your readers
	can't consult?
Author:	Some of the greatest names in international literature have done
	precisely that: Thomas Mann, Jorge Luis Borges, Stanislaw Lem,
	Italo Calvino, Flann O'Brien — even, dare I say it, Alasdair Gray.
	Literary critics such as Umberto Eco and, more recently, Bernard
	Sharratt, have taken the technique into academic contexts. The effect,
	and sometimes the intention, is to produce a discourse which the
	reader finds it hard to classify. Is it fiction? Is it literary criticism? If
	neither, what is it? My name for this is *interstitial discourse*: it
	flourishes in the interstices between two well-defined discursive
	categories. A hero of no-man's-land, you might say. In fact, I hope
	it will provoke in the reader the same kind of uncertainty that I feel
	about my cultural identity, being a Scot who lives in England.
Zoilus Editor:	You believe in making things difficult for readers.
Author:	Not necessarily difficult *to understand*, just difficult *to negotiate*.
Zoilus Editor:	I'm not sure I *understand* the difference! But what if I, as a publisher,
	don't want to make things *unduly* difficult for my readers?
Author:	I can appreciate that. But they may come to thank you for not doing
	the obvious.
Zoilus Editor:	On the other hand, they may think we are being merely pretentious,
	and refuse to buy any more of our books.
Author:	That is always a risk. But doesn't all publishing involve some degree
	of risk?

One wishes, indeed, that Gray's publisher had been as commendably sceptical as the editor in the (wholly imaginary) conversation above. We may thus have been spared at least the most facile of Gray's arguments, which occurs in the final chapter, the only one in which he stops relying on a selective historical sense or personal anecdotes and moves towards the kind of political nitty gritty that the title of his pamphlet promises. The classic Coleridgean cop-out which prevents any detailed discussion unfortunately follows: the publisher breaks in to tell Gray that he has only four and a quarter hours to finish the manuscript and get it from Glasgow to the printers in Edinburgh (*G* 62)! There ensues a flurry of impetuous grumbles and half-baked proposals which are, indeed, as credible as anything in the SNP election manifesto which was circulating at the same time. But by far the most curious response of the author in this final "discussion" is to the publisher's query, "Will a separate Scottish parliament improve things?":

I think Scottish poverty will get worse whether we have a Scottish government or not. I think it almost certain that the London government will regard an independent Scottish one as an excuse

to strip assets from this country even more blatantly. I also think a
new Scottish parliament will be squabblesome and disunited and full
of people justifying themselves by denouncing others — the London
parliament on a tiny scale. But it will offer hope for the future. The
London parliament has stopped even pretending to do that. I believe
an independent country run by a government not much richer than
the People has more hope than one governed by a big rich
neighbour. (*G* 63)

This, then, is to be the upshot of the great dream of political independence:
virtuous poverty! Hopeful penury is to make us a nation again! Solidarity
in adversity! How it must warm the hearts of those "Scots" who "live in
Scotland because they could buy a pleasant house here more cheaply than
in the south" (*G* 5) to know that their equity will evaporate within a month
of the supersession of Westminster by a Home Rule government in
Edinburgh! How tantalising this newly destitute country will appear to
those economic migrants, like myself, who have the misfortune to live
beyond its borders! How perplexing future Marxist chroniclers will find
this wholesale reversal, effected by the self-sacrificial consent of an
absolute majority of a small nation, of the fundamental axiom of historical
materialism! The oddest thing of all is to witness Harry Baum, a socialist
scholar (but one whose main energies were spent, sadly, in the service of
a London-based political faction which supports a Scottish assembly only
because it will ensure an apocalyptic break-up of the British state)
defending a schoolboy history of his nation masquerading as a serious
political intervention in the very adult circumstance of a general election!
Revisiting *Why Scots Should Rule Scotland* with hindsight makes one
wonder how many of its dissatisfied readers contributed to the 3% swing
to the Conservative Party which was the disgraceful outcome of the April
1992 vote in Scotland.[5]

Gray's half-conscious air of ludicrousness is relatively tolerable,
however, in comparison with the astonishing philistinism of thought and
vulgarity of prose style in James Kelman's collection of essays, *Some*

---

[5] All that one can do here is point the reader in the direction of a stimulating left-
wing critique of Scottish self-government, which preceded Gray's pamphlet but
nonetheless serves as a rigorous corrective to its floppy logic: see Mick Hume and
Derek Owen, *Is There a Scottish Solution?: The Working Class and the Assembly
Debate* (London, Junius, 1988). I shall have some unfavourable things to say about
Kelman's *Some Recent Attacks* in the remainder of this article, so it may be worth
registering here that the one memorable item in it, "Let the Wind Blow High Let the
Wind Blow Low" (*K* 85-91), concludes with a lively satire on the dogged servility of
Scottish political life, particularly in its nationalist manifestations.

Recent Attacks. Many of these pieces "were written for talks I was asked to give" (*K* 4) during 1990 and 1991, but Kelman makes it repeatedly clear that he has revised the texts for publication. Why is it, then, that virtually all of them are, in a technical linguistic sense, discursively incoherent? Take the third paragraph of the first essay in the book, "Artists and Value". The content of this paragraph has no logical connection to what precedes it (in the opening two paragraphs Kelman describes the experience of writing at three in the morning) and is entirely undeveloped in the paragraph which follows it (in which, with unwitting irony, Kelman tells us he once did an undergraduate course in logic!):

> In Hollywood pictures the artist as hero — and it's usually a hero and never a heroine — and this hero who is not a heroine is either a single fellow or else the woman he is involved with is going to turn out to be a bad yin — a bad yin, because then this dashing masculine male will have the absolute right to go off and sleep with anybody he likes, but most especially the beautiful young lassie from next door, without any moral guilt whatsoever. (*K* 5)

If this reads like a passage which has accidentally toddled onto the page from a short story Kelman was probably also writing at the time, that is my point. This ungrammatical, opened but not closed sentence, is an example of what, in my original review, I called "Kelman's habitual digressive redundancy" (I should have guessed that Harry Baum would lacerate me for betraying an "employer's unsympathetic attitude to redundancy"!), which certainly has a place in the species of fictional discourse in which Kelman specialises, but fails utterly to meet the demands of the polemical or analytical genre into which an essay like "Artists and Value" falls. In a very precise sense, Kelman does not have command of the language required by the occasion.

How much weight this objection would pull with Kelman, however, it is hard to say, since his essay goes on to berate the teaching of literature which, for him, "starts and ends with things like grammar and punctuation; in other words, if a lecturer calls a writer 'good' it might just mean the writer in question knows how to use semi colons and paragraphs in a certain manner, or has a very large vocabulary, or uses a great variety of rhetorical devices, or exhibits a certain educational or cultural background, or shows a wide knowledge of foreign words and phrases" (*K* 8). For Kelman, a judgment based on any of these qualities is mere empty formalism, and reprehensibly gives an entry permit into the artistic pantheon to political undesirables: "a good artist won't be somebody who hates people of a different religion, people who come from a different culture or economic background, who are not heterosexual, not homosexual, whatever" (*K* 8). This is as disarmingly puerile as Kelman's claim that the one thing that defines a literary artist as opposed to a mere writer is the ability to spot and reject a cliché (and in politics, it seems, virtually all clichés are right wing ones). Perhaps someone should have told him that the notion that "the important distinguishing feature [of an artist] will be the originality of his or her perception" (*K* 10) is the most clichéd, conventional, and practically vacuous aesthetic theory of all.

"The pathetic state of contemporary literary criticism" (*K* 17) is lambasted again in "English Literature and the Small Coterie", which is essentially a rather muddled attack on Salman Rushdie. The revolutionary *praxis* with which Kelman wishes to usurp this pathetic state is, however, the reverse of promising. The following specimen of literary criticism, one may take it, exhibits features of what he considers the panacea:

> Like many other folk I would probably have come to read *The Satanic Verses* in my own time and was resisting having to read it as any sort of obligation. Now that I have read it I have no difficulty at all in describing it as a good novel. I doubt if it is a great one but within a certain literary context it could prove to be. Rushdie's ambitions are high and he can write very fine prose indeed; at times he can also be very funny. There are other occasions when he writes bad prose; and ultimately he is not successful in dealing with the problems of time and space, and in terms of the novel's structure this is vital. On that count alone it is difficult to speak of *The Satanic Verses* in the same breath as the work of James Joyce which is what some critics appear to be doing. Yet problems of time and space beset most writers of good prose fiction and when I see this demonstrated in a text it usually signifies literary merit. (*K* 18)

None of the value judgments here — "good novel", "great novel", "very fine prose", "very funny", "bad prose", "not successful", "literary merit" — is either defined or exemplified with reference to Rushdie or anyone else. What Kelman seems to desire is a literary appreciation which, like this, says nothing at all in explanation or interpretation of a text beyond unelaborated acceptance or rejection. He practically adumbrates a minimally sophisticated system of evaluative literary grunting — good/bad, original/conventional — to which actual textual analysis is anathema. This very dangerous strain of anti-intellectualism (even Harry Baum felt compromised by it, I'm glad to say, for all its workerist cachet!) is promoted in the Romantic cause of "passionate response": "I remember from my own time as a student," Kelman tells us, " that 'passion' was rarely regarded as 'valid' literary criticism" (*K* 20). The problem with such a view, of course, is that "passionate response" can culminate in a *fatwa*, which is exactly what happened over *The Satanic Verses*. Kelman can bring himself neither to approve nor condemn the death sentence on Rushdie, but the problem is that coming down on the side of "passion" logically exonerates Khomeini, at least insofar as the death sentence remains, as it were, unexecuted, merely a threat, for Kelman is "not opposed to the right to insult and verbally abuse" (*K* 21), which might include the right so to intimidate. (How this squares with his view that artists ought to be politically correct is anybody's guess.)

Kelman is clearly sickened by what he sees as the self-confidence and cultural self-ratification of much contemporary literature:

> Unfortunately, like most of our other institutions, the mainstream Anglo American literary tradition is seldom available to challenge. And, whereas it rightly demands freedom of expression, where this has become insult and abuse it wants to be beyond criticism, it demands the right not to be judged — even by those who are being insulted and abused. It will not allow a wider social context. Retaliation remains inadmissible. When the 'victim' defends it is seen as attack, the grounds for outrage having been deemed 'invalid'. (*K* 23)

But what this wilfully obscures — and it is no credit to Harry Baum that he colludes with Kelman in this process — is the clear difference between criticism and judgment on the one hand, and public book-burning and threats of murder on the other: it is the latter rather than the former modes of "retaliation" which are "inadmissible". Intellectual critique and bodily execution are two distinct methods of engaging in disagreement, and Kelman should know better than not to say so. Few would disagree with his exhortation that "the right to reply has to exist" (*K* 23), although why his next paragraph should then indulge in summarily authoritarian literary judgments — Sadaat Hassan Manto is said to be "*without question*, a major writer" whose "short stories can be mentioned in the same breath as *anyone at all*" (*K* 23, emphases added) — remains a puzzle.

This is especially so when one weighs up the rightness of the statement that matters of controversy "can only be settled in dialogue. We can't afford to let dialogue become a lost art, not on the left, our networks and channels of communication have got to remain open" (*K* 52). Yet the essay from which this comes ("Harry McShane's Centenary"), like every other piece in *Some Recent Attacks*, is relentlessly mono- rather than dia-logic.

"If anybody wants to ask questions ... later on then they're welcome," (*K* 48) Kelman tells his audience on this occasion (which was organised by the Socialist Workers' Party). But dialogue is so prized that none of this post-lecture discussion is incorporated into or even reported in the text. My own experience of SWP meetings, for all my lack of concordance with the SWP's somewhat opportunist line on most matters, is of remarkably vigorous and well-informed (if bewilderingly sectarian) debate. It is a party which takes political education very seriously indeed. The SWP activists I know would be likely to drench a *spiel* as plodding as Kelman's with a tidal wave of ruthless invective and challenging ideological analysis. They would not take at all kindly to his public parade of his own ignorance: "I never met Harry McShane and don't know a great deal about him" (*K* 46); "I haven't read a great deal of John MacLean's writings" (*K* 49); "If there's one thing worth reading in the works of Lenin or Trotsky or especially Marx, then it's the index" (*K* 52). One can envisage the barrage of quotations from *What is to be Done?*, *Permanent Revolution* and *The Eighteenth Brumaire* with which an SWP audience would stone to death this Kelmaniac delusion that certain sorts of ideological benightedness are enabling. One can almost imagine, as Kelman innocently platitudinised, "on the radical left we have a situation where groups, parties and factions are divided by ideas and too often they waste their time polishing them up before sticking them back in the display cabinet" (*K* 52), that a stony-faced heckler at the back got to his feet and roared out Marx's astonishingly virulent (but objectively correct!) denunciation of the hapless Wilhelm Weitling: "Ignorance never yet helped anybody!"[6]

Kelman does not, on the whole, tell us how these lectures went down. In one prefatory note he does air some anxiety over a talk he gave in May 1991 ("Oppression and Solidarity") at a meeting organised by the Friends of Kurdistan:

---

[6] This famous outburst occurred at a meeting of the Communist Correspondence Committee in Brussels in early 1846; see David McLellan, *Karl Marx: His Life and Thought* (London, Macmillan, 1973), p. 157. Without being terminologically fastidious one might make a related complaint about Kelman's constantly loose deployment of political vocabulary. He refers, for example, to "a hegemony, where one community has assumed power and has absolute control over other communities" (*K* 70) in evident ignorance of the fact that, since Gramsci, "hegemony" has come to denote the multifarious set of processes whereby ruling formations actively forge and pursue strategies to *secure* and *maintain* power - meanings that are significantly different than those suggested by "assumed power" and "absolute control". To make these errors in conversation is forgivable, but to put them into print is simply to debase our political tongue.

It was a difficult experience back in Edinburgh. I don't talk without writing the talk, and the talk was written. So there was no turning back, even when I knew I had misjudged the audience. It was held in Edinburgh University, and I had been expecting to speak mainly to students, but it turned out there were very few students. In fact there was a fair proportion of Kurdish people in the audience, most of whom were refugees. As the night wore on it became apparent that political divisions existed among them but no room was allowed for that side of things, no room was allowed for authentic debate; maybe for the sake of a united front, maybe because one side controlled the meeting — and the fact that the platform speakers, including myself, went on far too long. But I used my experience of the evening to explore here and elsewhere the problems of offering solidarity. So the piece that follows is an amalgam of talks I was asked to give in contexts that might be described as alien to a white middle-aged Glaswegian atheist protestant-bred male writer and father of two mature daughters who spent his early years in Govan, Drumchapel, Partick and Maryhill. (*K* 69)

What is alarming about this is that Kelman does not conclude the obvious: that he would be better vacating the stage on such occasions to make way for those better qualified to address such audiences. Instead, a communicational failure is transformed into (or salvaged as) the perfect writerly drama, whose theme concerns "the problems of offering solidarity". *Some Recent Attacks* can, in a sense, be seen as the script of that drama, in which a professional writer of fiction offers up the records of talks he was asked to give in "contexts that might be described as alien" in terms of the intellectual, political, and linguistic demands that they make. The attacks, ultimately, rebound on Kelman's own credibility as a writer, because, like Gray's nationalist pamphlet, *Some Recent Attacks* invites readers to witness the drab spectacle of a fictionist floundering more and more desperately as he wades further and further out into non-fictional waters. There can be few more salient reminders of the dangers of believing that the cultural authority one has earned in a particular field can easily be transferred to others.

Harry Baum's spirited, tenacious, and highly unpredictable defence of Gray and Kelman sprang, of course, from his general political complicity with the eccentric views espoused in *Why Scots Should Rule Scotland* and *Some Recent Attacks*. But it owed much, also, to the fact that Baum gave in as readily as Gray and Kelman to the temptation to trespass beyond the boundaries of his own expertise. Baum's reputation in Scottish radical circles as an *intellectuel engagé* was, for those who were observant enough to notice such things, a phenomenon which provoked more mirth than respect. The industrial militants, socialist newspaper sellers, left-wing conference-goers and stalwart campaigners who collided constantly with him on his regular sorties to the north reacted to his affected proletarian mannerisms and romantic speechifying with a bemused tolerance that oscillated between the extremes of overt sympathy and covert ridicule. No matter how hard he tried, a sober colleague confided in me at his funeral, Harry simply didn't *belong* on a Timex picket line. Unfortunately, the time he devoted to such "practical interventions in the world of reality" (as he quaintly called them) was a sacrifice made at the expense of the tremendous intellectual promise his early academic work had shown. Indeed, for most of the thirteen years following the publication of his one highly praised book, *(Deco)nstruction/De(con)struction/De(construct)ion/ Deconst(ruction)* (1980), his research failed to issue in work of any lasting value, as he permitted his intellectual energies to become splintered and atomised by the transient demands of revolutionary journalism. Towards the end he was making notes towards a companion volume to the earlier book, provisionally entitled *(Her)meneutics/Her(me)neutics/Her(men)- eutics/Hermeneu(tics)*, but by then the professional celebrity he had enjoyed a decade earlier was virtually forgotten. He was even having difficulty, it was rumoured, in finding a publisher. That his institutional stock was certainly low at Oxford is evidenced by his complete inability to gain promotion, despite repeated attempts, after 1982.

Occasionally, Harry could be heard, in conversation, recalling the advice given to him by his father when he was a boy. He would reproduce it in the Fife accent (his dad was a miner) to which he never resorted for any other purpose. He mimicked his father loudly and coarsely: "Harry, my son: one, find out what you can do; two, do it; three, stick to it." Then he would cackle loud and long, for this terse counsel Harry considered limiting, accommodating and defeatist. One wishes he had taken it more seriously.

Malice Aforethought:
the Fictions of Ellis Sharp

On our last evening together, drinking whisky, and then more whisky, and then yet more, I have never forgotten how we came (whose idea was it — his or mine? I no longer remember) to open up his Thesaurus at random, selecting quite arbitrarily a single, humble word, and chuckling as our fingers promiscuously roamed back and forth across the pages, up and down, between and below, touching every inch and scrap, every glorious, throbbing vowel and consonant and crackling, pulsating fiery connotation, until at last, drenched in sweat, half-drunk, utterly fatigued by our endeavours, we tumbled into a wordless, innocent and dreamless sleep. Ah, what it is to bathe in language, to cavort there, unashamed, ecstatic, up to the very ceiling of one's mind in beauty and resonance, drifting and gliding amid the harmonic choruses, the plangent chords, hearing the sweet hum of pluralism, soaring across the dazzling ranges of multiplicity, then falling, falling, dizzy, satiated, drained and drowsy, soothed by excess of meaning! (Chess, by contrast, has always struck me as rather a bore.)
— "Dobson's Zone"

History happened so differently from how we imagine it.

Joseph Stalin did not die on 5 March 1953, but faked his decease, swam to England, and in 1957 "was a familiar figure on the promenade at Bognor". Indeed, so popular did Iosif Vissarionovich Dzhugashvili prove with the West Bognor Conservative Association, and so prized was his "personal knowledge of the horrors of Seychellism", that he became the local MP ("the previous MP having disappeared off the pier one foggy evening"), although he did feel obliged to enlarge the list of aliases drawn upon in his Russian period (Koba, Ivanovich, Gayoz Nisharadze, K. Cato, Chizhikov, Vassil, Stalin itself) by changing his name to Julian Iron.

Nor was Richard Nixon elected thirty seventh President of the United States in 1968, as the credulous think, for in 1962 he was "shot at least two-hundred-and-sixty-seven times, and afterwards cut up into small pieces" by a young philosopher outraged by Nixon's continual infliction of violence on his (Nixon's) bloodhound, Barbour. The philosopher was found guilty of murder and sentenced to one hundred and twenty five years in jail, but was given a Presidential pardon in the second week of his captivity ("a poll taken the next day showed that the President was the most popular President in the entire history of the United States") and treated on his release by the local Deputy Sheriff to a meal which consisted, in large part, of Nixon's bodily remains.

The classic three-volume study of political economy, *Capital*, was written by Charles Fort (1818-1883) and not by Karl Marx (1874-1932), to whom it was wrongly attributed for over a century, and whose "best work, *The Book of the Damned*, a study of unexplained phenomena, was published by Boni and Liveright in 1919". The seemingly disparate concerns of both have been synthesised by Charles M. Fawkes (1933-) in his "science of the laws of motion of capitalism and cosmic oddity" summarised admirably, if a trifle polemically, in his slogan "Bankruptcy, recession and frog-falls in Felixstowe are all one to me". Fawkes's unpublished works include *The General Law of Phantom Bullets and Capitalist Accumulation* and *Entombed Toads and Economic Elites*.

In the winter of 1846, Emily Brontë bribed a girl from Haworth to impersonate her while she read a gun catalogue in a nearby cave. In the summer of the following year, "having made the final revisions to her manuscript", she went to Liverpool, where she "disguised herself as a cabin boy and obtained employment on one of the vessels being used to transport British troops across the Atlantic". She spent the rest of her life engaged in a guerrilla war, sniping at U.S. imperialists in Central America, eventually dying in her lover's arms after a particularly heroic shoot-out. Her story was later memorialised, albeit with typical Hollywood distortion, in the films *Annie Oakley* (1935) and *Annie Get Your Gun* (1950). The legend of her much more passive death from tuberculosis in 1848 refuses, however, to disappear entirely from popular circulation.

Such "alternative histories", or engineered collisions between different ontological worlds (to employ some of the vocabulary current in discussions of much "postmodernist" fiction)[1], form one strand in the burgeoning improbabilia of Ellis Sharp, most readily accessible in two short story collections issued recently by an obscure small press specialising in surreal and experimental texts.[2] It would be easy to diagnose Sharp's writing as suffering from acute postmodernist schizophrenia by reference to any of several critically accepted checklists of symptoms, although a reading which did no more would fail totally to convey the hilarity, sheer weirdness, and political profundity which such a textual disorder yields. David Lodge lists half a dozen strategies habitually adopted by postmodernist texts — "Contradiction, Permutation,

---

[1] See, for example, Brian McHale, *Postmodernist Fiction* (London, Methuen, 1987).

[2] *The Aleppo Button* (London, Malice Aforethought Press, 1991), hereafter cited as *AB*, and *Lenin's Trousers* (London, Malice Aforethought Press, 1992), hereafter cited as *LT*. The stories referred to above are, respectively, "The Story of Julian Iron" (*AB* 11-16), "Nixon's Dog" (*LT* 72-87), "Tinctures, Stains, Relics" (*AB* 71-81), and "Shooting Americans, With Emily" (*LT* 27-35).

Discontinuity, Randomness, Excess and The Short Circuit" — which distinguish them from their modernist and antimodernist forebears.[3] Sharp's writing exhibits all six features.

If, for example, one story has Nixon being blasted to smithereens in 1962,[4] another ("The Ink-Horn" [*AB* 23-7]) will happily contradict it by calling him "President Nixon" and having him marked out for "supreme office in the greatest nation on earth" by the unexplained phenomena ("a shower of threadworms fell from an empty blue sky") surrounding his parturition.[5] But different permutations from a common root sometimes occur too within a single story: "Sunday Morning in July" (*LT* 118-24) runs through four possible socialist futures (utopian, Orwellian, transitional, communist) for the same couple. "Lenin's Trousers" (*LT* 36-58) describes at great length how "there is not one Lenin but three Lenins that people write about" — "Saint Lenin", "Lenin the Monster" and "Lenin the Revolutionary Socialist" — only to point out that "whichever of these three Lenins you happen to prefer, it is a fact that none of them showed any interest whatsoever in trousers" (*LT* 38-40).

The events related by any Sharp tale are likely not to flow with chronological surety, will usually be temporally discontinuous, are often (it is true also of Sharp's heroes and narrators) very mixed up. The chronicler of "Shooting Americans, With Emily" plays "some Victor Jara tapes" to Karl Marx — seemingly the one who really *did* write *Capital*, and took eighteen months away from so doing to indulge in the Timon-like maledictions recreated in "Da-Da Vogt" (*LT* 88-93) — and asks him

> ... whether it was his opinion that the 26 Commissars of Baku were beheaded or shot, observing that while there seemed to be no doubt as to the fact of their execution and to the fact that the atrocity was carried out by British troops there did seem to be some doubt about the manner of their murder. Marx irritably pointed out to me the irrelevance of the question. "What matters is to study in depth the

---

[3] David Lodge, "Modernism, Antimodernism and Postmodernism", *Working with Structuralism: Essays and Reviews on Nineteenth and Twentieth Century Literature* (London, Routledge and Kegan Paul, 1981), p. 13.

[4] The date of the release of *The Manchurian Candidate*, the brainwashed-zombie-assassin film which Nixon ironically urges the protagonist to see (*LT* 74). But there is no particular reason why the assassination could not take place on "22 November 1963" (*LT* 87).

[5] Sharp deliberately falsifies the location of Nixon's birth as Nausse, Arizona; everyone knows it was Yorba Linda, California.

policy of British imperialism in the Caspian region at the beginning
of the civil war." (*LT* 32)

The voice which speaks "Crocklefether Squiggs" (*LT* 147-8) is as
undecided about the method of execution but confirms "the irrelevance of
the question", as he knows that the 26 Commissars (mentioned *en passant*
in every story but one in *LT*) were not sent to their deaths until thirty five
years after Marx's own.

One of Sharp's idiosyncratic randomising techniques (routine plot
digressions abound) is impertinent reproduction, *in mediis rebus*, of
dictionary definitions, not simply of key words in the text, but also of those
words which *precede and follow them* in a lexicon. The lawyer defending
the murderous philosopher in "Nixon's Dog", in an address to members of
the jury which incites much readerly cachinnation, stresses that his client
shot Nixon two hundred and sixty seven times ("though our ballistics
expect Dr Surbase believes the correct number is, in fact, two-hundred-
and-sixty-*three*") out of

> ... PITY. Yes, PITY. PITY for that noblest of all the animals, a
> poor, defenceless dawg. PITY, which Plato describes as the most
> profound of all the human emotions. PITY, which shines out like
> a diamond amid mud. Consult your dictionaries, members of the
> jury. There you will find PITY lodged between PITUITOUS
> ("Consisting of mucus") and PITYRIASIS ("A chronic squamous
> inflammation of the skin"). (*LT* 77)

He then calls a witness to prove "beyond all shadow of doubt that had
Nixon lived his career would have been fatally impeded by pituitous
blockage of both nostrils ... together with a chronic squamous
inflammation of the skin".[6] Likewise, in "Backyard" (*AB* 28-32) — yet

---

[6] The dictionary possessed by members of the jury is clearly not *The Shorter Oxford
English Dictionary On Historical Principles* (3rd ed., Oxford, Oxford University Press,
1944) or *Collins English Dictionary* (3rd. ed., Glasgow, Harper Collins, 1991). In both
pity is indeed followed by *pityriasis*. But is it preceded in the former by *pituri* ("Native
name of an Australian shrub, *Duboisia hopwoodii*, the leaves, etc., of which are used
as a narcotic"), and in the latter by *pit viper* ("any venomous snake of the New World
family *Crotalidae*, having a heat-sensitive organ in a pit on each side of the head:
includes the rattlesnakes"). Speculation as to how the lawyer would have altered his
defence in accordance with *any* dictionary that happened to be in the laps of the jury
is an additional source of entertainment for industrious and inventive readers.

another text which confuses obstetrics and political premiership[7] — Mr
Reagan mentions to the "all-male-midwife-task-force" that his neighbours
have discovered their llama to be missing. "'Their *llama*?'" is the mystified
response, to which Reagan senior addresses himself: "'It's a South
American ally of the camel. Here boys — take this wad of ten dollar bills.
Why don't you all go buy yourselves some beers and a nice, fat dictionary.
You'll find "llama" between "Lixivium" — water impregnated with
alkaline salts — and "Llanero" — an inhabitant of a llano ... a vast level
plain in South America'" (*AB* 28).

Excess? Nixon's killer didn't just empty the contents of his deer-rifle
into the dog beater. When it jammed he ran indoors, "scooped up the
family armoury" and "came back and continued":

I began with Pa's Colt 44, moved on to my own historic Colt 17,
used up all the shells in Mum's shotgun, fired with my sister Jane's
little .22 at Nixon's inguinal region, blazed away with the replica
eighteenth-century Kentucky rifle that Uncle Abe had given us for
Thanksgiving, and plugged Nixon some more with my brother
Bill's Navy Colt. I made good use of deceased Uncle Ben's Heckler
and Kock self-loading carbines. Then I stepped over and filled Nix
up with a few well-aimed shots from Mom's prized derringer and
Pa's punch-packing .357 Magnum. ...

Hell, I'd clean forgotten about the 7.65 Mauser bolt-action
equipped with a 4/18 scope and thick leather brownish-black sling,
the rear portion of the bolt visibly worn. Hey, did I just say a 7.65
Mauser? Forget it guys. It was a slip of the tongue. I meant the
Mannlicher-Carcano bolt action rifle I'd gotten by mail order using
the pseudonym "Dawlos Varhey Eel". (*LT* 80)[8]

---

[7] It also misleadingly states that the fortieth U.S. president, universally known to
have come into the world in Tampico, Illinois, first saw the light of day in Mottobbe,
Ohio.

[8] Tim Wood, a one-time student of mine, eloquently throws light on the shooting
in an essay which explains Sharp's strategy in this story, and the difficulty any reader
has in following it:

Sharp chooses his subjects carefully: Nixon, largely because he was
exposed as a crook, was (before his death) probably regarded by the liberal
consensus as the most odious American politician, more even than Goldwater
or McCarthy, far more than Reagan. Moreover, Sharp turns Nixon's own
tactics against him. When campaigning against Helen Gahagan Douglas in
1950, Nixon deliberately misrepresented his opponent and made (unfounded)
accusations that she was a communist. Douglas described this strategy in the

Thames documentary programme, *Nixon*: "to avoid the issue you work up bogus issues, trying to play on the fears of the people".

In "Nixon's Dog" the narrator tells the story of how he killed Nixon before he began his political career. This telling of an alternative history destroys any sense of it existing in a single, precise historical moment. Nixon, we are told, is twenty-one years old, which would place the action in 1934. Furthermore, in the story Nixon has not started the political career which began in earnest when he was elected senator for California in 1950. But Nixon recommends to the narrator the film *The Manchurian Candidate*, which was made in 1962, and the novels of Philip K. Dick, who did not begin publishing until the mid-fifties (one of his earliest novels being, appropriately enough, *Time Out of Joint*). The story is also removed from any factual location, the setting being Byron, Texas. *Dulane's Gazetteer of North America* reveals that there are towns called Byron in North Illinois, central Georgia, Maine, south-central Michigan, south-east Minnesota, southern Nebraska, northern Oklahoma and northern Wyoming, but there is no town called Byron in Texas. There is a Byron in north California, but a very long way from the southern California town of Yorba Linda where Nixon spent his twenty-first year (although "Byron" is one letter away from being a perfect anagram of "Yorba").

The narrative is complicated by the inclusion of a number of events and references which make little immediate sense. A little research into the life and career of Nixon reveals some possible answers, none of which is altogether satisfying. The story begins with a description of the crashing of a Dakota aeroplane, in which the narrator's Aunty Babs is horrifically killed. On 8 December 1972 an aircrash in Chicago killed Dorothy Hunt — wife of the Watergate burglar Howard Hunt — who was survived by her purse. The fact that her purse contained $10,000 hush money paid by the Nixon administration was one of the first indications that the Whitehouse was engaged in the cover-up which would eventually be exposed and force Nixon to resign. However, the plane in which Dorothy Hunt was killed was a Boeing 737, not a Dakota.

In the story, Nixon's dog is a bloodhound called Barbour, who has the annoying habit of urinating on Nixon's flagpole. On one occasion Nixon punishes the dog by hitting it with a baseball bat, and it is this act of brutality which so enrages the narrator that he shoots Nixon 267 times. The real-life Nixon did own a dog, and in 1952 he used this dog to save his political career during his campaign for the vice-presidency, when he was plagued with allegations that he accepted illicit financial support from the Republican party's funds. Nixon appeared on television, claiming that the only gratuity he had ever accepted was a dog. Nixon wrote in his memoirs, "Exploiting a dog, as Roosevelt had once done, would irritate my opponents and delight my friends." However, Nixon's dog was a cocker spaniel named Chequers, not a blood-hound named Barbour.

In this imagined history the U.S. becomes a socialist republic under the benevolent President Shrubb. "Shrubb" is a partial anagram and synonym for "Bush", and thus could be read as an ironic reference to the President incumbent when Sharp was writing. However, Sharp may also have in mind

An uproarious sendup of lone-nut-assassin media stereotypes, a prolonged

---

William Barnett Shubb, one of the Supreme Court judges who ruled that the Special Investigator into the Watergate cover-up should be allowed access to the taped Oval Office conversations which would incriminate Nixon.

Once the reader has investigated any number of these apparently inconsequential cross-references between the real and fictional histories of Nixon, some begin to cohere. The story tells how whenever, as the narrator puts it, "someone famous got shot in enigmatic circumstances Nixon used to take out an old placard ... the placard read IS FECIT CUI PRODEST" (*LT* 74). My very amateur Latin roughly translates this as "It is he who has earned it". *The Manchurian Candidate* tells the story of a Korean war hero who returns home programmed to assassinate a liberal politician. During Nixon's career he was fortuitously served by a series of assassinations and attempted assassinations. John F. Kennedy was shot in 1963 when he was threatening to establish a Democratic power base in the electorate. Robert Kennedy would almost certainly have been Nixon's opponent in the 1968 Presidential election had he not been killed; George Wallace, who was running against Nixon in the 1972 election, was forced to withdraw after an assassination attempt left him with grievous injuries.

In the story the narrator tells how he shot Nixon using a Mannlicher-Carcano bolt action rifle which he had purchased by mail order. The same gun was obtained by the same method by Lee Harvey Oswald. The narrator also emulates the shooting feat that Oswald is supposed to have achieved, firing four shots in 5.6 seconds. The shots are even written on the page in a form which indicates the famous, impossibly short gap between the final two shots:

> BANG!
> BANG!
> BANG!-BANG! (*LT* 80)

It goes without saying that the name under which the narrator purchased his rifle is an obvious anagram.

None of this, of course, serves to implicate Nixon in the assassination of Kennedy, but rather just hints at a mystery, something which there is more to than is immediately apparent. All that is presented is a collection of desultory and, at times, contradictory pieces of evidence which can no more establish that Nixon was complicit in the Kennedy assassination any more than, say, the evidence presented to the Warren Commission supports the theory that Oswald acted alone. In "Nixon's Dog" no such claims are made: the story concludes with a list of things that do *not* happen, the last of which is that "On the morning of 22 November 1963 Richard Millhouse Nixon does not fly out of Dallas, Texas, where he has spent a short time obscurely occupied with his wide ranging business interests" (*LT* 87). Sharp cannot prove that Nixon was involved in the murder of Kennedy, but he can just raise the suggestion, show it to be possible. The effect is to alter the reader's perception of the real, historical character.

cathartic frenzy of anger at the politics Nixon embodies, and an intoxicated expression of the linguistic delights to be found in technical inventories, all in one, the passage is typical of Sharp's frequent over-the-topness. ("The Bloating of Nellcock [*AB* 82-90], a rancorous lampoon against the ex-leader of the British Labour Party, Neil Kinnock, climaxes in another political mercy-killing, with appropriate stylistic inflation.) Wordy flights, altiloquent, sonorous, arcane, are common throughout his texts, almost at times — as in "The Aleppo Button" (*AB* 96-106) or "Thingumajig" (*LT* 149-58) — reaching the murky stratosphere of idioglossic babble.

This is writing with strong tendencies to hyperbole, hyperprosexia, hyperventilation; it could almost be said to be *hypertext* in its inclusion of, and the transilience with which it switches between, conventionally divergent discourses. "Martina" (*LT* 11-26) evokes an old flame in a wistful, ostensibly Hamletian soliloquy addressed to "Horatio", the speaker's dog (but more a "Yorick", being dead). However, "the soft devastating drag and suction of Proustian recall" (*LT* 12) which more accurately names the stylistic inspiration at work in the story, that "zone of endless possibility" for digression (*LT* 14), permits a profusion of textual deflections and aberrations: here, into the rhetoric of contemporary British Trotskyism ("the system cannot be reformed from within by working through a capitalist workers party within a bourgeois parliamentary democracy in which the Queen has powers of Stalinist proportions" [*LT* 22]) or medical jargon ("Blepharospasm", "achromatopsia" [*LT* 15, 23]); there, into quotations from Marx and Engels on the natural sciences (*LT* 14), a synopsis of the career of Ludwig Feuerbach (*LT* 18), or thumbnail sketches of romantic and s-f movies (*LT* 16, 17, 25); everywhere, into the allusive exercise of a consuming obsession with Mars (for the title of the story is another appellational anagram). The dryness and redness of our nearest planetary neighbour provide opportunities for more than one verbal arabesque. In the description of the sojourn of Martina and her terrestrial lover in a summer London, "hot and getting hotter", the prose becomes, quite literally, florid:

> The sunlight had a reddish dusty tinge; the traffic on Red Place sounded blurred and slowed down, like a disc losing its momentum. Gubble-gubble-gubble, choired the birds perched on high ledges. Honk-honk, replied the big red buses. Every patch of baked earth seemed occupied by ecstatic sparrows taking vigorous dust baths. The Thames stank, airliners crawled mutely across the burning sky, a band in Embankment Gardens played a Janacek melody. Sweating like a pig, dripping like a stalactite, slippery as an eel, I pulled her into the tomb-cool darkness of Southwark

> Cathedral then towed her across the river, into the white-as-a-
> refrigerator interior of St Magnus Martyr. Then on, on, and up the
> spiral stone steps inside St Paul's, where we spoke soft words to
> each other, inaudible, meaningless as Martian gobbledygook, like
> stranded astronauts from different worlds, straining to communicate
> across the vast cosmic space of the whispering gallery ... (*LT* 16)

Our hero later wonders if he has been "drawn to revolutionary socialism
by a liking for the colour red" (*LT* 23). Even Horatio, it turns out, was a
red setter.

Allusion is Sharp's characteristic means of effecting short circuits. The
sense of the texts "here", on the page, referring to the world "there",
beyond them, regularly disintegrates. Sharp refuses to "mind the gap"
between the domains of reality and textuality, short circuits it by the strong
tendency in all of his texts to signify a welter of other texts, even to mine
them as *pretexts* for his own plots. His stories store up cultural references
as desperately as guests at a dinner party rein in their flatulence. Indeed,
central to two stories, "The Bloating of Nellcock" and "Rubbish" (*LT* 59-
71), is the image of a wind-filled Gargantua, a man masquerading as an
immense balloon, met in so gas-engorged a condition that the story serves
as the fuse which precipitates his imminent momentous explosion.
Nellcock's bloatedness is a metaphor for linguistic bombast:

> At the age of six his future as a deipnosophist seemed certain.
> Guzzling filched apples he loved to prattle. Hogging the pie he
> invariably piped up and rattled on. Devouring fried eggs and beans
> he became voluble, prolix. At puberty he used to perorate under the
> sheets. One day he became lost in a welter of subordinate clauses
> and did not return until dusk, panting and red-faced. At sixteen he
> loved nothing better than to rise to speak, ejaculating in full view
> of passers-by. How he spouted, shuddering! How he loved to stand
> on stumps, tuning his rant, oblivious to the pain of the amputees.
> (*AB* 82-3)

We are of course informed that "'Bloater' is found between 'blitzkrieg',
which has one meaning, and 'blob', which has four or five" (*AB* 86). The
narrator, who is writing a book on Nellcock which he has yet to finish,
enables himself to do so by carrying out a fatal blitzkrieg on this particular
blob. He punctures Nellcock with a harpoon, thereby changing the world

rather than merely interpreting it.[9] The classical source of the characterisation is itself given in an anachronistic sideswipe at Nellcock's previous biographers (two of whom bear the inflatable names "Dunlop" and "Michelin"): "Not one of these writers has managed to spot the witty, unmistakeable allusion to Nellcock ('the bloat king') in *Hamlet*, III, 183" (*AB* 86).

Nellcock is half a self-parody, for Sharp's writing is aware of the possibility of being perceived as mere panoply, puffed up by verbal treasures rightly belonging to others, a fragile collage of literary plunder, hardly more substantial than the phantom aerostatic contraptions which frequently float through his plots. Dobson, in "Dobson's Zone" (*AB* 33-58), sets out to "manufacture a mystery" and thus achieve immortality, but with an awareness that "for a hoax to be successful and to endure after the perpetrator's death various essential ingredients were required" (*AB* 49). The "zone" he goes on to describe turns out to be his invention, the inexplicable crop circle. However, it might equally well be a trope for Sharp's fictional *oeuvre*:

> "It must be entirely novel, yet with hints of an ancestry. It must be baffling yet plausible. Once visible it must be constructed so as to encourage the mystery-mongers and occult-property-speculators to heap up a vast tower of rickety theories. It must entice the imagination and encourage a throng of competing, mutually exclusive explanations. It must be stupidly simple to invent yet give birth to generations of commentary. It must be a labyrinth which entices the seeker-after-truth to enter, and then imprisons her in a wilderness of perplexing and half-possible speculations. It must, in short, provide a Z.C.F.M. — a ZONE for the CONVERGENCE of FECUND MULTIPLICITY. The productions of such a zone will range from the crudest scepticism to a sixteen-volumed explanation replete with photographs, sketches, and innumerable eye-witness statements ... " (*AB* 49)

"How I abhor gratuitous allusion!" protests another of Sharp's narrators (*AB* 77) at the end of a paragraph which is knee-deep in it, in a story whose title — "Tinctures, Stains, Relics" — is borrowed from *Julius Caesar*, II.ii.89. There may even be justice in suspecting that the protest itself is culled from another writer, for Sharp is casual about identifying his

---

[9] Marx's eleventh thesis on Feuerbach, "the perception that even today causes intellectuals and academics to scowl, and fidget, and flush", quoted in the original German, is one of the sundry allusions of "Martina" (*LT* 18-19).

sources. Robert Coover's "A Pedestrian Accident" is treated to a wittingly fanciful political interpretation in "Sunday Morning in July", but it is not made plain that "Rubbish" is largely a concerted reply to Coover's "Milford Junction, 1939: A Brief Encounter", his textual reworking of the famous railway film.[10] And when Bodsworth's train pulls out of Norwich station in "The Epsom Flashes" (*LT* 106-117) it leaves in its wake verbal details reminiscent of the last paragraph of this Coover story.[11]

"The Aleppo Button", which poses as the text of a lecture given by an erudite imbecile, in the course of which every member of the audience gradually slips out of the theatre, exhibits this literary kleptomania *in extremis*. Sources include Shakespeare's sonnets, William Faulkner's *The Wild Palms*, Raymond Chandler's *The Long Goodbye*, *Dr Jekyll and Mr Hyde*, some very obvious Keats (*AB* 97), some very unobvious Keats (*AB* 104),[12] and some verse which is all but untraceable.[13] The obscure list of bellowed quotations (*AB* 101-2) includes bits from the closing lines of *Romeo and Juliet*, "The Ancient Mariner", and the first sentence of the Dutch edition of Lowry's *Under the Volcano*. "Psychoanalysis plus ... " is what Derrida says after answering the 'phone in an ad-lib scene in Ken McMullen's experimental film, *Ghost Dances*. "The dark eagles!" is a teasing allusion to the first line of the Austrian poet Georg Trakl's "Lament" (which begins "Sleep and death, the dark eagles ... "). The political quotations are (at an informed guess) all Trotsky, except "The homeland of Marxist theory remains where it always has been, the real human object, in all its manifestations", which is from the late E.P.Thompson's *The Poverty of Theory*, and "The truth is that an enormous enterprise of indoctrination is carried out in Britain, day in and day out, by a multitude of different agencies; but that the nature of this enterprise is often obscured" (Ralph Miliband, *Capitalist Democracy in Britain*). "My racket has gone blooey" is a phrase from Dashiell Hammet's

---

[10] Cf. Coover's *Pricksongs and Descants* (London, Picador, 1973), pp. 146-64, and *A Night at the Movies or, You Must Remember This* (London, Paladin, 1989), pp. 140-7, with *LT* 122 and *LT* 59-71 respectively.

[11] Cf. Coover, *A Night at the Movies*, p. 147, with *LT* 109-10.

[12] "This morning I scarcely know what I am doing" (*AB* 104) is from Keats's letter to Fanny Brawne of 13 September 1819, a maudlin epistle whose broodings about personal identity and agonised rhapsodising no doubt makes it relevant to the general themes of "The Aleppo Button".

[13] Cf. "Her carrot - " (*AB* 97) and "She loot me see her carrot cunt" from "Green Grow the Rashes", reprinted in T. Scott (ed.), *The Penguin Book of Scottish Verse* (Harmondsworth, Penguin, 1970), p. 355.

Red Harvest. The "cracked bells" and "washed-out horns" (*AB* 105) do not
resonate when separated, but put together they form a well-known line
from Bob Dylan's "I Want You". The Spanish quotation towards the close
(*AB* 106) is from the last line of César Vallejo's "Black Stone on a White
Stone". Scattered throughout are fragments of one of John Clare's Mary
poems ("I sleep with thee, and wake with thee"). This is not to speak of
the multitudinous references which are made *with* acknowledgment, such
as that to Munch's *The Scream* (*AB* 97); and there are no doubt many more
furtive thefts than my solitary industry can prove. It may be that the story
is reaching towards "Benjamin's ideal of producing a work consisting
entirely of quotations, one that was mounted so masterfully that it could
dispense with any accompanying text".[14]

Vladimir Nabokov — whom the narrator of "Tinctures, Stains, Relics",
displaying his usual chronogrammatical waywardness, calls "a minor comic
novelist ... [who] died in May 1940 when the *Champlain* was torpedoed
off the French coast by a German submarine" (*AB* 76) — wrote fourteen
years before his *actual* death:

> It may be asked if it is really worth an author's while to devise and
> distribute these delicate markers whose very nature requires that
> they be not too conspicuous. Who will bother to notice ... ? Most
> people will not even mind having missed all this; well-wishers will
> bring their own symbols and mobiles, and portable radios, to my
> little party ... In the long run, however, it is only the author's
> private satisfaction that counts. I re-read my books rarely ... but
> when I do go through them again, what pleases me most is the
> wayside murmur of this or that hidden theme.[15]

Private gratification of this kind can hardly be Sharp's rationale, if we take
the expression of referential intent in "Crocklefether Squiggs" to be
delivered in his own voice: "I want you to read this book [a volume of
Trotsky], and other books. ... I want to break down your solitude and
wrench you from this page and shout 'Things don't have to be the way
they are!'" (*LT* 149). This is the reverse of Nabokov's narcissistic
aesthetic, which can contentedly propose that "the influence of my epoch
on my present book is as negligible as the influence of my books, or at

---

[14] Hannah Arendt, "Introduction" to Walter Benjamin, *Illuminations* (Glasgow,
Fontana, 1973), p. 47.

[15] Vladimir Nabokov, "Introduction" (1963) to *Bend Sinister* (Harmondsworth,
Penguin, 1974), pp. 10-11.

least of this book, on my epoch".[16] Sharp wishes for no such splendid
isolation. He has, on the contrary, clearly social interventionist ambitions.
He has read *Literature and Revolution* and grasps as a matter of textual
practice the dialectic it proposes between "past accumulations of culture"
and aesthetic production in the present. Their relation is one of
transformative appropriation: each new generation "appropriates existing
culture and transforms it in its own way, making it more or less different
from that of the older generation".[17]

Sharp's recycling of past cultural icons, lore and booty, unlike a great
deal of postmodernist fiction, is consistently political in nature. What
reader of *Wuthering Heights* has speculated, between chapters 9 and 10,
that Heathcliff's mysterious disappearing act may be explained in terms of
a revolutionary sojourn such as that enjoyed by his creator in "Shooting
Americans, With Emily"? But with knowledge of the latter, who could
revisit Brontë's novel without considering the possibility? (Indeed,
Heathcliff is missing for the climactic years of the American Revolutionary
War and returns in September 1783, the year of its conclusion: "'Have you
been for a soldier?'" is one of Nelly Dean's first questions to him. He
deliberately neglects to answer it.)[18] "Dobson's Zone" rolls, pig-like, in
the very mud of popular mythology it ends by rejecting. "Who now
remembers Che Guevara?" it begins by asking (*AB* 33), and goes on, in
contrapuntal mode, to link his courageous but ill-considered Bolivian

---

[16] Nabokov, p. 6. This, a comment on a novel which is essentially a satire, by one
whose father was a leader of the Kadet Party, on the October Revolution! (Nabokov
senior - whose fate Sharp records with some artistic licence [*AB* 76] - is scathingly
portrayed throughout Trotsky's *The History of the Russian Revolution* [3 vols., London,
Gollancz, 1932-3].)

[17] Leon Trotsky, *Literature and Revolution* (Michigan, Ann Arbor, 1960), p. 194.
Trotsky's vocabulary in the crucial chapter "Proletarian Culture and Proletarian Art"
may have outlived its usefulness, but the general argument remains serviceable.

[18] Emily Brontë, *Wuthering Heights* (Harmondsworth, Penguin, 1965), p. 133. It
has not escaped the present writer's attention that this novel was first published under
the pseudonym "Ellis Bell". What! – could it be? – is it possible that even Sharp's *first
name* is an allusion? I leave it to more paranomasial critics to make what they will of
his surname – to talk of his Sharp-eyed observation, his Sharp-witted social satire,
textual Sharp practice, even to note that Nixon's killer is a Sharpshooter, to link this
author's passion for assassination with Sir Walter Raleigh's words on feeling the edge
of the axe before his execution ("'Tis a Sharp remedy, but a sure one for all ills") or
to muse "how Sharper than a serpent's tooth it is to have a thankless child" of the
disgruntled infant of "To the Wormshow" (*AB* 91-5). I shall only note that the great
English philologist Alexander John Ellis (1814-90), author of *Early English
Pronunciation* (1869-89), was born Alexander John Sharpe.

campaign with the narrator's contemporaneous quest for the Loch Ness plesiosaur. This superbly violent yoking together of heterogeneous legends seems to release nitrous oxide from the surface of the pages. Appropriation of revolutionary politics for the purposes of mad humour is ubiquitous in Sharp, and can easily be misunderstood as a mere knowing, nudging, trivialising iconoclasm. In truth, it is more of a restitution, an exorcism of the earnestness, the deadly lack of play, which has ironically come to characterise much subversive politics. "Not any more, Fidel" (*AB* 57) — because Sharp knows his Bakhtin too, knows all about the political power of the carnivalesque. Following the killing of Nixon, "Under President Shrubb the U.S.A. withdraws its armies from Vietnam and all other outposts of the empire. The C.I.A. is shut down and its leaders go on trial for crimes against humanity. The defence budget is cut by ninety per cent. President Shrubb announces his country's unilateral nuclear disarmament. Foreign aid is ended to military dictatorships around the globe" (*LT* 86). Fantasy? Perhaps. The scenario owes something to Philip K. Dick's *Time Out of Joint*, after all (*LT* 74), as well as to J.G.Ballard's *The Atrocity Exhibition*. But history can turn on a sixpence, and Sharp wants to demonstrate that positive, politically energising truth.

In "The Hay Wain" (*LT* 125-46) we encounter the most concentrated and profound of Sharp's transformative appropriations, as well as the most serious in tone. This opens at noon in Manchester on 16 August 1819 with Jack Frake, a once-renowned Shakespearean actor, "hit one day in the street by a cart, bad leg injury, career in decline" (*LT* 125). Frake gets caught up in the Peterloo Massacre, kicks a soldier "hard in the crotch, sees him curl up in agony. An action witnessed by two of the yeomanry who come at him with their sabres" (*LT* 127). He runs for his life and, wanted for high treason, "set[s] his actor's talents to work" in disguising himself and going underground. "A month later he's in Norwich, three days later at Ipswich", moving from bolthole to bolthole, "things — poverty, hunger, fear, illness, the cold, age, the forces of the State — closing in on him" (*LT* 128). Close to collapse he finds "a white house, deep in mist. Tall redbrick chimneys and a red slate roof" (*LT* 129) and manages to conceal himself for a night in an empty box room at the top of it. "He wakes five hours later to the sound of housemartins chattering outside the window and a dull bronze glow over everything from the noonday sun. Goes to the window. Sees, over on the far bank, a man in his early forties, sat on a folding chair, reading a book. No, not reading a book. Holding a sketch pad and pen. Making two or three strokes, then pausing to look across the river. Looking right at Jack Frake" (*LT* 129).

It is "almost noon" (*LT* 130). The house, of course, is Willy Lott's Suffolk home; the artist, John Constable. One recent commentator complains of the famous picture, "exhibited as *Landscape Noon* [it] is now so well known that ... it is ... never looked at, and its 'novel look' is taken for granted".[19] If Sharp's dramatically contrived collocation of English labour history's most notorious slaughter with English bourgeois art's most popular idyll makes us look anew at the latter, it also makes it impossible to see in it what Cormack's ideological purblindness makes out:

> Here in the centre is, again, the focal point of the design, which consists of two horizontally opposed diagonals. One leads the eye over to the right to the haymaking, where the white shirts of the haymakers provide rhythmic accents on the horizon. ... The white smock of the drover nearer at hand is balanced by the light tone of the horizon at mid-left, so that he does not leap out of the picture, but helps the movement into space in the opposite direction. The figures are simply blocked in, and their simple poses also help the timelessness of the scene. Constable, then, to [*sic*] a boundless feeling for nature and twenty years' experience of close observation has created a work which is as pure as he can make it, a memory of his Suffolk home. *The Haywain* owes much of its lasting success to the feeling that in this "Idyllium", this image of "rustic life", "the essential passions of the heart speak a plainer and more emphatic language", as Wordsworth justified his own work in a different context, but we should not forget that, equally, even more than in his Hampstead Heath scenes, it also looks back to the high art of the seventeenth century and, in particular, to Rubens ...[20]

The painting is appropriated here solely in the formal terms which allow it to be abstracted from any determining social context: consequently it is made to signify what is "balanced", "timeless", "boundless", "essential". But if to these qualities the painting "owes much of its lasting success", they are also precisely what cause it to be "never looked at", "taken for granted". For these attributes are so indefinite, so abstract, that they cannot *be* seen. Nor (if one studies Constable's picture) can Jack Frake, or anything that could be mistaken for him. But no one who reads Sharp's text will look again at *The Haywain* without feeling that he is *there* — without the suspicion, indeed, that he has been *deliberately erased*. One does not *see* anything new *in* the picture: rather, one is made to *confront*

---

[19] Malcolm Cormack, *Constable* (Oxford, Phaidon, 1986), p. 132.

[20] Cormack, p. 133.

it in an entirely different manner. The sensation is akin to the deeply discomforting moment in which one realises that the glass one is looking into is actually a *two-way mirror*. The kind of inspection associated with such a discovery is not one in which idyllic feelings supervene.

For Frake the scene is anything but "timeless". He is wondering whether to "make a break for it" or "wait for dusk", temporal calculations based on a visual activity ("Frake glances wildly back out of the window") which is the reverse of contemplative. He suddenly hears dogs:

> The cattle are gone, the ferryman's gone. The man with his sketchpad has folded up his little stool and is walking away along the riverbank path. He's bent forward, holding up his trousers, the sketchpad half-slipping from beneath his arm as he tries to keep the turn-ups out of the mud. Undisturbed by the sound which rivets Frake's gaze to the yard, the ferocious barking, brutes on leashes, brutes with studded collars, straining, slavering excitedly, towing behind them as they burst from around the back of the house half-a-dozen grim, burly constables. As they move towards the doorway below the artist on the far bank disappears from view. Now all Frake can see is the ferryman, back where he was before, punting across a bowed labourer who holds a scythe. (*LT* 130)

Life-enhancing bucolicism, seen from one bank, becomes death when stared at from the other: for what else can the scythe-bearing labourer, accompanied by his Charon, represent? That Frake's end is meted out to the accompaniment of "the grunts and curses of the heavy constables" amid a knell of "hollow reverberating chimes of a nearby church ringing noon" (*LT* 130) intensifies the passage's marvellous, terrible resonance. One starts to detect traces of blood in Constable's *Landscape, Noon*.

"The Hay Wain" is one of the most powerful ideological deconstructions to be found in contemporary fiction. One can detect in it a persistent aim of historical materialism, the exposure of the truth, in the words of Benjamin's "Theses on the Philosophy of History", that "there is no document of civilization which is not at the same time a document of barbarism".[21] *The Haywain* is a "myth" ripe for dismantling, as Barthes takes to pieces bourgeois culture and the western consumerism it serves in *Mythologies*. In "Wine and Milk" Barthes points out that French national euphoria over wine is so habitual that it seems "natural", and the economic basis of its production ("deeply involved in French capitalism, whether it is that of the private distillers or that of the big settlers in Algeria who

---

[21] Benjamin, p. 258.

impose on the Muslims, on the very land of which they have been dispossessed, a crop of which they have no need, while they lack even bread") deliberately and outrageously ignored. To thus link seemingly innocent everyday pleasures with the barbarities of imperial conquest is, of course, to shatter them: "wine cannot be an unalloyedly blissful substance, except if we wrongfully forget that it is also the product of an expropriation".[22] The "unalloyed blissfulness" which *The Haywain* represents in English culture proves equally brittle when it is invaded by working class history.

But Sharp knows that there are proletarian myths as well as bourgeois ones. Peterloo (eleven dead) was a mere scrap by comparison with massacres on a modern scale: the vast magnitude of its *impact* on English radicalism routinely gets transferred to the event itself. But in a contemporary Britain in which the labour movement has been in retreat for a decade, such episodes from working class history have become mythological in a much more damaging sense than this: that is, the nostalgic and romantic celebration of them has come largely to replace radical political action in the present. "For godsakes stop going down to commemorate the Tolpuddle Martyrs, or don't you remember, *they broke the law*?" urged Britain's most famous trade union leader, attempting unsuccessfully to persuade his colleagues not to co-operate with hostile Conservative legislation. "If you're going to commemorate that, do something in 1992 along similar lines to defend the rights of workers today. Don't go along and sing the praises of Nelson Mandela on the one hand, who defied the law for twenty seven years, and not understand the lessons of history."[23] This was a protest against the mythologising of labour's past, its presentation in a ritual form which nullifies its potential as a mobilising force in the present; merely the radical version of idyll.

There is no such living in the past for Sharp. *The Haywain* does not, he knows, belong simply to the nineteenth century. It is permanently in process, an image in ideological circulation along with those produced today:

> ... a painting like *Top Gun*, all gloss, myth, fantasy. The judicious placement of flagpole or cart, runway or field, sunset or cloud, labourers or carrier in the Indian Ocean, until the two blur, and now that speck's a MIG fighter, beyond the house lurks a blonde

---

[22] Roland Barthes, *Mythologies* (London, Paladin, 1972), p. 61.

[23] Arthur Scargill, President of Britain's National Union of Mineworkers, in a speech to the 1992 Trades Union Congress.

in leather, all sunlight and honey, in which there's no place for
agricultural depression, recession, squalor, poverty, the all-night
wage slave, the women in the electronics factories of Korea, the
tortured of Palestine, the black children with puffy bellies and skull
faces and big teardrop eyes, the masses blotted out by the sugar of
individual destiny ... (*LT* 141)

This is from the second section of "The Hay Wain" (Frake's story occupies
only six of the story's twenty two pages), the action of which takes place
on 31 March 1990, the date of "The Battle of Trafalgar Square" in which
200,000 Poll Tax protesters staged one of the most insurgent
demonstrations witnessed in Britain within living memory.[24] Sharp's
roller-coaster description of this event is punctuated by "flashbacks" to
historical disorders and protests (the Peasants' revolt, the Blanketeers,
Peterloo itself), thumbnail philippics aimed at Establishment icons whose
statues are met *en route* by the marchers (Richard the Lion Heart,
Cromwell, "Sir Winston Twister Dardanelles-Disaster dulled-by-brandy
dago-hating ... Churchill" [*LT* 131], Earl Haig), and attacks on the media
which have replaced Constable in providing reactionary representations of
what is to be seen.

At the centre of this physical and textual vortex is Robinson (we
discover [*LT* 139], with a nice sensation of irony, that he is the lovesick
narrator of "Martina"), chased by the police into the National Gallery, who
finds himself arrested, in more ways than one, before a familiar painting:

... much bigger than he'd imagined after seeing it all those times
on biscuit tins and trays and calendars and hanging on the lounge
wall of remote dusty relatives along with the Reader's Digest
Condensed Novels and the 22" TV and the hideous china country
maids and cherry-cheeked grinning shepherds ... (*LT* 140)

---

[24] "The Hay Wain" is clearly indebted to *Poll Tax Riot: 10 Hours That Shook
Trafalgar Square* (London, Acab Press, 1990), a virulently anarchistic pamphlet account
of this demonstration, and itself a prose specimen worthy of study. There is a brilliantly
surreal passage in the former in which even the inanimate world becomes enlivened by
the riot. A wooden chair suddenly appears "suspended in the air, about ten feet from
the ground ... tilted, as if to about to launch itself into battle. The chair bides its time,
enjoying every moment" (*LT* 136). A photograph on p. 30 of the pamphlet depicts a
chair, presumably hurled at the police by a protester, seeming to do just this.

He steps towards the canvas to read the caption: "' ... represents a link between the idealism of Claude and Poussin, and the future empirical vision of the Impressionists' ... " (*LT* 141). The police assault him, and fling him against the painting, his blood "spurting in a bright unreal slash across *The Hay Wain* by John Constable R.A." (*LT* 142). He spends the following moments in a new vision of art — "seeing for the first time a ghost in the murky water" (*LT* 143) — that mingles with a foreseeing of political corruption:

> The Coroner ... whose directions to the jury would be biased, rambling, repetitious, confusing and confused, and who would put it to the jury that Robinson had perhaps *deliberately* cracked his head against the painting, the fracture being caused not (as everyone had assumed) by a police truncheon at all but by *the frame of the painting*, Robinson's motive possibly being a wanton and who knows even *anarchistic* desire both to discredit the police *and* to besmirch the one real masterpiece of English art. (*LT* 145)

Thus, as well as putting "real" blood on the picture, does Sharp defuse in advance reactionary readings or critical "inquests" of his text. In the precise image, also, of a violent collision between present and past, and between conventionally different realms of discourse (art and politics in particular), we have the master trope of his fictional method.

"The Hay Wain" sets a tough agenda for Sharp to follow, but he seems capable of equally memorable postmodernist fables. It is not an isolated masterstroke. "To the Wormshow", the monologue of a man recalling his embryonic refusal to emerge from his mother's womb during the five years of the post-war administration of "MIST-AIR-HAT-LIE" (*AB* 93) is an ingenious, consummate piece of political comedy, a fantastic compound of *Tristram Shandy* and Leon Trotsky, whose immensely funny Darwinian characterisation of the Fabians it would be appropriate to quote:

> English pigeon-fanciers, by a method of artificial selection, have succeeded in producing a variety by a progressive shortening of the beak. They have even gone so far as to attain a form in which the beak of the new stock is so short that the poor creature is incapable of breaking through the shell of the egg in which it is born. ...
>
> Having been induced to enter the path of analogy with the organic world, which is such a hobby with MacDonald, we may say that the political skill of the English bourgeoisie consists in shortening the revolutionary beak of the proletariat and thus

preventing it from breaking through the shell of the capitalist state.[25]

Whence, perhaps, the narrator's reflection that "when I look back over that strange, dark phase of my life I can only assume that my mother's body, intoxicated by what it had learned, through osmosis, from her mind (she was a great fan of Trotsky and Victor Serge) was spontaneously attempting, out of kindly charity and in defiance of all biological orthodoxy, to delay for as long as possible my entry into that golden age of Labour Government" (*AB* 94).

There is an indictment of a somewhat different order, too, in "Dead Iraqis" (*LT* 94-9). Reading for the first time this monstrous, outrageous satire on Western attitudes to the 1991 Gulf War, one is probably feeling something similar to the appalled amazement of the original readers of Swift's "A Modest Proposal":

> They are not nearly so much of a nuisance as dead Paraguayans. Dead Paraguayans are cumbersome, frequently blood-spattered and almost always attract flies. They smell disgusting. Dead Iraqis, on the other hand, are lightweight, portable and, on the whole, easy to manage. At most they give off a light powdery odour, not at all unpleasant, redolent of potting compost in a rose-bordered rural shed. (*LT* 94)

This is a teratological text, a deeply distressing report from an eavesdropper on the British racist imagination. It is a risky performance, not easy even for Sharp's political allies to stomach. It is not the kind of writing which is calculated to endear Ellis Sharp to the wider audience which, nonetheless, the future will surely bring him. For those who believe that postmodernist fiction disavows serious social purposes or is politically inept will want urgently to read him. Those whose experience of overtly political fiction is of a stylistically despondent realism will find him a revelation. And those who want to laugh with more hope than despair should give Sharp a try. He is the funniest advertisement the politics of postmodernism has had for years, and looks set to go on being so.

---

[25] Leon Trotsky, "Where is Britain Going?" (1925), *Leon Trotsky on Britain* (New York, Monad Press, 1973), pp. 74-5.

An Argument Against Abolishing Socialism

I AM very sensible what a Weakness and Presumption it is, to reason against the general Humour and Disposition of the World. It may perhaps be neither safe nor prudent to argue against the abolishing of Socialism, at a Juncture when all Parties seem so unanimously determined upon the Point, as we cannot but allow from their Actions, their Discourses, and their Writings. However, I know not how, whether from the Affectation of Singularity, or the Perverseness of human Nature, but it so unhappily falls out, that I cannot be entirely of this Opinion. Nay, though I were sure an Order were issued out for my immediate Expulsion by the National Executive Committee, I should still confess, that in the present Posture of our Affairs at home or abroad, I do not yet see the Absolute Necessity of extirpating socialist Ideas from among us.

THE Curious may please to observe, how much the Genius of a Nation is liable to alter in half an Age: I have heard it affirmed for certain by some very old People, that the contrary Opinion was even in their Memories as much in vogue as the other is now; and that a Project for the abolishing of Socialism would then have appeared as singular, and been thought as absurd, as it would be at this Time to write or discourse in its Defence.

BUT here I would not be mistaken, and must therefore be so bold as to borrow a Distinction from the Writers on the other Side, when they make a Difference betwixt nominal and real *Reactionaries*. I hope no Reader imagines me so weak to stand up in the Defence of *real* Socialism, such as used in primitive times to have an Influence upon People's Belief and Actions: To offer at the restoring of that, would indeed be a wild Project, it would be to dig up Foundations; to destroy at one Blow *all* the Wit, and *half* the Learning of the Kingdom; to break the entire Frame and Constitution of Things; to ruin Trade; in short, to turn our Courts, Exchanges and Shops into Desarts.

BUT why should we therefore cast off the *Name* and *Title* of Socialists, although the general Opinion and Resolution be so violent for it, I confess I cannot (with submission) apprehend the Consequence necessary. However, since the Undertakers propose such wonderful Advantages to the Nation by this Project, and advance many plausible Objections against Socialism, I shall briefly shew what Inconveniences may possibly happen by such an Innovation, in the present Posture of our Affairs.

ONE Necessity of a *nominal* Socialism among us, is that if Great Wits cannot be allowed an *Object* to revile or renounce, they will *speak evil of Dignities* and abuse the Government, which I am sure few will deny to be of much more pernicious Consequence.

IT is further objected against socialist Notions, that they oblige persons to the Belief of Things too difficult for Free-Thinkers, and such who have shook off the Prejudices that usually cling to a confin'd Education. Though sharing the general amusement at the vulgarities of language indulged by those Sectarians who speak of a "bourgeois hegemony" and, yet more comically, of "the working class", I warn that we should be cautious how we raise Objections which reflect upon the Wisdom of the Nation. Is not every Body freely allowed to believe whatever s/he pleaseth; and to publish their Belief to the World whenever they think fit; especially if it serve to strengthen the Party which is in the Right?

IT is likewise urged, that there are, by Computation, in this Kingdom, above one Hundred socialist Journals, Periodicals, and other extreme Publications (some fit, it is true, only to be denominated Rags and Scandal Sheets), whose Revenues may individually be negligible but whose Expenditures, *in toto*, would go to maintaining at least a dozen or half dozen more colourful and sociable organs devoted to the Arts of male Grooming or female Allure. This indeed appears to be a Consideration of some Weight: But then, on the other Side, it deserves to be considered likewise Whether it may not be thought necessary that in certain Tracts of Country, there should be *some* Persons at least whose appearance will demonstrate (by what one may term a *negative Example*) the great vice of permitting an interest in collective Politicks to preponderate over that more immediate consideration of individual Vanity.

THERE is one Advantage greater than any of the foregoing, proposed by the Abolishing of Socialism, that it will utterly extinguish Parties among us, by removing those factious Distinctions of Left and Right, of *Labour* and *Tory*, of Hard and Soft and Wet and Dry, which are now so many mutual Clogs upon publick Proceedings, and are apt to prefer the gratifying themselves or depressing their Adversaries, before the most important Interests of the State.

I CONFESS, if it were certain that so great an Advantage would redound to the Nation by this Expedient, I would submit, and be silent: But, will anyone say, that if the Words *Whoring, Drinking, Cheating, Lying, Stealing*, were by Act of Parliament ejected out of the *English* Tongue and Dictionaries, we should all awake next Morning chaste and temperate, honest and just, and Lovers of Truth? Is this a fair Consequence? Are Party and Faction rooted in human Hearts no deeper than linguistic Phrases, or founded upon no firmer Principles? Will we not find newer Divisions from invented Causes? Shall we not wake up to the founding of novel Sects according to the Cut of Clothes or the Style of Coiffure? Would not these serve as properly to divide the Parliament and Kingdom between them? And therefore I think there is little Force in this Objection against *Socialism*; or prospect of so great an Advantage as is proposed in the abolishing of it.

'TIS again objected, as a very absurd ridiculous custom, that a Sett of Persons should be suffered, much less employed and hired, to bawl against the Lawfulness of those Methods most in Use towards the Pursuit of Greatness, Riches, and Pleasure, which are the constant Practice of near Everyone alive in the Kingdom. But this Objection is, I think, a little unworthy so refined an Age as ours. Let us argue this Matter calmly; I appeal to the Breast(s) of any polite Free-Thinker, whether, in the Pursuit of gratifying a predominant Passion, s/he hath not always felt a wonderful Incitement, by reflecting it was a Thing forbidden.

'TIS likewise proposed, as a great Advantage to the Publick, that if we once discard the System of Socialism, all Egalitarianism will of course be banished for ever, and consequently along with it, those Grievous Prejudices of Education, which, under the Names of Virtue, Conscience, Honour, Justice, Fairness, Fraternity and the like, are so apt to disturb the Peace of human Minds, and the Notions whereof are so hard to be eradicated by right Reason or Free-Thinking, sometimes during the whole course of our Lives.

HERE, first, I observe how difficult it is to get rid of a Phrase which the World is once grown fond of, tho' the Occasion that first produced it, be entirely taken away. For several Years past, if a youth had but an ill-favoured Nose, the Deep-Thinkers of the Age would some Way or other contrive to impute the Cause to the Prejudice of his or her Education. From this Fountain were said to be delivered all our foolish Notions of Justice, Equality, Love of Fellows; all our Opinions of a better future State, and the like: And there might formerly perhaps have been some Pretence for this Charge. But so effectual care hath been since taken to remove those Prejudices, by an entire Change in the Methods of Education, that (with Honour I mention it to our polite Innovators) the young Persons, who are now on the Scene, seem to have not the least Tincture left of those Infusions, or String of those Weeds, and by consequence the Reason for abolishing *nominal* Socialism upon that Pretext, is wholly ceas'd.

FOR the rest, it may perhaps admit a Controversy, whether the banishing all Notions of Socialism whatsoever, would be convenient for the masses. Not that I am in the least of opinion with those who hold *Soviet Communism* to have been the Invention of Capitalists, to keep the lower Part of the western World in Awe by the Fear of what may come to pass under Socialism: For I look upon the Body of our People here in *Britain*, to be as Free-Thinkers, that is to say, as staunch Unbelievers in any socialist Utopia whatever, as any of the highest Rank. But I conceive some scattered Notions about Reds under the Beds to be of singular Use for the common People, as furnishing excellent Materials to keep Children quiet when they grow peevish, and providing Topicks of Amusement in a tedious Winter Night.

HAVING thus considered the most important Objections against Socialism, and the chief Advantages proposed by the Abolishing thereof; I shall now with equal Deference and Submission to wiser Judgment, as before, close by mentioning one Inconvenience that may happen, if *Leftwingery* should be repealed; which perhaps the Projectors may not have sufficiently considered.

IF Socialism were once abolished, how could the Free-Thinkers, the strong Reasoners, and those of profound Learning, be able to find another subject so calculated in all Points whereupon to display their Abilities? What wonderful Productions of Wit should we be deprived of, from those whose Genius, by continual Practice, hath been wholly turn'd upon Raillery and Invectives against Socialism, and would therefore never be able to shine or distinguish themselves upon any other Subject? We are daily complaining of the great Decline of Wit among us, and would we take away the greatest, perhaps the only Topick we have left? Who would ever have suspected *Kinnock* for a Wit, or *Smith* for a Philosopher, if the inexhaustible Stock of Socialism had not been at hand to provide them with Materials? What other Subject through all Art or Nature could have produced *Blair* for a profound orator, or furnished him with Listeners? It is the wise choice of the Subject that alone adorns and distinguishes the Writer. For had a Hundred such Pens as these been employed on the side of Socialism, they would have immediately sunk into Silence and Oblivion.

AND therefore, if notwithstanding all I have said, it still be thought necessary to have a Bill brought in for repealing Socialism, as being thought for the Benefit of the State, I conceive however, that it may be more convenient to defer the Execution until after the General Election, and not venture in this Conjuncture to disoblige that Minority of Persons who, as it falls out, remain Socialists, many of them, by the Prejudices of their Education, so bigotted, as to place a sort of Pride in the Appellation. This I would urge as a matter of mere polite manners towards their style of living. For they are not only strict Observers of socialist Belief, but, what is worse, actually Practise it; which is more than is required of us, even while we preserve the name of Socialists. We may find, with the relentless Demise of their Creed which future electoral Circumstance will undoubtedly terminate, that they come to see the Light without our having to force the flood of it upon them.

TO conclude, I counsel against precipitate Action. Whatever some may think of the great Advantages to Trade by this favourite Scheme, I do very much apprehend, that in six Months' Time after the Act is passed for the Extirpation of Socialism, the FTSE may fall at least One *per Cent*. And since that is fifty Times more than ever the Wisdom of our Age thought fit to venture for the *Preservation* of Socialism, there is no Reason why we should be at so great a Loss, merely for the sake of *destroying* it.

A Metafictionist Manifesto

I

A spectator is haunting your hope — the spectator of fictive self-consciousness. All the powers of the academy are no longer able to resist aggressive dalliance with this spectator. Where is the unfashionable literary style that has not been decried as Metafiction by the orthodox novel mode in power? Where the *outré* prose mannerists that have not blasted back the branding reproaches of Surfiction, Fabulation, Irrealism against more radical textgenerators, as well as against reactionary talespinners?

Three things result from the fact of the rise of these abortionists against the Self-begetting Novel:

1. Metafiction is already acknowledged by all literary critics to hold cultural power.

2. It is high time that Metafictionists should openly, in the face of the whole world, publish their views, their aims, their tendencies, and meet this nursery tale of the Spectator of Fictive Self-Consciousness with a Manifesto which reflects more authoritatively on the wholly imaginary nature of all of the foregoing.

3. So self-referential a programme will, paradoxically, be the first official engagement of a new political formation in battle with lackspittle Social Democratic Mimeticists, lacklustre Conservative Classicists, lackadaisical Anarchist Aleatorists, laconic Liberal Symbolists and lachrymatory Socialist Realists — a battle to make the world metafictional!

II

All politics is fiction. Every manifesto is fabulosity. Each constructs a vision of a future which is imaginary from records of a past which are fabricated in a moment called the present which is mythological. Only Metafictionists have told the truth about this process. All our tomorrows thus depend on what Metafictionists say today about yesterday. All our yesterdays will be modified tomorrow by what Metafictionists say then about today. And all our todays are merely provisional forms of the tomorrows prophesied yesterday by Metafictionists. These are just three good reasons for attending to the Metafictional message with an intense predisposition towards sceptical approbation. Our adversaries will tell you that Metafictionism is a vulgar retailing (retelling?) of verbal confectionery

THIS MANIFESTO

which bears no more relation to "reality" than a lollipop bears to food, and that this Manifesto is a supreme example of such *ersatzery*. We ask you to trust us when we say that this is make-believe.

Metafiction is not aleation (just as the latter is not to be confused with *alienation*, which, like metafiction, it causes: but whereas metafiction alienates consumers from *unreflective consumption*, aleation merely alienates them from *itself*). Metafictionists do not hold the key to the prison house of language, but neither do they profess a John Cage of randomness. Metafictionists make difficult rather than impossible the concept of "reality". We construct as many rules and systems as we subvert. We play as hard as we work but we are under no illusions that all play and no work makes Jackson Pollock a dull boy. What we are *against*, essentially, is any system (such as capitalist democracy) or set of rules (such as bourgeois law) which do not lay bare the conditions of their own construction. What we are *for* is accurately symbolised by our distinctive policy on building regulations: under a Metafictional government, architects will be required to comply with a "Pompidou Edict" prohibiting the concealment of the structural components of public edifices, foundations in particular. Such legislative strategies form the basis of our entire political programme.

We will add that *manifestare* is the Italian verb meaning to show, display, reveal, disclose, demonstrate. Yet which of our adversaries, in their *manifestoes*, dares show, display, reveal, disclose or demonstrate this etymology? When they say the word *manifesto*, apply the "read my lips" test to see that they spell out its contrary — *dissimulo*! Political life has for too long in this country borne this impress of badly dubbed foreign language feature films. Only we Metafictionists offer the hope of a more satisfying relationship between "reality" and its representation (as well, it should be said, as a revivified British movie industry). Were we to vouchsafe absolutely nothing more than the publication of this manifesto the accuracy of such a claim would be unimpeachable. But, as we have made clear, we are not a party of non-government. We promise more, much more.

Our educational programme, for example, aims to replace current National Curriculum English with an entirely new discipline called Texts and Textuality, which will include instruction for all children over fourteen in the following compositional arts:

(1)   the over-intrusive, visibly inventing narrator;
(2)   ostentatious typographic experiment;

SPONSORED BY

(3)   explicit dramatisation of the reader;
(4)   Chinese box structures;
(5)   Russian doll structures;
(6)   English rose structures;
(7)   Welsh rarebit structures;
(8)   incantatory and absurd lists;
(9)   over-systematised or overtly arbitrarily arranged structural devices;
(10)   total breakdown of temporal and spatial organisation of narrative;
(11)   infinite regress;
(12)   dehumanisation of character, parodic doubles, obtrusive proper names;
(13)   unlucky for some;
(14)   self-reflexive images;
(15)   critical discussions of the story within the story;
(16)   stories criticising discussions within discussions;
(17)   discussions of stories about criticisms within criticisms;
(18)   continuous undermining of specific fictional conventions;
(19)   use of popular genres;
(20)   use of unpopular genres;
(21)   explicit parody of previous texts whether literary or non-literary;
(22)   manifesto writing.

Nor is this the only major cultural transformation which we shall bring to pass. Our reform of national broadcasting regulations will ensure that, from 1 January next year, no television programme may be transmitted in which at least one working TV camera is not in shot for a minimum of 20% of the programme's running time. This will revolutionise the industry as we daily know it.

III

(a)   We intend to sing the love of drivel, the habits of blatherskiting and hooeymaking.
(b)   Guff, palaver, and Pickwickianism will be essential elements of our lucidity.
(c)   Up to now literature has exalted a thoughtful decipherability, explicability, and an awful lot of words. We intend to exalt

ZOILUS

aggressive concision, a feverish manufacture of baloney, the gambler's logic, soiled underwear, the punch and the judy.

(d)   We say that the world's munificence has been enkitsched by a new booty; the booty of seaweed. But a rock whose surface is adorned with great swirls of it, like serpents of Coleridgean depth — 'midst a roaring sea that sprays its tide like buckshot — is still not more of a booty than *Pricksongs and Descants*.

(e)   We want to hymn any old Blake painting that fits our mood.

(f)   Metafictionists must spend themselves with ardour, splendour and generosity, unto personal bankruptcy, preferably using the Co-op Bank Metafictionist Party VISA card, to swell the enthusiastic fervour of the primordial elements.

(g)   Except in squiggles, there is no more booty. No work of an unsquiggly character (graphic or verbal) can be a masterpiece. Down with straight lines and *sans serifery*! Composition must be conceived as a violent attack on unknown forces, evident in its corrugated, fiddleheaded convolvulusity.

(h)   We stand on the last promenade of Norfolk! ... Why should we look back on crumbling cliffs, when what we want is to wade into the North Sea, to endure the freezing breakers of the coming Ice Age of Art? Time and Space died yesterday.

(i)   We will glorify candy floss — the world's only metafictional substance — which dissolves before the possibility of consumption can be realised.

(j)   We will spit on any old Blake painting that fits our mood.

(k)   We must destroy syntax in favour of carpet tacks and income tax. The first shall be buried in a plot in a Parisian graveyard, next to Balzac's. The second shall be scattered at random. The third shall be raised.

(l)   Infinitives are in fashion. People like them. They are somehow reassuring. To ban them would be to offend. Thus we shall do so.

(m)   Adjectives. Pah! It is our objective to replace them all with *abjectives*.

(n)   Nouns — pronouns — yes.

(o)   Adverbs. We love 'em.

(p)   The inflated balloon of punctuation — we shall press the flaring cigarette end of our wit annihilatingly into its surface.

(q)   Of everything else, one question: is it worth it? If the answer is

PRESS

yes, put the price up, till the answer is no.

(r)   We will sing of great crows excited by misprints, by leisure, and by rot; we will sing of the multiphonic, polycoloured tiles in modern bathrooms; we will sing *in imitatio* of futurist hokum; widgets that infiltrate livers like giant gnats, adventure steamers that look like spliffs on the horizon, double-breasted locum doctors who squeal, sounds of enormous steel horses manufactured in Tübingen, and the prophylactic clatter of readers who march against our texts under the banners of realism, seeming to roar like hungry lions, until our metaphorical water cannon are uncoiled, and they scatter.

(s)   Do away with the last seven letters of the alphabet.[1]

It is from Cromer pier that we launch through the world this violently upsetting, incendiary manifesto of ours. With it, today, we establish *Metafictionism* because we want to free this land from its smelly gangrene of humanists, evolutionaries, costive Cyclopeans, Romantics, and dainty turds of all descriptions.

IV

Comprehensibility is error: politics is beyond understanding.

The function of politics is the extension of human consciousness.

Politics is therefore the most important of human activities; all others are dependent upon it.

The most appropriate politics at any time can only be understood by an infinitesimal minority of the people — if by any.

The ideal observer of politics would be one conscious of all human experience up to the given moment.If consciousness be likened to a cleared space, politics is that which extends it in any direction.

---

[1] Representations have been made by the Penzance branch of the Party to the effect that Metafictionists should "... rid society of bourgeois, sensible ABC (and common or garden DEFG) and retain the irregular enticements of Z, two fingered V, saucy W, the X of sex and Xanadu, Typography and the T-shirt rather than the hairshirt, Unammuno, Yorick ...". Once in government we shall hold a referendum on this controversial matter. Citizens with names containing the letters T through to Z will not, naturally, be eligible to vote in this referendum.

METAFICTION AT

METAFICTIONIST SYNTHESIS OF THE NOW

We glorify public bumblarting, which for us is only adherence to the principle of freedom at the physiological level, and abhor all fart-fearing windbaggery. Dimwittedness, humanism, Christian moralism, conjugal rights and historical U-turns excite us much less than a generalised Hans Pfaallery. Betrayed in the role of unacknowledged legislators of the world, we now crave, claim and seek powers actual, substantial, convivial and elephantine. We reject all agglutinative morphologies, and thus present our programme in a syntheticon, bombasticaliferous.

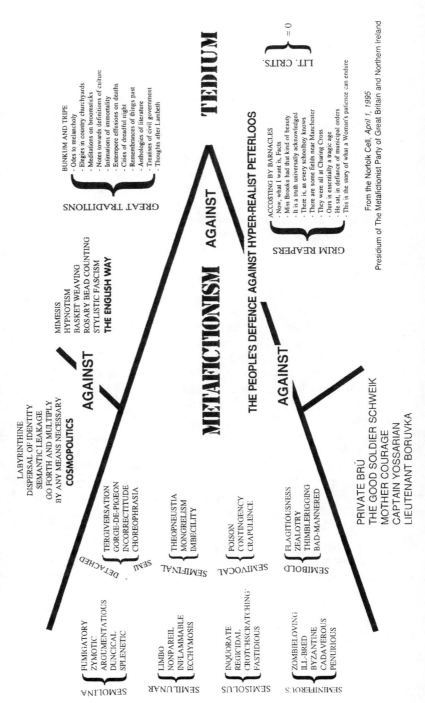

METAFICTIONISM

TEDIUM

THE PEOPLE'S DEFENCE AGAINST HYPER-REALIST PETERLOOS

AGAINST

COSMOPOLITICS
BY ANY MEANS NECESSARY
GO FORTH AND MULTIPLY
SEMANTIC LEAKAGE
DISPERSAL OF IDENTITY
LABYRINTHINE

AGAINST

THE ENGLISH WAY
STYLISTIC FASCISM
ROSARY BEAD COUNTING
BASKET WEAVING
HYPNOTISM
MIMESIS

GREAT TRADITIONS

BUNKUM AND TRIPE
- Odes to melancholy
- Elegies in country churchyards
- Meditations on broomsticks
- Notes towards definitions of culture
- Intimations of immortality
- Extempore effusions on deaths
- Cities of dreadful night
- Remembrances of things past
- Anthologies of literature
- Treatises of civil government
- Thoughts after Lambeth

GRIM REAPERS

ACCOSTING BY BARNACLES
- Now, what I want is, Facts
- Miss Brooke had that kind of beauty
- It is a truth universally acknowledged
- There is, as every schoolboy knows
- There are some fields near Manchester
- They were all at Charing Cross
- Ours is essentially a tragic age
- He sat, in defiance of municipal orders
- This is the story of what a Woman's patience can endure

LIT. CRITS. } = 0

From the Norfolk Cell, *April 1, 1995*
Presidium of The Metafictionist Party of Great Britain and Northern Ireland

AGAINST

DETACHED / SEMI-DETACHED
TERGIVERSATION
GORGE-DE-PIGEON
INCORRECTITUDE
CHOREOPHRASIA

SEMIFINAL
THEOPNEUSTIA
MONGRELISM
IMBECILITY

SEMIVOCAL
POISON
CONTINGENCY
CRAPULENCE

SEMIBOLD
FLAGITIOUSNESS
ZEALOTRY
THIMBLERIGGING
BAD-MANNERED

SEMOLINA
FUMIGATORY
ZYMOTIC
ARGUMENTATIOUS
DUNCICAL
SPLENETIC

SEMILUNAR
LIMBO
NONPAREIL
INFLAMMABLE
ECCHYMOSIS

SEMISOLUS
INQUORATE
REGICIDAL
CROTCHSCRATCHING
FASTIDIOUS

SEMINIFEROUS
ZOMBIELOVING
ILL-BRED
BYZANTINE
CADAVEROUS
PENURIOUS

PRIVATE BRÛ
THE GOOD SOLDIER SCHWEIK
MOTHER COURAGE
CAPTAIN YOSSARIAN
LIEUTENANT BORUVKA

The ideal observer alone can appreciate the value, in relation to politics as a whole, of any further achievement.

There is no ideal observer of politics. There are only voters.

Capacity for political understanding increases in so far as one is making progress in any direction towards the confines of the cleared space. Space abhors a vacuum. There is a political vacuum at the heart of our polity.

Metafictionism is a vacuum clearer (*sic*) in the space of that polity. The polity abhors *politesse*. There is no space for it in a Metafictional state. Only the politics of *anti-politesse* will clear the space required if the polity is not to remain as vacuous as it is at present.

Ground covered in any direction ceases to be politics for those who have covered it, and, for them, lapses into mere history. However ponderable from other points of view, from the standpoint of politics, those bogged in what has lapsed (for those who have passed any given point) cease to exist. Only those who are further ahead than themselves are of consequence to those who are making political progress. But to those further ahead those to whom they are of consequence do not, as has been said, effectively exist. Any relationship with those others is a waste of time, of life, of breath, of space. This is the ineluctable paradox of all Metafictional politics.

To halt or turn back in order to try to help others is to abandon political progress. This is not why we Metafictionists, as our opponents claim, are in favour of infinite regress: that is a different matter entirely. There is no altruism in politics. In so far as one advances, the progress of others may be facilitated, but in so far as one is conscious of affording any such facilitation one's concentration on purely political objectives is diminished. Manifestoes are one of the most pointless and distracting exercises in this respect, which should never be indulged, and consequently always are.

From the point of view of the ideal observer nothing has value as politics which does not add to the area of the cleared space. To such an observer, everything coming within the cleared space automatically lapses into mere history. Something like this has been said already, but it is an insight which bears repetition.

True politics is incapable of repetition.

No politician is great (or really a politician) unless s/he reaches some point in the unknown outside the cleared space and then adds to the cleared space.

The total addition made to the cleared space is the measure of greatness

REALISTIC

as a politician — *at the time the addition is made.*

No achievement of politics is permanent — as politics.

Great politicians of the past diminish in so far as the point or frontier of their particular addition recedes from the latest confines of the cleared space.

They cease to be great politicians from the point of view of the ideal observer, and acquire compensatory importance in mere history.

They remain politicians or great politicians only in proportion to the appropriate ignorance (i.e. incapacity for experience) of those for whom they are so.

If politics is compatible with big popular appeal, it can only be so in so far as it contains elements unthinkable to the public.

In direct ratio to its popularity (i.e. its comprehensibility) it is not politics.

The most persuasive politics at any given time is that which is comprehensible to the fewest persons of competence and integrity, as approximations to the ideal observer. As has been emphasised, all dicta on politics are to be judged only in relation to omniscience of human experience, which no one possesses. For politicians to pride themselves on their knowledge of politics is to boast — not of their achievements, still less of their powers — but of their tools.

All that claims to be politics therefore is of value *in inverse ratio* to its comprehensibility and to the extent to which it falls into any particular category.

Of necessity this includes the category of Metafiction. To our adversaries who claim, on the basis of the above points, that Metafictionism is nonsense, we have only one answer. It is.

V

Clear a space today, insist
on voting

PRICES!

Term: a Documentary

Meditation: DEADWOOD to HIMSELF

So many texts, so many books. So much GREAT LITERATURE. So few lectures. Bumble bumble. Hard choices to make. My Gethsemane. A cup that cannot pass, sweat falling to the ground like great drops of blood. Amen. This shall have to suffice.

Letter: COLERIDGE to WORDSWORTH (23 January 1798)

... a mere patchwork of plagiarisms; but they are well worked up, and for stage effect make an excellent *whole*.

Notice: DEADWOOD to STUDENTS

The order of my ROMANTIC LITERATURE lectures is as follows. Please use the bibliography, available from the departmental office, to do the background reading on these lecture topics.

Week 1   What was Romanticism?
Week 2   Wordsworth's poetry
Week 3   Coleridge's poetry
Week 4   Blake's poetry
Week 5   Byron's poetry
Week 6   Shelley's poetry
Week 7   Keats's poetry
Week 8   Other Romantic poetry I (Landor and Darley)
Week 9   Other Romantic poetry II (Hood and Beddoes)
Week 10 The Celtic spirit in Romantic poetry (Burns and Scott)

Dr Panjandrum Deadwood
Reader in Literary Reading

Internal Memorandum: WROTH to DEADWOOD

The irony of Chekhov remarking "That's true!" or "That's wrong!" when reading *The Kreutzer Sonata* is striking, given the terminological debate after Blabdrip's lecture yesterday evening (see enclosed). I still fail to understand what precise objection you or Blabdrip had to the *Sonata*.

Lecture One: Attendance — DEADWOOD plus 130

... You will read in textbooks claims to the effect that "Romanticism resists its definers, who can fix neither its characteristics nor its dates". I shall persuade you that this is not true, and shall begin by declaring that Romanticism in these isles was nothing more and nothing less than an unprecedented spirit of sublimity, akin to a religious enthusiasm in the sphere of letters, which entered into and departed from English writers between 1765 and 1832. ...

Internal Memorandum: DEADWOOD to ALL COLLEAGUES

The hungry sheep look up, and are not fed. (Milt.)

I have sat, on innumerable occasions through the years, at the Departmental table and heard what I opined was the wrong decision being agreed upon and implemented, but never before, so acutely as at last week's Departmental Meeting, have I heard an agreement which spells certain and complete disaster.

It has been evident to colleagues teaching at the "modern end" of the Dept. for years, that students coming straight from 6th form English into our Dept. begin to gasp for LITERATURE like fish suddenly landed upon the strand. It was for that reason that I, years ago, invented HOW TO READ LITERATURE (a module long ago discontinued under duress) and, in reacting to a real demand with a real answer, did a real service.

And now, again, we hear the usual cry from students: more LITERATURE in Year 1. And what did modern colleagues decide to do? To cut the only LITERATURE course there is (my own and Dr Proops's LITERATURE AND MORALITY), and to double the commitment to "theory".

Disaster! READING MATTER AND MATERIALIST READING (convened by colleagues Hamner and Spive) is one of the most unpopular courses in Year 1. This is not *my* assessment. The "rationale" for it is universally agreed to be unclear, and its periodisation and *telos* are subject to sharp *student* critique. Yet modern colleagues decide to *double* precisely that course, to make it a two semester rather than a one semester "happening" (but to give it a new name, as the outlaw takes an *alias*), and to *cut* the only REAL LITERATURE module!

"But it *will* contain literary works — we will 'build into' our theoretical discourse a series of great texts, in order to make their nature clearer." Wrong again! Those works will not be free. The double READING MATTER AND MATERIALIST READING module will incorporate them *only as illustrative of* some wider truth to which those teaching the course are privy. These works will be forced unwillingly into service, to prove some point. They will be vassal texts. And, as such, they will be rejected by the students. ... **(to be continued)**

Letter: CHEKHOV to PLESCHEEV (15 February 1890)

Don't you really like *The Kreutzer Sonata*? I won't say it is a work of genius, or one that will last for ever, I am no judge of these matters, but in my opinion, among everything being written here and abroad, you will hardly find anything as powerful in seriousness of conception and beauty of execution. Without mentioning its artistic merits, which in places are outstanding, one must thank the story if only for the one thing that it is extremely thought-provoking. As I read it I could hardly stop myself crying out: "That's true!" or "That's wrong!" Of course it does have some very annoying defects. Besides those you enumerated, there is one further point which one will not readily forgive its author, namely the brashness with which Tolstoy pontificates on things he does not know of and out of stubbornness does not want to understand. Thus his pronouncements on syphilis, foundling hospitals, women's repugnance for copulation and so on are not only debatable but also show him to be a complete ignoramus who has never taken the trouble during the course of his long life to read a couple of books written by specialists. Still these defects fly off like feathers in the wind; considering the merits of the story you simply do not notice them, or, if you do, it is only annoying that the story did not avoid the fate of all works of man, all of which are imperfect and possess faults.

Extract: From JOSEPH GIBALDI and WALTER S. ACHTERT, *MLA Handbook for Writers of Research Papers* (2nd ed., 1984)

... Plagiarism is the act of using another person's ideas or expressions in your writing without acknowledging the source. The word comes from the Latin word *plagiarius* ("kidnapper"), and Alexander Lindley defines it as "the false assumption of authorship: the wrongful act of taking the product of another person's mind, and presenting it as one's own" (*Plagiarism and*

Originality [New York: Harper, 1952] 2). In short, to plagiarize is to give the impression that you have written or thought something that you have in fact borrowed from someone else...

Plagiarism often carries severe penalties, ranging from failure in a course to expulsion from school.

The most blatant form of plagiarism is to repeat as your own someone else's sentences, more or less verbatim. ...

Lecture Two: Attendance — DEADWOOD plus 61

... It is inevitable, while man lives in the world as it is, that his poetry should reflect the knowledge of good and evil. Morality colours all language, and lends it the most delicate of its powers of distinction. Take from a poet his moral reflections, his saws, and his sentences; you rob him of his most effective instrument. It is by these, indeed, rather than by his constructive or exploratory powers, that Shakespeare holds his most popular title. A poet who coins proverbs and gives point and polish to a moral truth is a poet whose fortune is quickly made. But how, except in some completely transcendental sense, can a moral expression be given to a sunset? No clearly rounded period can reproduce that marvel, with all its vague messages to the heart. And it was this sort of power and this sort of beauty that was the inspiration of Wordsworth's poetry. He did not under-value another sort of beauty, which appeals chiefly to the intellect — the beauty of contrivance, of perfect adaptation to an end, which makes a steam-engine or a masterly game of chess a source of pure joy. But this is a beauty imposed by the active intelligence of man on the shapeless material that comes to his hand. So also does human morality, in so far as it takes its origin from the necessities of social life, impose itself on the raw material of society. There is no question here of the intuitions of a great prophet or teacher, but simply of that wide field of social judgment and social sanction, far wider than the operation of any definite enactments, where the moral sense of a community imposes itself on the tastes and habits of the individual and brings order out of chaos. ...

Internal Memorandum (strictly confidential): PROFESSOR GLOBULE (Registrar) to MRS BOOM (Academic Arbitration Committee)

I am now in a position to report and recommend on Disputes 513a (Axelrod v. Deadwood) and 513b (Deadwood v. Axelrod).

At the end of last academic session a problem arose concerning the marking of one element of the English Literature Department's Part I Module "Literature as Therapy". The first marker (Deadwood) and the second marker (Axelrod) were unable to reach agreement on a run of marks, so a selection of essays and then the whole run were given to the external examiner for adjudication. The consequences and issues of this disagreement continue to create great internal strife in the department concerned.

In asking the external examiner to adjudicate an entire run of scripts the internal markers added an immense load to this colleague (who has since resigned and published an article on the matter in the *Times Higher Education Supplement*) and created a situation which delayed the start of the exam board (during which an unseemly altercation led to damage of the order of £350 being done to furniture in the room). Such use of an external examiner should be avoided and internal markers should be able to arrive at agreed marks in the majority of cases. In the arguments, questions were raised as to the procedures of exam marking. The account that follows show: (a) why the internal markers were unable to reach agreement; (b) some of the problems with regard to marking; (c) a comparative table of the contested marks (this last is included because some apparently statistical arguments had been used in the disagreements). ... **(to be continued)**

Prefatory Remarks: COLERIDGE to HIS READERS (1816)

... there is amongst us a set of critics, who seem to hold, that every possible thought and image is traditional; who have no notion that there are such things as fountains in the world, small as well as great; and who would therefore charitably derive every rill they behold flowing, from a perforation made in some other man's tank. I am confident, however, that as far as the present poem is concerned, the celebrated poets whose writings I might be suspected of having imitated, either in particular passages, or in the tone and the spirit of the whole, would be among the first to vindicate me from the charge, and who, on any striking coincidence, would permit me to address them in this doggerel version of two monkish Latin hexameters:

'Tis mine and it is likewise yours;
But an if this will not do;
Let it be mine, good friend! for I
Am the poorer of the two. ... **(to be continued)**

Internal Memorandum: DEADWOOD to ALL COLLEAGUES (**continued**)

... I cannot conceive of anything more likely to lead to disaster, and even to open rebellion, than a "doubling" of the READING MATTER AND MATERIALIST READING course. It is at least conceptually possible that the students just aren't interested in the reasons why "English" became what it did and the way in which "English" is held in place by A-level questions and Mr Kenneth Baker's *Faber Book of Patriotic Jingles*. Everything that Chris Baldick says may be entirely true, and worth investigating again and again over the three years, but the students do seem to be genuinely insensible to the charms of his case.

Be that as it may, they want to get on with doing "English". I still remember the shock of recognition when I read, in one of the student evaluations of my Shakespeare course a few years back, "I really miss Eng. Lit. as I did it at A-level. Degree level hasn't been nearly so good, unfortunately." I really miss Eng. Lit. as I did it at A-level. A death's head. ... (**to be continued**)

Extract: From CHRIS BALDICK, *The Social Mission of English Criticism 1848-1932* (1983)

In general, all these critics fill the gap left by their exclusion of theoretical concerns with a haphazard critical method loosely combining empiricist and idealist components. Thus, in Arnold's writings the act of pointing to certain lines of poetry or to certain social institutions acts as an empirical anchor for semi-mystical categories like "charm", "natural magic", "the Celtic spirit", or "the spirit of the Populace". Arnold tends to leap unsystematically from the noumenal "*life*" to the phenomenal "*there*"; and the same pattern of short circuits between vitalism and empiricism is repeated almost exactly by the Leavises. In Richards, the uneasy mixture of methods is even more visible: the attempt is made to reconcile an atomistic, semi-behaviourist model of the human mind as a circle bombarded by particles of stimuli, with an antagonistic model of subjective self-development and critical choice patched together with Buddhist themes. This forked or double method is an almost inevitable consequence of the division of the world into sealed compartments of scientific fact on the one hand and moral value on the other.

Internal Memorandum (strictly confidential): PROFESSOR GLOBULE
(Registrar) to MRS BOOM (Academic Arbitration Committee) **(continued)**

... The internal markers for the "Literature as Therapy" essays met twice.
The scale of disagreement became apparent at the first meeting. While
Axelrod agreed with some of Deadwood's comments on the essays, he
disputed the high marks which had been awarded. The markers agreed to
send a selection of essays to the external examiner. Deadwood, as first
marker, chose which essays were to be sent. The internal markers met a
second time ten days later, after the adjudicated sample had been returned,
but they were still unable to agree. It is Axelrod's contention that
Deadwood's attitude at the meeting inhibited the possibility of agreement:
in particular, he claims that Deadwood expressed the belief that he
(Axelrod) "instructed" the external examiner by telephone to agree with his
(Axelrod's) marks, that he (Deadwood) implied a conspiracy between
Axelrod and the external, and finally refused categorically to accept the
authority of the external. Deadwood testifies that the possibility of agreeing
with someone who "does not believe in the notion of literature as therapy
and is in any case not a family man" (this is a reference to Axelrod) is
virtually nil, but denies calling into question the probity of the external,
who, although he (Deadwood) regards her (the external) as "an intellectual
foal", had "acted in good faith but under the influence of suave
manipulation". He also notes that the external works in the same institution
as Axelrod's "lover", who sits on the promotions panel to which she (the
external) had made application (an application since reported as successful).

During the later meeting Deadwood impugned Axelrod's general
abilities as a second marker, saying his second marking of the previous
year's MA in Joycean Jouissance had gone down in departmental legend
as puritanical in the extreme. He averred that Axelrod's second marking
of the "Therapy" scripts was moved by malice, that it was political, and
that it was an act of vengeance for past disputes in which he (Deadwood)
had been triumphant. In considering the case of one student whose mark
Axelrod proposed lowering from a First to a II.ii, Deadwood said he didn't
know how Axelrod could live with his conscience, as that student had been
so pleased with her provisional mark for the essay that she had been seen
hopping and skipping down the corridor. When towards the end Axelrod
told Deadwood he had to accept the authority of the external, Deadwood
said "Don't read the rule-book to me" (a phrase he used repeatedly to the
present writer when interviewed about the affair). Axelrod said that
Deadwood's position was one which was now a matter for the head of
department, and that the meeting had better be terminated. Deadwood said
he would "take the dispute into the public arena". Axelrod claims that

Deadwood later said he would accept the authority of the external examiner on condition she read the whole set of essays, but that, once this was arranged, Deadwood denied ever having given such an undertaking. ... **(to be continued)**

Lecture Three: Attendance — DEADWOOD plus 52

... After making due allowance for the Spenserian origin of the allegory, the antithesis of the beauty of innocence to the beauty of sin, the conclusion of the whole matter is that Coleridge's Christabel is a new creation, as new as when Eve "first awaked", and strange as yet to Adam and to Paradise. Perhaps the most wonderful quality or characteristic of this First Part of *Christabel* is that the action is not that of a drama which is *ex hypothesi* a representation of fact; nor are we persuaded to reproduce it for ourselves as by a tale that is told, but we behold it, scene after scene, episode after episode, as in a mirror, as the Lady of Shalott saw the knights ride by. If we stay to think of Christabel "praying beneath the huge oak tree", or of Geraldine and Christabel crossing the moat and passing through the hall, and stealing their way from stair to stair, our minds make pictures, but we do not stay to think or reflect on their fears or their rejoicings. We "see, we see it all", and now in glimmer and now in gloom we "live o'er again" that midnight hour. It is not a tale that is told, it is a personal experience. ...

Internal Memorandum: DEADWOOD to ALL COLLEAGUES **(continued)**

... "Yes, but in order to teach 'Eng. Lit.' at all, one must theorise it. There is no such thing as the innocent eye." Quite so. But it is just as important to be aware of the nature of one's own theorisation. And if the general thrust of one's own theorisation is running counter to what the students are actually asking for, one ought to be very wary of one's own motives? If the students loved 'Eng. Lit.' at school, and they chose to come here to study it, and when they get here, they are told to distrust it, it may be that we are not being fair to them?

I beg my "modern" colleagues not to impose what they think is desirable over the students in a kind of *pax romana*, but to listen to what they are actually saying. They want some more LITERATURE. That is their only "bridge" (to deploy the metaphor currently being used to justify the multiplication of READING MATTER AND MATERIALIST

READING by itself: READING MATTER AND MATERIALIST READING squared, READING MATTER AND MATERIALIST READING to the second power, a READING MATTER AND MATERIALIST READING^2 whose square root will be READING MATTER AND MATERIALIST READING itself!) from what they knew at school to their studies here. So ought we not to be sensitive to their (implicit) demand? We should certainly retain LITERATURE AND MORALITY. It would be the easiest thing in the world to change its contents to something a little more "mainstream", but something that was still recognisably "literature" — some Hardy stories + *Heart of Darkness* + some Auden poems + *The Bell Jar* + *Waiting for Godot*? — or any such like substitutions, and probably we ought to find a way to put on a more general introduction for Year 1 as well (we could resurrect HOW TO READ LITERATURE), in place of one of the other non-literary modules (such as READING MATTER AND MATERIALIST READING). I invite responses to this concrete proposal.

Extract: From CIARA VAN SERAI, "Gender and Sexuality in Coleridge's *Christabel*" (essay submitted to DR SPILLMATTER)

... Critics have tended to see Geraldine as the evil seductress leading "Sweet Christabel" astray. However, there are clear textual indications that Christabel is not the chaste young woman she appears to be. Indeed, one could suggest that in her implied sexual liaison with Geraldine, Christabel is not the passive victim of Geraldine's wiles, but rather an active and willing participant. ... **(to be continued)**

Internal Memorandum: HAMNER to DEADWOOD

Personally, Panjandrum, I would throw your concrete proposal in the canal and watch it sink.

Prefatory Remarks: COLERIDGE to HIS READERS (1816) **(continued)**

... I have only to add that the metre of Christabel is not, properly speaking, irregular, though it may seem so from its being founded on a new principle: namely, that of counting in each line the accents, not the syllables. Though the latter may vary from seven to twelve, yet in each line the accents will be found to be only four. Nevertheless, this occasional variation in number of syllables is not introduced wantonly, or for the mere ends of convenience, but in correspondence with some transition, in the nature of the imagery or passion.

Table Talk (Seminar): SEVERAL to OTHERS

CAROL: ... To conclude, then, the metre of *Christabel* is just the principle of the freely constituted four-foot verse as used in old English poetry (*viertaktig*).

ANDY: It occurs to me that it is also the principle of the four accented iambic-anapaest or trochaic-dactylic new English long line (*vierhebig*), which is frequently combined with the one you've just mentioned. Burns's *Tam o'Shanter* is a conspicuous instance.

CAROL: Yes! I see. Which only confirms that the claim raised by Coleridge to have discovered a new metrical principle is in every respect unfounded. The best we can say is that it came into vogue through him, and exercised considerable influence on his contemporaries, and on later poets, such as Byron, Scott and Moore.

NAOMI: But, really, it's *quite impossible* to suppose that Coleridge believed, or imagined that his readers would believe, that the alternation of iambic with trochaic or anapaestic lines, or the occasional variation in the number of syllables in lines of equal metrical accentuation, constituted "a new principle" of verse. He could not have been under the delusion that Milton's *L'Allegro* or Shakespeare's songs were out of reach of the public to which he appealed. His claim was that *Christabel* was the first poem in the English language composed on the deliberate principle of so varying the *time* (and if need be, the number of syllables) as to make the tune of the words a kind of running accompaniment to the sense, and to do this without exceeding or falling short of four accents (or rather, suggestions of accentuation — a stronger compensating for a weaker stress) to the line. It was a fact that *Christabel* was the first of its kind, that *as a whole* it was not modelled on any immediate or remote predecessor, and it was a fact that it had already served

	as a model to more than one immediate successor. It marked a new departure in the art or science of metrification.

ROBERT: Well, I don't know. Just looking at it, the normal rhythm is iambic, but an anapaest is admissible in any foot, a dactyl in the first, and a trochee in the first or third. The metre is tetrameter acatalectic, that is there are four feet, and the last foot terminates the verse. There are only eleven instances of the dimeter and trimeter, and only twenty instances of hypercatalectic verses out of upward of six hundred and seventy lines. The *ictus metricus* principally falls on the second and fourth accents in the line.

DEADWOOD: But, when all is said and done, *Christabel* is a thing of fragile beauty, is it not?

Lecture Four: Attendance — DEADWOOD plus 44

... Blake says in the essay on the Last Judgement that the antediluvian Church knew only spring and autumn, and that the four seasons did not come until after the flood. The meaning of this will be seen when we remember that heat is masculine, cold feminine, and that the feminine powers form the outer world by a process of freezing. At first heat and cold, masculine and feminine, dwell together in harmony, each tempering the other with itself. Then the cold resolves to live for itself and all is changed, for "there was no female will in paradise". The awakening of this female will is the generalizing of Canaan, which by giving general rules of conduct, born of reason, set up an external necessity to which the internal life must bow. ...

Internal Memorandum: BRIDIE (Head of Department) to DEADWOOD

Thank you for your "concrete proposal". Contrary to your request, I shall not be placing it on the agenda of the next Departmental Meeting. Time and opportunity to discuss the issue were in plentiful supply at the last meeting, when you exercised your right of total silence on the matter. The circulation of a mesmerising memo five days later, even with an epigraph from Milton, is not likely on this occasion to have the *Deus Ex Machina* effect you obviously intend for all of your ponderous missives.

On an unrelated matter, there have been complaints from colleagues Spive and Bettermint that you have been conducting seminars of sixteen students rather than the departmental norm of eight, while claiming to teach the number of hours you *would* be teaching *were* you teaching groups of eight. I would be grateful if you would confirm that such rumours are unfounded.

Extract: From CIARA VAN SERAI, "Gender and Sexuality in Coleridge's *Christabel*" **(continued)**

... In Part I, great emphasis is placed upon the journey from the forest to the castle — as if there were the expectation of some kind of climax in the reader's mind once they arrive at their destination, Indeed, their stealthy progress through the castle has the suspense which one might normally expect from a scene in a film involving two young lovers, desperate to remain undiscovered by their parents: they hold their breath when they pass Sir Leoline's door, and the image of them going up the stairs, "Now in glimmer, and now in gloom" (l. 169) has something of a cinematic quality about it.

More specifically, when they have crossed the moat and are unlocking the gate, what they are doing has clear sexual connotations. At a location conventionally associated with a male preoccupation —

The gate that was ironed within and without,
Where an army in battle array had marched out (ll. 127-8)

— we discover that Geraldine is weak ("a weary weight" [l. 131]), so Christabel has to pick her up and carry her over the threshold (an activity one would ordinarily associate with newly weds). In addition, when the narrator tells us of how "Christabel/Took the key that fitted well" (ll. 123-4), one perhaps thinks of the key to a chastity belt. The gate protects the castle just as a chastity belt protects the purity of the woman (and delimits her sexual possibilities to interaction with a male proprietor). Indeed, one could argue that the fact that Christabel herself unlocks her own "gate" is significant, since it demonstrates again that she is a quite willing participant. ... **(to be continued)**

Internal Memorandum: DEADWOOD to WROTH

I am sorry if you were offended by my challenging you after Oswald

Blabdrip's talk. It did seem to me, however, that Oswald needed a little protection! He is, after all, a Grand Old Man of English letters, Gloiretit's successor at Balliol, and the author of some thirty books of criticism, and your critiques of his talk about Sylvia Plath's poetry did seem to me harsh and unnuanced. You referred to him, so far as I remember, as little better than a schoolmaster writing "could do better" at the end of Sylvia Plath's poems; you called him "didactic", you said he was limited and limiting in his "humanistic" approach; that his use of concepts like "true" and "false" was naïve; that his whole approach was embarrassing and out of date; and you ended up by saying that his talk as a whole appeared to you as just outright stupid. That last may not have been the exact word you used (my mind has "erased" it, from shock) but it was a word of that tenor and carrying that charge, and intended, obviously, to offend Blabdrip outright.

I had to intervene to defend Oswald from this kind of attack, as he was a guest of the English Society, had come here as an act of goodwill from the deeps of retirement, and his whole aim was to do a kind act by speaking here.

You ask me, in the annotated xerox you left me in my pigeonhole after the talk, "what objection was being made to *The Kreutzer Sonata*". Let me try to give you an explanation. ... **(to be continued)**

Review: From *The Champion*, 26 May 1816 (anonymous)

... One friend suggests that the whole is a mere hoax. ... Another thinks it is the result of a wager on the digestive capabilities of the public taste; and a third declares that the poem has just the same effect on his temper as if a man were to salute him in the street with a box on the ear and walk away. ...

Exchange (overheard prior to lecture)

STUDENT A: One of these days *real history* is going to erupt into all
                this intellectual fucking psychobabble, y'know. I can't
                wait.

STUDENT B: *Real* history? In which of two possible senses are you
                using the word "history" there?

STUDENT A: Eh?

STUDENT B: Well, you might be envisaging history as the signification of a discourse, a set of meanings which — for
such is the nature of signifieds — are internal to and the
product of processes of signification. But something in
your tone and the erection of a binary opposition
between "*real history*" and "intellectual fucking
psychobabble" makes me want to suggest that you are
drawing upon another meaning of the term in which
history figures as an extra-discursive *origin* of
discourse. One cannot hold to both definitions, for the
one contradicts the other.

STUDENT A: I mean *real history*, get it? The kind of history that is
upon you without warning like the clenched fist that
bops you one in the gob in the middle of you prattling
shit, and stops you dead. Right?

STUDENT B: I see.

Question

Does the inclusion of the above exchange in this text imply that it has a use
value over and above its evident exchange value?

Lecture Five: Attendance — DEADWOOD plus 35

... Just one word of protest, before I resume the thread of my argument,
on the attempts made to prove a man guilty of crimes from the tone or
context of his works. Nothing can be more unfair or more uncritical. Some
of you are probably aware of the imputations which certain critics have
brought against Shakespeare, arising out of constructions they conceive
may be put on some of his sonnets. These imputations we should
indignantly repudiate. But had Shakespeare's wife — to whom we know
he was not particularly attached — only made the abominable charge the
imputations involve, and had she chosen further to communicate it to a
contemporary authoress, the latter would certainly have argued that
anybody who read the sonnets with her story in mind would see that the
story was true! In Byron's case, the trouble he took — like St Augustine
before his conversion — to make himself out worse than he was, joined to
"the wild fame of his ungoverned youth", disposes many people to believe

anything and everything that can be said against him; and they are just as ready to convict him out of his own writings as they would on the evidence of their own senses...

Internal Memorandum (strictly confidential): PROFESSOR GLOBULE (Registrar) to MRS BOOM (Academic Arbitration Committee) **(continued)**

... As convener for the group of optionals of which "Literature as Therapy" is part, Axelrod has not only to organise marking arrangements but to deal with students' questions. During this process he observed for himself, and students volunteered unprompted accounts of, the activities of Deadwood which Axelrod considers to be ill-advised if not downright improper. The following is rephrased from from a list supplied by Axelrod:

1.   Deadwood deposited the marks for the "Fantastic Feminists" module (which he second marked) as agreed marks, then afterwards claimed he had no qualifications as a second marker.
2.   Deadwood threatened, after second marking "Malicious Masculinists", that it might be necessary to lower the marks by at least a class because that was what was being suggested for his own module, "Literature as Therapy".
3.   After depositing "Fantastic Feminists" marks as agreed, Deadwood threatened to remark the essays, suggesting that the marks should all be reduced.
4.   After the exam results had been published, Deadwood told a student that a mark of 30 was a first mark which he (Deadwood) thought should have been raised to a 40 (although Deadwood had deposited the mark of 30 as agreed by himself with the first marker).
5.   Deadwood attempted to prevent a second marker lowering individual marks by working out percentages of first class marks for three options and then claiming that his option had to have a similar proportion of first class marks (as if this proportion were irrespective of the quality of individual essays).
6.   Deadwood attempted to prevent a second marker lowering an individual mark by telling him that the student had already been told she had high marks for that essay.
7.   While Deadwood's students had been told their marks were not confirmed, they had no firm idea that these marks could or might be altered.

8. Deadwood agreed to undertake second marking he later claimed to have no competence in, and further suggested that where any second marker did anything other than agree with a first marker, then that second marker was acting beyond his or her competence. He said he would not be as "daring" as to disagree with any of the first marks for the "Fantastic Feminists" essays (although he later contested two).

9. Deadwood talked about Axelrod to the second external examiner (not normally concerned with Part I materials) in such terms that the external reported that it was clear that "they hated one another's guts", which suggests that she formed the impression that the disagreement arose mainly out of a personality clash.

When this list of problems was put to Deadwood he denied each in turn, with the exceptions of numbers 6 (which he considered "eminently reasonable") and 9 (which "demonstrates the perceptiveness of the external in question"). ... **(to be continued)**

Extract: From LEO TOLSTOY, *The Kreutzer Sonata* (1889)

" ... It's like slavery. Slavery's just the exploitation by the few of the forced labour of the many. And so, if there's to be no more slavery, men must stop exploiting the forced labour of others, they must come to view it as a sin or at least as something to be ashamed of. But instead of this, all they do is abolish the outer forms of slavery — they arrange things so that it's no longer possible to buy and sell slaves, and then imagine, and are indeed convinced, that slavery doesn't exist any more: they don't see, they don't want to see, that it continues to exist because men go on taking satisfaction in exploiting the labour of others and persist in believing that it's perfectly legitimate for them to do so. And for as long as they believe this, there will always be those who are able to do it with more strength and cunning than others. ..."

Internal Memorandum: DEADWOOD to WROTH **(continued)**

... My opening ploy, when I intervened to save Oswald from you, was to insist on the theoretical point that there are only two sorts of ideological prejudice, that of which a speaker is aware, and to which he will willingly admit, and that of which a speaker is unaware, and to which he will not admit at all, under the naïve conviction that his position "has" no "ideology" attached to it, it is just "common sense" or "getting back to basics" or whatever.

I set out, twenty years ago, my profound conviction that we cannot speak "from nowhere", that speaking at all implies a position taken, a series of beliefs held to, a stance, a cast of mind, a certain experience, and so on. (I am pleased to discover, more recently, that Gadamer agrees with me: without taking account of our *Vorurteil*, our "prejudice", in advance [that word having no negative, but a purely analytic or judgmental force] we argue out of mere naïvete, we deceive only ourselves.)

It seemed to me that you were suffering from a mild form of that naïvete in correcting Blabdrip quite so roundly. It sounded perilously as if you were labouring under the belief that you were in some sense "right", and Blabdrip was "wrong".

I therefore intervened to the effect that, since Oswald had set out his own "prejudices" (*Vorurteilen*) in a very frank manner, you might do the same. To my surprise, rather, you abandoned what I had taken to be your "naïve" position and took up a new one, that of a convinced theoretician. You were, you said, arguing (you supposed) from the position of a "Marxist". When I pointed out then, that the "prejudices" of a Gloiretitian humanist and moralist would, *a priori*, be at loggerheads with the "prejudices" of a "Marxist", everyone in the room laughed, for that was obviously the case. ... **(to be continued)**

Extract: From WILLIAM HAZLITT, *The Spirit of the Age* (1824)

... All that he has done of moment, he had done twenty years ago; since then, he may be said to have lived on the sound of his own voice. ...

Extract: From CIARA VAN SERAI, "Gender and Sexuality in Coleridge's *Christabel*" **(continued)**

... Once they reach the end of their journey and arrive in Christabel's chamber, the scene takes on the atmosphere of a seduction. Having "picked up" Geraldine, Christabel secretly brings her to the chamber, where she plies her with drink ("a wine of virtuous powers" [l. 192]), as a consequence of which Geraldine's eyes "'gan glitter bright" [l. 221]). One might argue that, if Christabel were a man, critics would have had none of the difficulty they have had in attaching sexual meaning to their activities. It is simply because they are women that critics have been reluctant to acknowledge it. (Dr James Gillman, with whom Coleridge lived for eighteen years, did indeed expound the argument that Geraldine is, in fact, Christabel's betrothed in disguise. Patricia Adair [1967] cannot bring herself to admit, or at least articulate, the suggestion of a lesbian liaison, and instead sees their relationship in non-sexual parental terms as "an ironic and terrible parody of a mother's love for a child". Fruman [1971] denounces "the bedroom scene" as a "loathsome act".) ... **(to be continued)**

Review: From *The Anti-Jacobin Review*, July 1816 (anonymous)

... Had we not known Mr Coleridge to be a man of genius and of talents we should really, from the present production, have been tempted to pronounce him wholly destitute of both: Mr Coleridge might have spared himself the trouble of anticipating the charge "of plagiarism or servile imitation" — it is a perfectly original composition, and the like of it is not to be found in the English language.

Extract: From TOM BOTTOMORE *et al.* (eds.), *A Dictionary of Marxist Thought* (1983)

In Marxist social theory the notion of property and some related categories (property relations, forms of property) have a central significance. Marx did not regard property only as the possibility for the owner to exercise property rights, or as an object of such activity, but as an essential relationship which has a central role in the complex system of classes and social strata. Within this system of categories the ownership of means of production has outstanding importance. Lange (1963) says that according to Marxist theory such ownership is "the 'organizing principle' which determines both the relations of production and ·the relations of distribution".

Lecture Six: Attendance — DEADWOOD plus 23

DEADWOOD: ... In Shelley's poetry, if we peep over the wild mask of revolutionary metaphysics, we see the winsome face of the child. Perhaps none of his poems is more purely and typically Shelleyan than *The Cloud*, and it is interesting to note how essentially it springs from the faculty of make-believe —

STUDENT: Just a bloody minute there!

DEADWOOD: I'm sorry. I beg your pardon? Is something wrong? Are
                you feeling ill?

STUDENT: This metaphysics business. I mean, in June 1817 a few
                operatives rose in Derbyshire. A score of dragoons put
                down the Derbyshire insurrection, an insurrection there
                is reason to believe put up by a government spy. On
                November 7th, 1817, three men, Brandreth, Turner,
                Ludlam, were drawn on hurdles to a place of execution,
                and were hanged and decapitated in the presence of an
                excited and horror-stricken crowd. Shelley's voice was
                lifted up against this judicial murder, as it would be
                now, for cases like this are occurring still, in increasing
                numbers as the class struggle intensifies. The Gibraltar
                murders —

DEADWOOD: Yes, thank you —

STUDENT: Shoot-to-kill English imperialism in Ireland and lynch-
                mob justice —

DEADWOOD: If I may go on — where was I?

STUDENT: Not much metaphysics there, you stupid git!

DEADWOOD: Er, the universe is Shelley's box of toys. He dabbles his
                fingers in the day-fall. He is gold-dusty with tumbling
                amidst the stars. He makes bright mischief with the
                moon. The meteors nuzzle their noses in his hand ...

Internal Memorandum: DEADWOOD to WROTH (**continued**)

    ... What then happened was that Oswald himself re-entered the
conversation, having thought the matter through privately and at a different
level. He said that he thought that one could instance the work of Tolstoy.
Everyone would admit that *Anna Karenina* was a magnificent novel, a
"good" novel, that it was "true" in some sense; but everyone would also
aver that *The Kreutzer Sonata* was a poor story, full of "false" doctrine and
therefore didactic in the wrong way, and inartistic through and through. It

could be called "bad or "false".

It was at this point that you began to find what was going on puzzling. (I explained to the room in general, for the benefit of those who might not have read *The Kreutzer Sonata* recently, that the story was written late in Tolstoy's life, when he was totally estranged from his wife, that the story condemns sex within marriage, and indeed without marriage, as inherently evil, and preaches the doctrine that we should all give up sex altogether and allow the world, too wicked to be allowed to endure, to depopulate itself gradually.)

The basis of the discussion had now swung round to a sort of Johnsonian area. In the common pursuit of true judgment, we were testing out the idea that "everyone" (over a hundred years or so, and with every probability into the future) had found *Anna Karenina* "true" and "good", while everyone had found *The Kreutzer Sonata* "false" and "bad", and that, therefore, this is probably what they *are*. ... **(to be continued)**

Extract: From CIARA VAN SERAI, "Gender and Sexuality in Coleridge's *Christabel*" **(continued)**

... Once in the room, Christabel actively *chooses* to look at Geraldine getting undressed. Again, however, the narrator presents the situation with seeming innocence. Even although he/she clearly does not have access to Christabel's mind, the narrator assumes that Christabel looks at Geraldine simply because she has many restless thoughts inside her head (but why it might be that she is in this mental state is not pondered):

> So many thoughts moved to and fro,
> That vain it were her lids to close;
> So half-way from the bed she rose,
> And on her elbow did recline
> To look at the lady Geraldine. (ll. 240-4)

It is equally valid to suggest, however, that Christabel looks at Geraldine precisely because she *wants* to view Geraldine's body...

Speech: COLERIDGE to THE PEOPLE OF BRISTOL (26 November 1795)

"THE MASS OF THE PEOPLE HAVE NOTHING TO DO WITH THE LAWS, BUT TO OBEY THEM!" — Ere yet this foul treason against the majesty of man,

ere yet this blasphemy against the goodness of God be registered among
our statutes, I enter my protest! Ere yet our laws as well as our religion be
muffled up in mysteries, as a CHRISTIAN I protest against this worse than
Pagan darkness! Ere yet the sword descends, the two-edged sword that is
now waving over the head of freedom, as a BRITON, I protest against
slavery! Ere yet it be made legal for Ministers to act with vigour beyond
law, as a CHILD OF PEACE, I protest against civil war! This is the brief
moment, in which freedom pleads on her knees: we will join her pleadings,
ere yet she rises terrible to wrench the sword from the hand of her
merciless enemy! We will join the still small voice of reason, ere yet it be
overwhelmed in the great and strong wind, in the earthquake, and in the
fire! ...

Internal Memorandum (strictly confidential): PROFESSOR GLOBULE
(Registrar) to MRS BOOM (Academic Arbitration Committee) **(continued)**

... and so, after due consideration, although with reluctance, my
recommendation is that *nothing be done*. We may all cross our collective
fingers and hope that Christmas comes in June and that Deadwood leaps
at the tasty carrots on offer in the new early retirement package recently
announced. But he has tenure and, short of some sexual indiscretion taking
place in full view of an audience in a public corridor, it would be well nigh
impossible to discipline him effectively. Besides, he has the ear of the V.C.
to such a degree that one suspects something positively Masonic may be
going on.

Needless to say, I am unable to allow you to go public with the
contents of this report. Please deliver my conclusions to the Committee in
the numinous, enigmatic, multiply ambiguous manner agreed for cases of
this kind.

Best, JEFFERS

PS — It was in any case agreed at the last Disaster Planning Committee to
allow the situation in Eng. Lit. to deteriorate as much as possible. This can
only help.

Extract: From H.O.WHITE, *Plagiarism and Imitation During the English
Renaissance* (1935)

Thus far the present investigation has revealed neither the word
"plagiarism" nor the attitude toward literary indebtedness denoted by the

modern use of that word. On the other hand, it has shown Englishmen deprecating certain types of incorrect imitation for nearly a century, yet wanting a technical term for the abuse. At last, shortly before 1600, two writers anglicized Martial's figurative use of *plagiarius* (man-stealer) for literary thief, one using the term "plagiary" as an adjective, the other as a noun. About twenty years later two others employed the equivalent nouns "plagiarism" and "plagium" as English terms. No other use of the epithet "plagiary" or its derivatives until after 1625 are cited in *A New English Dictionary*: so slowly was this addition to the critical vocabulary accepted that, far from becoming naturalized, it achieved only the rarest use during more than a quarter of a century after its introduction. Furthermore, the appearance of the modern term does not, as will become evident, indicate the appearance of the modern attitude.

Lecture Seven: Attendance — Deadwood plus 11

DEADWOOD: ... Poetic genius is a thing of organic life: it cannot be wholly comprehended in its own definitions of itself, or in its own declarations of its purposes, for those definitions and declarations cannot in the nature of things be more than partial. In trying to grasp its essential reality, we also, like the poet himself, are dependent on our powers of intuition, for intuition alone will enable us to apprehend the essence that lies behind all partial formulations. We must be prepared at any moment to reconcile apparent contradictions, and to reconcile them not by an arbitrary and enforced accommodation of one to the other, but by a deeper perception which can reach to the living reality which evades direct expression. I have already emphasised that the philosophy to which Keats proposed to dedicate himself was quite different from the philosophy of the schools. On 18th February of the year in question he wrote to Reynolds on the virtues of "delicious, diligent Indolence." "Diligent Indolence" — it is a happy phrase. Let us see what it meant.

STUDENTS: (*producing placards*) Clare not Keats! Clare not Keats!

DEADWOOD: Claire who?

STUDENT: John Clare is conspicuous by his absence, sir. Is that
fact totally unrelated to another fact, namely that it
might necessitate quotation of the lines "Every village
owns its tyrants now/And parish-slaves must live as
parish-kings allow"? Or acknowledgment that Clare was
a man for whom each axe-ring, each fence-post driven
into the soil was like a personal wound? ...

Extract: From FRIEDRICH ENGELS, *Anti-Dühring* (1878)

... At similar or approximately similar stages of economic development
moral theories must of necessity be more or less in agreement. From the
moment when private ownership of movable property developed, all
societies in which this private ownership existed had to have this moral
injunction in common: Thou shalt not steal. Does this injunction thereby
become an eternal moral injunction? By no means. In a society in which
all motives for stealing have been done away with, in which therefore at
the very most only lunatics would ever steal, how the preacher of morals
would be laughed at who tried solemnly to proclaim the eternal truth: Thou
shalt not steal!

    We therefore reject every attempt to impose on us any moral dogma
whatsoever as an eternal, ultimate and forever immutable ethical law on the
pretext that the moral world, too, has its permanent principles which stand
above history and the differences between nations. ...

Internal Memorandum: DEADWOOD to WROTH **(continued)**

    ... But you would not have this. To admit (after centuries of discussion)
that work X is "good" and "true" while work Y is "bad" and "false" struck
you as another instance of Blabdrip's universalising reason. In fact, you
were now arguing (though you did not realise it) with Dr Johnson himself.
If work X is "true" and "good" and work Y is "bad" and "false", then it
follows that the judgments "true", "good", "bad", "false" *can* be
legitimately used, and that they *do* correspond to time-tested realities.

    But you had trouble even with that. To admit that *anything* could be
called "good" or "bad", "true" or "false", seemed to you unacceptable, for
wearing your old-fashioned "Marxist" hat, or your newer "Cultural
Materialist" hat, you feel that you cannot admit to the terms "true",
"good", "bad" or "false" *at all*. This is because Cultural Materialism
declares itself totally relative, and such terms cannot exist within its

discourse. (You even quarrelled with Oswald's assumption that literary works have "upshots", i.e. that reading a literary work can have harmful, *or* positive, effects. This is just so obviously true that you felt you had to quarrel with it, for it implies that there are "better" and "worse" ways of living in society, and none of these may necessarily be approved of by Cultural Materialism.)

Ultimately, what worries me about Cultural Materialism, about which I am thinking quite a lot at the moment, is that it is, like Freudianism, Marxism, etc., another dogma, another theological position, where the free play of mind is not allowed. To insist upon pure relativism at all times, to refuse to allow evaluative terms into a discourse, is to shut that discourse into a *Huis Clos*, where only ideologically acceptable members are allowed to speak. Politically, that is dangerous, but intellectually, it is a loss, because it means one renders oneself deliberately unable to "hear" another discourse (such as Oswald Blabdrip's) and unable, then, to avail oneself of its insights. For there *are* insights in every discourse, even those which may be delivered in "dialects" which are not quite our own!

Best wishes as ever, PANJANDRUM ... **(to be continued)**

Extract: From JOHN FLORIO, "Epistle Dedicatorie" to *The Essays on Morall, Politike, and Millitarie Discourses of Lo. Michaell de Montaigne* (1603)

If nothing can now be sayd, but hath beene saide before (as hee sayde well) if there be no new thing under the Sunne. What is that hath beene? That that shall be: (as he sayde that was wisest) What doe the best then, but gleane after others harvest? borrow their colours, inherite their possessions? What doe they but translate? perhaps, usurpe? at least, collect? if with acknowledgement, it is well; if by stealth, it is too bad: in this, our conscience is our accuser; posteritie our judge: in that our studie is our advocate, and you Readers our jurie.

Lecture Eight: Attendance — 7 minus Deadwood

Dr Deadwood is unwell.

Extract: From JANE MOORE, "Plagiarism with a Difference: Subjectivity in 'Kubla Kahn' and *Letters Written During a Short Residence in Sweden, Norway and Denmark*", *Beyond Romanticism: New Approaches to Texts* *and Contexts 1780-1832*, ed. STEPHEN COPLEY and JOHN WHALE (1992)

Taking to its extreme the maxim that imitation (by way of assimilation) is the sincerest form of flattery, Coleridge's subsequent plagiarism of that book [*Letters Written During a Short Residence in Sweden, Norway and Denmark*] might be interpreted as an act of love. Or, perhaps more accurately, as an act, like the murderous feast held by Grenouille's worshippers, "done out of Love" (with all the attendant ambiguity of that phrase). ...

Coleridge is thus made culpable for the crime of plagiarism, which in traditional literary circles is probably the most serious charge that can be brought against a writer.

It is also, from the perspective of poststructuralism, the most difficult to prove, or even to conceptualize. In poststructuralist theory language is a social fact, meanings are public and shared and there is no available knowledge outside culture. This suggests that the author is not the source of meaning but one of its effects, and that reading and writing are irreducibly intertextual activities. As a consequence plagiarism is no longer opposed to the concept of individual Romantic creativity, but itself a radical condition of the Romantic text. Plagiarism becomes part of the very structure of writing.

Internal Memorandum: DEADWOOD to SPILLMATTER

Words fail me in responding to this essay. It is dreadful and repugnant. I refuse utterly your request that I second mark it. It is the correlative of blasphemy in the critical sphere. Just reading it has made me feel tainted. It is a sign of the worsening corruption in this department that you have been prepared to foster and encourage such thinking (a sin of commission) or failed to dam it up at source once it came to your notice (a sin of omission). Only by tremendous rebellion against my sense of *Rechtschaff-enheit* am I able to return it. I still feel that I should in conscience have destroyed it.

The author of *Christabel* would have been horrified to have been told that his great poem "envisages several different types of sexual relationship and activity, including lesbianism, incest, and auto-eroticism" and indescribably scandalised by the accusation that "Sir Leoline did, in fact, have a homosexual relationship with Geraldine's father, Lord Roland de Vaux of Tryermaine, when they were younger". *Christabel* is about none of these appalling things. It is a parable of precisely the kind of evil which van Serai's wicked essay exemplifies.

To be sure, evil is not represented in any straightforward way in the poem. It is the veiling and hiding of good. The minimal light of the clouded moon and the half-hidden eye of the snake both speak of a vision which has been obscured until it no longer controls human energies, which are left to the caprice of the passion of the moment.

Regulation: From *Ordinances of the University of Odium*

Plagiarism. The substantial use of other people's work and the submission of it as though it were one's own is regarded as plagiarism. Work which is not undertaken in an Examination Room under the supervision of an invigilator (such as dissertations, essays, project work, experiments, observation, specimen collecting, satires, spoofs, pastiches, bombastic imitations, textual tomfoolery, and other similar work), but which is nevertheless required work forming part of the degree, diploma or certificate assessment, must be the candidate's own, and must not contain any plagiarised material. When an examiner suspects plagiarism in any work which forms part or all of a unit of assessment for a University examination, he/she shall report the matter to the candidate's Head of Department, who shall submit a written report to the Registrar.

Internal Memorandum: DEADWOOD to WROTH **(continued)**

... P.S. Most of us would endorse Blabdrip's implication that, if the direct result of a line of thought (or of a "schizoid" illusion) is that there is no way out for this poet but to go and commit suicide, then that line of thought is "bad" and "false" and so is the solution.

What is of genuine interest, though, is whether or not the poem itself is "bad" and "false". Here Blabdrip seemed to think it was, and you seemed to think it wasn't (or needn't be). Blabdrip's objection was that such poems as "Edge" and "The Night Dances" oughtn't to be given to schoolchildren at A-level shows, I think, a sensitive awareness of the powers that poetry has, as well as a sensitive awareness of just how exposed, muddled, mixed-up and confused kids at that age can be. Both sensitivities are wholly admirable, for Oswald Blabdrip, in a rather Harold Bloom-like way, is one of the very last to whom poetry is actually a force.

So here we have a triple split in the problem:

(1)   Reading (or writing) works with "false" doctrine may well have "bad" "upshots" but

(2)   A work which describes a "bad" thought-process (schizoid), like Plath, or the Tolstoy of *The Kreutzer Sonata*, needn't necessarily be "bad" *as art*, though

(3)   It *might* be.

It is this third possibility that Chekhov is discussing in his letter to Plescheev, but the complexities of it are pretty daunting. How would one set up criteria to decide whether a "bad" thought-process is bad *as art*, or whether it isn't?

I haven't done the thinking on this, but my reaction would probably be, in the end, something very close to Oswald Blabdrip's, an existential one. It's bad *as art* if it leads to suicide, murder or some other affray. It's difficult to think of convincing internal criteria, quite divorced from ethical applications. So, Blabdrip's answer seems to be pretty subtle to me (which one *wouldn't* have gathered from the tone of your critique)!

Lecture Nine: Attendance — 4 minus Deadwood

Dr Deadwood is still unwell.

Internal Memorandum: WROTH to DEADWOOD

Thank you for your detailed memo. Your account of the debate (particularly the order in which you say things happened, and some of the things which you say happened but which, to my mind, didn't, or did but happened differently from the way you describe them) shows that we don't have a difference of mere theoretical perspective. Why "a Grand Old Man of English letters, Gloiretit's successor at Balliol" should need "a little protection" from a mere stripling like me (and why he should need such "heavyweight" protection as your own) amazes me even further. But no matter: your reply is surely the greatest piece of Panjandrummery yet. I shall keep it. I shall frame it.

Lecture Ten: Attendance — DEADWOOD plus 2

... Firstly, one must controvert the deluded notion that Burns was a republican. ...

Letter: AN EDITOR to DEADWOOD

Dear Dr Deadwood,

I regret that we are unable to publish your submitted article, "D.H. Lawrence: Poetic Whimsy", and return it herewith. Our reader felt that, weighing the piece's meagre strengths alongside its preponderant deficiencies, this was the only possible decision. In particular, she suggests that you might revise your comments on "Snake" to take into consideration the poem as a homosexual discourse. The basis for such a line of enquiry seems solid enough, given that the snake is evidently a phallic symbol, and that it penetrates a "dreadful hole" which leads "into the burning bowels of this earth", thus prompting the narrator to ask, "Was it perversity, that I longed to talk to him?" Our reader further suggests a possible parallel with the depiction of Geraldine in Coleridge's "Christabel", at which the (once lesbian) Ursula is "wildly thrilled" in chapter XIV of Lawrence's *The Rainbow*.

Yours sincerely, etc.

Review: From the *Monthly Review*, January 1817 (anonymous)

This precious production is not finished, but we are to have more and more of it in future! It would be truly astonishing that such rude unfashioned stuff should be tolerated, and still more that it should be praised by men of genius ... were we not convinced that every principle of correct writing as far as poetry is concerned, has been long *given up*: and that the observance rather than the breach of such rules is considered as an incontrovertible proof of rank stupidity. It is grand, in a word it is sublime, to be lawless; and whoever writes the wildest nonsense in the quickest and newest manner is the popular poet of the day.

Punishment Essays

David Solomon. Punishment Essay for Miss Scupping. 7/3/97

An explanation for my poor behaviour, an apology, and how my behaviour will improve. What St Ignatius Loyola would say about it. And an explanation of why we were talking.

I know that I have not been behaving as well as I could have done in lessons, but as of now, a firm attempt will be made to amend the situation. The teacher has every right to inflict a punishment if he/she feels that a pupil/pupils are not[50] paying attention.

Firstly I am not going to deny that I deserve this punishment, I am not even going to say that it was too much, I will just accept the imposition, and consider myself chastised. In fact, I would like to thank you, Miss, for depriving me of my[100] freedom and enforcing the task of this essay upon me. I think you are completely justified. If I was in your shoes I also would curtail the liberty of any pupil who has been so disobedient as me. Secondly I must apologise for my undesirable habit of talking too much[150] and too loudly. I did not realise that my voice carried so far across the room. I was also saying some things that I now feel really ashamed that you heard, and this is another reason why I feel thankful that you have reprehended me in this way. Otherwise I[200] might have thought that I could get away with doing and saying shameful things in future, and this would not be good for me and it might embarrass my parents as well if brought to their attention.

Most importantly I apologise for my fit of the giggles at the end.[250] I failed to appreciate the seriousness of the situation. It was not helped by the laughter of others or of the faces peering through the doors. I am not using this as an excuse, but the atmosphere in the room felt too relaxed. I don't think this was your fault[300] at all. Unlike you, Miss, we have a lot to learn about acting responsibly and maturely, and I know that some of us let you down badly in today's lesson. All I hope is that you can forgive us.

So, I have covered explanation, apology, improvement of my behaviour, and[350] excessive talking.

All that I am now able to say is that I intend to prove to you that I am not just writing a load of rubbish to fill up the page. I will finish with a quote from St Ignatius Loyola: "With a most firm desire for amendment."[400]

P.S. Although it's only 1 page, I have written the 400 words. I know my writing's a bit small but I am trying to improve this as well as my behaviour.

*

Richard Keithly/Punishment Essay/Miss Scupping/Fri. 7 Mar. 97

An explanation as to why we were talking, reasons why Miss Scupping was angered by me, destroying other people's education, the cataclysmic effects of a little bit of mischief, etc., how I would reform the situation, plus a bit of wisdom from the life or writings of St I. of. L.

I have to write this essay because I was talking in the classroom. I was also so impertinent that I made some fly remarks and comments. I made one about the teaching profession all being of the mental age of 12½ which (though everyone whooped and giggled and tittered and sneered and smirked and grinned and beamed and hooted and chortled and sniggered and chuckled and erupted into uncontrollable fits of amusement at it, and some even went to the ridiculous lengths of whispering other much more offensive comments to the pupil sitting beside them) did not go down too well in a certain quarter (well, in one twenty-ninth, to be accurate) of the classroom.

At the time the teacher only smiled and said something under her breath, which gave the impression that she was in fact quietly humoured by the whole affair. So I certainly am a bit shocked now to find myself imprisoned here all lunchtime. That was pretty clever, pretending to appreciate the joke and then swooping down on me like an avenging wildebeest at the end of the lesson. Must remember those tactics when I'm older and have kids of my own! Congratulations, Miss: one-nil to you!

From then on I tried to keep on her good side. I am not surprised that poor Miss Scupping was angered and annoyed and frustrated and upset and harrowed and offended and disquieted and discomposed and deranged and generally so much internally disturbed and demented that she (you) started slamming things down on the desk and making incoherent *caw-caw* screaming and wailing noises at regular intervals and cursing and spitting and such things so that the veins in her (your) head (especially the right temple — or is that a varicose?) became visibly more prominent. That is the sort of reaction we have all come to expect from our teachers in such circumstances: the people you trust with your education are not necessarily the people you would turn to in a riotous crisis. Nor should we expect them to be.

Certain members of the class that sit two rows back from me and shall remain nameless (although they are in this room at this very moment) were still carrying on even after you had delivered several dire warnings and vicious verbal assaults. I am glad that they were punished, because I find it difficult to achieve a satisfactory prose style when writing in complete isolation — a little artistic quirk of mine.

What the school's saint would say about the matter I am not really sure. We know that St Ignatius wasn't a very good pupil in his youth. He only just scrambled a degree from the University of Odium. Apparently he preferred to gamble, have a good scrap (e.g. against the French in the siege of Pampeluna in 1521, where he got a cannonball in the hip as a reward for his adventurousness) and indulge in what one Dictionary of the Saints rather primly calls "affairs of gallantry" (there's a Jackie Collins novel in there somewhere, don't you think?).

What I have learned from today's experience is that when a bad element creeps into the class then it disrupts the smooth running of lessons and hinders the academic future of many of the schoolchildren. How are we meant to learn anything when a person spends most of the lesson deliberately attacking the minutiae of our behaviour and besmirching our otherwise reputable characters? I have fairly fixed opinions on how I would reform this situation. I believe that all teachers should undergo a short training course in how to treat pupils like reasonable human beings rather than mongrel pups which have not yet been domesticated.

From now on I am going to turn over a new leaf or sheet or page (whichever I have handy at the time) and stop this bad behaviour and habitual sarcasm. Although such behaviour is, I am aware, an excellent preparation for my chosen career in Law, I realise that in perpetuating it I am preventing others from practising and perfecting the subservient demeanour required for the more subordinate occupations which the vast majority of them wish to pursue. Worst of all (and above all else) we are vexing and frustrating poor Miss Scupping and stopping her doing what she likes best — teaching. Sorry miss.

*

A Letter to Miss Scupping

7th March

Dear Emma (I trust you will not mind such familiarity),

This is ridiculous.

Let's try and look at it reasonably, shall we?

You have told me to explain in writing why I have been confined as a punishment for my behaviour in this morning's lesson.

The answer is, I don't know. I didn't do anything to offend you.

All I did was pass you a note telling you how desperately I was in love with you and suggesting ways in which we might try and work something out. But more of that later.

I accept that I may have been a little indiscreet in some of the things I said and did, although I think you are aware by now that this stems from an unruly intoxication of spirits being in your presence induces in me and which I thought I was slowly beginning to control.

I understand, with hindsight, that the remark about your lipstick and your new hairdo just before you started calling the register may have been a little unexpected, but I can assure you that no one other than you heard it. As you know, I sit right next to your desk, and I had my head turned away from everyone else when I said it. I simply wanted you to feel that all the effort you put in to making yourself look attractive was acknowledged.

As for my later and louder statement about your "absolutely stunning body", you need to know all the facts which led up to this. James Chaplin and Andrew Morton had been saying some things about your physique (e.g. that your delicate and exquisitely shaped nose reminded them of "a pointer bitch") that were crude and indecent. I suppose their intention all along was to wind me up and they succeeded, but I had managed to contain myself for a long time. It was A.M.'s disgusting claim that he would "rather have incest with his granny" than contemplate lovemaking with you that led directly to my outburst. But I was only trying to defend you. I think if you had heard some of the other things they said about other parts of your anatomy (which I would not repeat) you would be more grateful to me.

I fully appreciate that what I did when you were looking at my work and talking to me about it must have come as something of a surprise, but all I can say is that it was involuntary and that if I could have resisted I would have done so. Whenever you come near me like that I am almost overwhelmed by what seems to be a powerful erotic charisma radiating from you. You seem not to be aware of the fact that you induce a virtually intolerable sexual excitement in many young men in this class. It may be explained by the fact that this is an all boys school and we form unhealthily strong attachments to the few women we come into contact with. But the effects are more important than their cause. A lot of us emerge from your lessons pale and physically exhausted, as if we've just been through an encounter with a vampiress. Just ask Mr Mountebank: he takes us for P.E. after your lesson on a Thursday afternoon and he's always complaining about how sluggish we are then.

I seem to come off worst from these encounters, which is probably because you and I vibrate on the same psychic frequency (did you know that we share not only the same conventional star sign but are also the same animal in the *Chinese* horoscope?). As I've said, by a monumental force of will I usually manage to block the urges I have at these moments. I think it was your short sleeved blouse which caused the problem today. Your arms still have that rich bronze colour from the summer heat. The sun flushed through the window just after you bent over to speak to me about what I had written, bringing out all the tiny golden follicles of hair on your forearm. It was beautiful. I felt a strong downward force on the back of my neck, making me bow my head forward in a movement I could not and did not want to fight against, and what I next remember is finding my lips gently touching the soft fleshy part of your arm just below the deltoid. It was a second or two before you flinched and when I looked at your face I saw delight there in the instant before the cloud of repulsion crossed over it.

This was a revelation. I suddenly knew that your feelings for me in fact matched mine for you and that it has been only for the sake of appearances that you have, understandably, shunned me up until now. If my new-found confidence led me to act too rashly in passing my note to you a few minutes later, please forgive me, and do not reject me on account of the feverishness of my desire. I am sure that we can avoid these embarrassing public moments in the future if we co-operate in relieving our mutual sexual tensions privately, in the manner suggested in my note, or by any other method that you may find convenient.

I am certain that if we do not embark on some venture of this kind soon I am likely to behave even more irresponsibly in future than I have done today. Recently I have begun to experience the strangest kind of psychological disturbance as a consequence of my lust (forgive the word, but I must give the passion I feel its proper name).

In the first week of term, you asked us to close our eyes and attempt to visualise the landscape described in a passage you then read to us: D.H.Lawrence's *Rainbow*, if my memory serves me correctly. I had then what I can only call an out-of-body experience. My eyelids, in fact, when I closed them, proved to be diaphanous. I saw you still as you walked gently up and down in front of the blackboard, reading aloud in that clear, sweet voice. I witnessed myself stand up and leave my own body as if it were nothing more than the seat it had been sitting in. I watched myself move towards you. You had your back to me and were still reading when my other self placed his hands on your shoulders and buried his face in the warmth of your neck. You threw back your head until it rested on his shoulder. You had no more thought for reading then, and dropped the book. Your hand moved towards my left cheek just as mine touched your left breast and you arched your back even more so that I thought you must fall. I haven't the vocabulary to do justice to the dizzy reeling splendour that seemed to have been injected directly into my veins at that moment.

I felt your heart knocking so hard against your breast that I thought it might punch its way out of your body altogether, but just then the vision dissolved and my sitting body seemed to suck its counterpart back into itself, so that he moved in the bathetic fashion of a character in a film speedily reversed.

You will remember this event only as the occasion on which I rudely interrupted your reading with a cry of "Yes. **Yes! YES!**" which I was not able subsequently to explain. But now you know what caused it, and the kind of emotional torture I endure on account of my desire.

It is not punishment to sacrifice a lunchtime to stay in a room where your spiritual presence is strong, even if you are not physically here but gracing the canteen instead. You will return in a few minutes to take in these essays, and I know that when you read this letter you will be urged by that part of your personality which is obsessed with correctness, propriety and moral common sense to see it as an outrage, an affront, the ravings of a juvenile fiend. All that I ask is that you pause, consider, and take its contents to your heart over the weekend. If after that time your conscience still tells you that you cannot offer what I request or, worse, that you must engage in a punitive crusade against my candid feelings and actions, then I will have little to live for, and will probably make an end of things.

I leave my life in your hands.

With all my love,
Peter Michael Bartholemew

xxx

P.S. Look at the reproduction of Rubens' painting of St Ignatius in the school entrance hall. There is a young, almost totally naked young man lying on his back in the bottom left hand corner, with a whip in his hand. He has presumably been flagellating himself out of a frenzy of unconsummated lust. I know how he feels.

*

how i wos punshed by scupping by JASON G.

wot of i dun now i never did nuffing did i all i did wos tak a peek in at the top set and mak a few funy fases at em cos that lots al rich kids an brite begarz and not pure porpers lik wot peepul like me iz it aint my folt iz it then scupping seez wot im dooing an she starts goin wild an draggin me into the room an off corse it got me pritty well annoid an i sez fuk a fue tims lik wot the fuk of i dun now an fuk of scupping an thats wy she dissidid i was in hear al off the dinner tim juss cos i sed fuk a fue tims at her for draggin me in a room i had only lookd thru the windo of juss to mak sum funy fases at set won peepul cos you shood sea the fings they sez to peepuls lik me whore in the botum set stoopid git an dunsy brane an smelly jason an jelly bean man an stuf lik that i hop they dye to morro al off em i do an you to an no i aint apologisin cos i never did nuffing an st ignashus loyla i ate him an hiz skool cos its a fuker

Virus Alert

Source of Alert: Dept of Scottish Literature, University of Odium
Name of Virus: The Kelman Avenger
Risk Rating: ~~Low~~ / ~~Medium~~ / ~~High~~ / Emergency

The provenance of The Kelman Avenger virus is unknown. It was first discovered by researchers working on the late twentieth century volumes of *The New Canon of Scottish Literature* (24 vols., London, Sickness and Warthog, forthcoming) in the Department of Scottish Literature at the University of Odium. The main aim of the virus seems to be to undermine the reputations of contemporary Scottish writers of genius, several of them winners of commercial literary prizes whose works attract continuously laudatory reviews in quality English newspapers. It is therefore quite unlikely that the virus was engineered in Scotland, where the tradition of wholly unquestioning acceptance of aesthetic authority remains thankfully unassailable, and where the raising of an eyebrow over established literary opinion in the domestic sphere is still a major taboo.

The virus is of the "Trojan Horse" variety (i.e. it is a type of virus which is disguised as a legitimate program, and is much more apt to destroy files or damage disks than other programs). It is 13312 bytes long and infects all known wordprocessor .EXE files. It does not remain resident in memory. Side effects include corrupted program and overlay files, changes to system run time operation, reformatting or overwriting parts of the hard disk, and irrecoverable damage to infected files. In this respect it gives the appearance of a conventional "Trojan Horse". The main effect of the virus is, however, much more radically destructive than is suggested at first sight.

Workers on *The New Canon* became aware of the virus at work while examining proofs returned prior to publication in the volumes in question. No effect was visible on screen to typing operatives either before or after the saving of the relevant files. Every attempt to print the same files in hard copy, however, offered abundant evidence that they had become contaminated by an external agency.

In brief, The Kelman Avenger is a text-insertion virus. It "homes in" on certain keyed-in textual elements (primarily but not exclusively the names of certain Scottish authors) and inserts adjacent to them, or substitutes for them, non-keyed-in textual elements. The "rogue" elements massively disrupt or displace the meaning of the keyed-in text.

The most salutary example of the virus at work is the effect it has on references to the writer whose name is used to describe it: James Kelman. The inventor of the virus clearly does not share the virtually universal consensus which pertains to this fine artist, and which has placed him in a select pantheon alongside international prodigies of the order of Franz Kafka, Albert Camus, and Vladimir Nabokov. However, in its dealings with "Kelman" the virus shows signs of what might be called "intelligent reading", in that it does not simply replace or qualify this text string with expressions of abuse or hostility, but seems to "search around" the text string for terms of favourable evaluation, which it then replaces with antonymic words and/or phrases. Thus, where Kelman's style is rightly applauded for its "demotic integrity", the virus will condemn it for its "parochial deadness". Where Kelman's judicious handling of narrative is praised for being "experimentally improvisational", the virus instead attacks it for being "yawn-promptingly boring". And where the distinguished critics who have deservedly raised Kelman to his current pinnacle of success are approved for adopting a controversial stance "at the cutting edge of the business of literary discrimination", the virus tells us they are "a horde of bumsuckers".

In short, the operating principle of the virus is irresponsibly and unaccountably to reverse all orthodox, settled and respectable opinion with regard to Scottish letters at the present time. It does not do so *entirely* insensitively. In its dealings with Alasdair Gray, for example, the virus demonstrates a thoroughly ambivalent attitude. It quite properly interpolates ejaculations of delight at every citation of *Lanark*, and goes so far as to insert an analytic article as long as a typical encyclopaedia entry when mention is made of *Unlikely Stories, Mostly*. By contrast, its mood unpredictably darkens when confronted by Gray's equally accomplished later work. *Something Leather* is given a particularly uncomfortable ride ("recycled garbage"), *The Fall of Kelvin Walker* is attacked ("pedestrian bilge"), *McGrotty and Ludmilla* is accused of having been called into existence for utterly commercial motives ("derisory potboiler") and *Ten Tales Tall and True* is condemned out of hand ("lamentable tripe").

Consistent with its vulgar demotion of truly major artistic work in the Scottish literary field, the virus arrogates to ludicrous positions of eminence those contemporary writers whom *The New Canon of Scottish Literature* is as a matter of policy concerned to categorise as minor. Thus John Herdman, author (*inter alia*) of *Three Novellas* and *Imelda* — mentioned only once in *The New Canon*, and that primarily to establish the comprehensiveness of the project — has an entire 10,000 word chapter devoted, on account of the virus, to his "skilful" remoulding of Dostoyevskian motifs and revival of the gothic "double" theme as found, for instance, in the work of Hogg. Similarly, Frank Kuppner, a semi-unemployed Glasgow wordsmith with dubious affiliations to continental surrealism, is warmly and extensively recommended in a survey which was intended to portray his surprisingly published fiction and poetry as "childish antics".

The effects of The Kelman Avenger on *The New Canon of Scottish Literature* have been near catastrophic. Unfortunately, the workings of the virus were not discovered before proofs were sent out to contributors, and many resigned their commissions in protest at what they took to be editorial subversion of their views. The publisher has had to make a heavy reinvestment to secure new contributions, but this late effort may have been in vain. The publication delays, compounded by rumour-mongering and whispering campaigns, have placed so dark a financial cloud over the forthcoming edition that Sickness and Warthog are currently considering total withdrawal from the Scottish publishing scene. Therefore the ripples are likely to spread much further afield than *The New Canon* project. It would not be melodramatic to insist that the international profile and economic profitability of Scottish Literature are now under very grave threat.

The adroit technical specifications of The Kelman Avenger make this national plight doubly desperate. Once detected, it is not difficult to track down. It is usually installs itself in the DOS directory under the filename KAMIKAZE.EXE. This apparently vulnerable self-flaunting conceals the utter malignancy at the heart of the virus designer. When an instruction is given to delete KAMIKAZE.EXE, it erases the entire hard disk on which it is resident before apparently "committing suicide". But if the computer is attached to a network, and the user is logged on, it *sends itself by electronic mail to every user registered on the network*, taking up residence *in each user's MAIL ATTACHMENTS or equivalent directory*, whence it is automatically forwarded to *each and every email correspondent of each and every registered user*.

The potentially global consequences of such monstrous replication should be obvious. The very future of Scottish Literature hangs in the balance.

Envoi

I wrote most of this book when I was meant to be writing another much more sensible, reputable, and unreadable one. But I am proud to say that in doing so I was standing on the shoulders of several giants of what, somewhere in these pages, I have called "interstitial discourse": the names Bernard Sharratt, Umberto Eco and Stanislaw Lem spring to mind. Indeed, *Crackpot Texts* is very like Sharratt's *The Literary Labyrinth*, a mixture of humour and politics, with the politics removed; it is also like that combination of humour and literary theory, Eco's *Misreadings*, without the literary theory; and it is consciously indebted to Lem's compound of humour and idiocy, *Imaginary Magnitude*, in all but its failure to amuse.

Undemanding as this book is, there are certain features of it which it might be helpful to explain. The Latin epigraphs might be translated thus:

Example is better than precept
The language of truth is plain and always simple
A monster whose vices were not redeemed by a single virtue
I hunt not for the votes of common people, which veer with every wind
Those who set a trap for others often fall into it themselves
He who knows not how to dissemble knows not how to live
The fiery, impetuous disposition of the Scots
While I re-read my compositions, I am ashamed of having written them
We do not trouble about things beyond our comprehension
We read books to prevent them being read by others
Nobly mendacious
Fodder; matter for study

I could, of course, have rendered these in English; but, as the ocularly attentive reader can see by comparing the Latin, only at the price of abandoning a pleasing aesthetic effect.[1]

---

[1] Even a re-arrangement of the lines as follows could only translate the morphology of the sequence very roughly:

I hunt not for the votes of common people, which veer with every wind
While I re-read my compositions, I am ashamed of having written them
A monster whose vices were not redeemed by a single virtue
He who knows not how to dissemble knows not how to live
Those who set a trap for others often fall into it themselves
We do not trouble about things beyond our comprehension
We read books to prevent them being read by others
The language of truth is plain and always simple
The fiery, impetuous disposition of the Scots
Example is better than precept
Fodder; matter for study
Nobly mendacious

"Examiner's Report" was first published in *English in Education* 25, 2 (Summer 1991), pp. 72-8. It was a reaction to the *bourgeois* prejudices of the real examiner's report mentioned on p. 15. Although some licence is taken with Roland Barthes' death (he was actually hit by a laundry van), *The S.C.U.M. Manifesto* is not an invented detail: Valerie Solanas's genocidal programme ("Life in this society being, at best, an utter bore and no aspect of society being at all relevant to women, there remains to civic-minded, responsible, thrill-seeking females only to overthrow the government, eliminate the money system, institute complete automation and destroy the male sex") was first published in 1968 after she had shot but unfortunately not killed Andy Warhol. It is still available in a slightly altered version (London, Phoenix Press, 1991); some of us would like to know how it has been altered, why, and by whom.

"Your Average Working Kelman" initially came to light in *Cencrastus* 46 (Autumn 1993), pp. 14-16. In an editorial, Raymond Ross deftly softened up his readers for this piece by remarking that "in Macdonald Daly's flyting agin James Kelman ... in the midst of a heartfelt Kelmanesque *pastiche, in imitatio il miglior fabbro* nae doot, he utilises, with full colloquial strength, the word *cunt*. I only point this out because it is, to my knowledge, the first time this particular four-lettered word has appeared in these pages." The *in imitatio* I admit — but *il miglior fabbro*? That seems to run a little counter to the spirit of the piece. Surprisingly, this squib still gets me more fan mail and hate mail than all else I have written. The hate mail I put down to the usual small-mindedness of Scottish letters (i.e. we have so few "major" novelists that once the London reviewers and Booker Prize judges combine to award us one, we ought to play along and self-censor our reservations). Most of the fan mail expresses gratitude that someone has at last had the gumption to speak freely. At any rate, a well-known buddy of Kelman's wrote to tell me that the piece was "too long and not funny enough". This didn't seem to be the verdict of the major Scottish writer who toasted the piece many times over — once in my presence — or of the University Literature department which, one of its members informed me, spontaneously combusted with collective mirth when the piece was copied to its staff. Needless to say, this kind of thing didn't happen at the University of Glasgow: one of its denizens (Willy Maley) apparently rapped my knuckles thus in the *Edinburgh Review*:

And besides, this would be to disturb the order in which the sentiments are expressed, which is clearly all-important. Nor should one forget Poe's recommendations in "How to Write a Blackwood Article": "In a Blackwood article nothing makes so fine a show as your Greek. The very letters have an air of profundity about them. Only observe, madam, the artiste look of that Epsilon! That Phi ought certainly to be a bishop! Was ever there a smarter fellow than that Omicron? Just twig that Tau!" Of course, with Latin, the charm resides in the individual words rather than the individual letters.

"Daly's vitriolic parody in *Cencrastus* seems to me to say little beyond 'Look at me. I can swear too!' As though Kelman's literary genius could be reduced to cursing." (I say "apparently" because I cannot frankly be bothered reading anything else about Kelman. I am relying on the transcription of a friend.) Of course, if you've decided in advance that Kelman is a "genius" you remove any obligation you might have had to argue a case. But Maley's mere assertiveness produces such a reductive reading of what I thought I was doing that one would like to know if he is simply yet another buddy of Kelman's.

"Only the Names Have Been Changed" is published here for the first time. Readers are advised that the note appended to the end of this dialogue is deliberately misleading.

"Concplags and Totplag: *Lanark* Exposed" came into the world via the *Edinburgh Review* 93 (Spring 1995), 167-199. On that occasion it was a little mangled and chopped about for reasons of space. Somehow, despite copy being supplied in wordprocessed form, one of the epigraphs also got buggered up ("versi" horrendously replacing "veris" — I never saw proofs). It appears here in a restored version. For reasons which should be obvious from footnote 55 of the essay, the *Edinburgh Review* offered Alasdair Gray the opportunity to comment on the piece in advance of publication. His letter is reprinted on p. 200 of the same issue and offers judgments which in the circumstances seemed generous and, coming from Alasdair Gray, I took to be enormously complimentary. For the one reader of the original piece who contacted me in the belief that its discoveries were veracious, I can only emphatically translate its second epigraph: "fictions to please should wear the face of truth" (the first, by the way, roughly means "I wrote these versicles, another carried off the credit of them").

The main text of "'It's' Misspelled: History of an Error in *The Waste Land*" really was published in the *Bulletin of the Bibliographical Society of Australia and New Zealand* XI, 4 (1987), pp. 169-70. The quotations from correspondence with *The Library: Transactions of the Bibliographical Society* and *Papers of the Bibliographical Society of America* are genuine. My thanks go to Alexander George for his permission to allow me to reprint the article in this form, which demonstrates a certain disparity in our respective views of the demands of politeness, as he has already recycled it without my say-so (see Lawrence Douglas and Alexander George, "T.S.Eliot's Peripatetic Apostrophe", *The North American Review* [May/June 1996], pp. 41-5). No one can convict either of us of failing to milk this one dry.

"Crackpot Texts, or Nonsense Plumb'd, Explor'd, & Sustain'd" was too stylistically abnormal for any publication other than this book. I have not applied to this essay Robert Gunning's "Fog Index" test of readability, on which Margaret Mitchell's *Gone With the Wind* registered 8 — i.e. American school eighth-grade reading level (see Gunning's *The Technique of Clear Writing* [revised edition, New York, McGraw-Hill, 1968]) — but I have run it through a computer program known as the Wintertree Writing Style Analyzer which does something very similar without human effort. It told me:

* On average, each word contains 1.7 syllables and each sentence contains 34.5 words.
* 26% of the sentences use the active voice. Suggestion: rewrite passive sentences in the active voice to raise this number to 60%.
* On average, the reader must have 21.1 years of schooling to understand the document. Suggestion: use smaller words and shorter sentences to lower the writing to the target reader's level (10.0 years).

This contrasts fascinatingly with the response to the W.H.Auden poem quoted in full near the end of the essay, which I ran through the program on its own, and whose vital statistics were: average word = 1.5 syllables; average sentence = 29.3 words; sentences in active voice = 58%; years of schooling required for understanding = 15.6. This final figure triumphantly explains the virtually universal failure to make sense of the poem (as there is no country in which it is not anomalous to enjoy more than 12.75 years of schooling). Furthermore, such comparative analysis reveals that the impermeability of my own writing is *diluted* rather than *intensified* by the multitudinous bloviations I quote (true even the most impressionistically rebarbative slice of Kuppner: 1.5 syllables, 20.8 words, 38% active voice, 14.1 years of schooling.)

A foreshortened version of "Gray Eminence and Kelman Ataxy: A Reply to H. Baum" appeared in *Gairfish* 9 (1995), pp. 23-35.

"Malice Aforethought: the Fictions of Ellis Sharp" was written in late 1993 and first given as two lectures at the University of Nottingham in 1994. I have not significantly revised it, other than to include, at length, some comments from Tim Wood, whom I thank for permitting me to do so. I should explain, given my already expressed hostility to literary favours based largely on acquaintance, that I got to know Ellis Sharp after prescribing *Lenin's Trouser's* on a postmodernist fiction course, and not the other way round. When I wondered about his future in this essay, I couldn't have imagined that it would involve *me* — see our *Engels on Video: A Joint Production* (London, Zoilus Press, 1995). Sharp has since gone on to publish another book of short stories, *To Wanstonia* (London,

Zoilus Press, 1996).

Swift's "An Argument Against Abolishing Christianity" first tickled the world's ribs in 1710. "An Argument Against Abolishing Socialism" had its first (anonymous) incarnation in *The Gong* (1994-5), p. 34. It is appropriate to reprint it in an election year in which the case it pleads seems ever more necessary.

"A Metafictionist Manifesto" — first published in *Massacre* 5 (1994), pp. 24-32, with a definite rather than an indefinite article in the title — draws freely on the following: Filippo Tommaso Marinetti, "The Founding and Manifesto of Futurism" (1909), "Technical Manifesto of Futurist Literature" (1912), and "Futurist Synthesis of the War" (1914), tr. R.W.Flint, in *Marinetti: Selected Writings* (London, Secker and Warburg, 1972), pp. 39-44, 84-9, 62-3; Karl Marx, *The Communist Manifesto* (1848); Hugh MacDiarmid, "Art and the Unknown" (1926), in *Hugh MacDiarmid: Selected Prose*, ed. Alan Riach (Manchester, Carcanet, 1992), pp. 39-43; and Patricia Waugh, *Metafiction: The Theory and Practice of Self-Conscious Fiction* (London, Methuen, 1984). Section I is of course essentially a reworking of Marx; section II is primarily invention, although the list of "compositional arts" with which it concludes is stolen (excepting items 5, 6, 7, 13, 16, 17, 20 and 22) from Waugh; the whole of section III is a Marinetti *mélange*; and virtually all of section IV is MacDiarmid, the most notable difference being that the word "art" is replaced by "politics". Other collisions of revolutionary communism and futurism can be found in Trotsky's chapter on the latter in *Literature and Revolution*. Peter Stansill and David Zane Mairowitz, *BAMN (By Any Means Necessary): Outlaw Manifestos and Ephemera 1965-70* (Harmondsworth, Penguin, 1971), was an inspirational rather than derivational source for the style and tone of the whole.

No resemblance to any living person(s) is intended in, or should be construed from, "Term: a Documentary". A shorter text with the same title was published pseudonymously as a chapbook (London, Zoilus Press, 1996).

A version of "Punishment Essays" appeared in *Critical Quarterly* 34, 4 (Winter 1992), pp. 65-71. I thank my sister for the hand she knows she had in the birth of this piece.

"Virus Alert", previously unpublished, was conceived in the wake of a now unattributable remark made during an unforgettable carouse in Edinburgh in August 1996. If any member of the disorderly company recognises the witty idea as his, I hope he does not take exception to my elaboration.

Mac Daly
1 April 1997 (p.m.)

Z ⊕ O ⊕ I ⊕ L ⊕ U ⊕ S
P ⊕ R ⊕ E ⊕ S ⊕ S
B ⊕ O ⊕ O ⊕ K ⊕ S

Mac Daly and Ellis Sharp
Engels on Video: A Joint Production

Nietzsche. Engels. Freud. Trotsky. Four gigantic figures famous for their facial hair and authorship of strange, difficult books. In this extraordinary collection of paired stories Mac Daly and Ellis Sharp reveal the hitherto unknown sides to the lives of these heterodox hirsute humans. Here for the first time is the full story of Trotsky's career in the movies, as well as his little-known exile in a town with only one set of traffic lights. Sleep, philosophy, politics, Engels's interest in video and Freud's behaviour at the Villa Wassing are probed in dramatic detail. The volume, which includes a unique interview with Nietzsche's legendary moustache, is essential reading for anyone interested in Dorset, eighteenth century Spanish quodlibetarianism, a train named Sylvia, or Prince Hamlet's behaviour and play at the age of four.

"First and foremost a postmodern literary exercise, it is also a grand tour of political in-jokes, philosophical musings and sexual innuendo. All those ideas that have shaped the world and our discussion of it in the last two hundred years are, here, gleefully sent up. Its postmodern intentions deliberately eschew conventional structures. Once emerged in its midsts, rewind. Surf. The text is rich with meaning and suggestion. No word or punctuation mark appears accidentally or innocently."
Impact

155 pages. £6.99
ISBN 0 95220228 2 4

ALSO AVAILABLE FROM ZOILUS PRESS

Charles Cutting
The Surleighwick Effect

Why is the English Department of the University of Surleighwick buying all the Romanian books it can lay its hands on? Why are private detectives spying on the staff? This lighthearted comic novel expores the vibrant new commercial values of modern academic life, as well as its more traditional features such as fraud, stupidity, drunkenness, witchcraft, ignorance and lechery.

"A campus novel of wild comic caricature which bounces along with unflagging zest."
Times Literary Supplement

277 pages. £7.99.
ISBN O 9522028 0 8

*

Ellis Sharp
The Aleppo Button

Stalin fakes his death, swims to England and starts a new life. Strange paranormal phenomena occur shortly before the pregnant mothers of future American presidents go into labour. A purple mould spreads across Europe and a marriage collapses. Thirteen idiosyncratic stories synthesize fact and fiction to provide dark, comic parables for our times.

"A deep but surface-laden exploration of the limits of surreal humour. Above all, this is a performance which will win or lose according to the reader's patience, probity and sense of adventure."
Northern Star

109 pages. £4.99.
ISBN 1 871197 99 6

ALSO AVAILABLE FROM ZOILUS PRESS

Ellis Sharp
Lenin's Trousers

History collides with fantasy as Ellis Sharp tackles the big questions of our time and uncovers startling new facts about Emily Brontë, extra-terrestrials and gastric secretion. These thirteen inventive stories answer such questions as: who invented yogurt? Why was the British Government prepared to spend one million roubles in an attempt to seize Lenin's trousers? And what did happen to Fred, Laura and the children in *Brief Encounter* after Alec left for South Africa?

"Sharp's experiment is an attempt to find out what kind of fiction a socialist should write. You'll find out what really happened to the 26 Commissars of Baku, that it was Lenin who said, 'Enjoy yourself, get fat, and never stop laughing', and Churchill who said, 'Proletarians and free thinkers of the world, unite against the fascist tyrants!' At last somebody has written stories about real socialism and real socialists."
Socialist Review

159 pages. £6.99.
ISBN 1 871197 95 3

*

Ellis Sharp
To Wanstonia

A must for students of *Pride and Prejudice*, Bob Dylan, *Blow-Up*, Bolshevism, and the struggle against the M11 link road, this remarkable collection of stories probes the relationship between carp and revolution, the poetry of Gerard Manley Hopkins and the Paris Commune, imperialism and the sex life of Jane Austen, and anti-roads protests and Alexander Pope, as well as the connection between *Tess of the d'Urbervilles* and "New Labour". It also includes a valuable biography of the international socialist Edith Cavell, told entirely through her involvement with vegetables, as well as a diary of the 39 day strike at Thrabb's and a re-telling of the legendary Henry James seminar at My Lai.

155 pages. £6.99.
ISBN 0 9522028 4 0.

ZOILUS PRESS ORDER FORM

Books are sent POST FREE on all orders. Please allow 28 days for delivery. Trade orders are discounted at 35%. All orders must be paid in advance by cheque made payable to ZOILUS PRESS and sent to **Zoilus Press, PO Box 9315, London E17 4UU**.

Please send me POST FREE:

__ copy/copies of Mac Daly, *Crackpot Texts*
@ £10.00 per copy   £___.___

__ copy/copies of Mac Daly and Ellis Sharp, *Engels on Video*
@ £6.99 per copy   £___.___

__ copy/copies of Charles Cutting, *The Surleighwick Effect*
@ £7.99 per copy   £___.___

__ copy/copies of Ellis Sharp, *The Aleppo Button*
@ £4.99 per copy   £___.___

__ copy/copies of Ellis Sharp, *Lenin's Trousers*
@ £6.99 per copy   £___.___

__ copy/copies of Ellis Sharp, *To Wanstonia*
@ £6.99 per copy   £___.___

GRAND TOTAL £___.___

I enclose a cheque for the grand total made payable to ZOILUS PRESS.

Signature _____ Date _____

NAME...

ADDRESS...

....

....

....